AF454306

# Remaking Sustainability

# John Morrison

# Remaking Sustainability

## Why the pushback will make it stronger

John Morrison
Eastbourne, UK

ISBN 978-3-032-23754-5    ISBN 978-3-032-23755-2   (eBook)
https://doi.org/10.1007/978-3-032-23755-2



This Palgrave Macmillan imprint is published by the registered company Springer Nature Switzerland AG.
The registered company address is: Gewerbestrasse 11, 6330 Cham, Switzerland

If disposing of this product, please recycle the paper.

*This book is dedicated to Fiona, thank you for a lifetime of love.*

# Preface

It feels that much is in flux now. The work of decades appears to have been thrown into the air, if not quite to the wind. Assumptions that once felt settled are being questioned again, sometimes thoughtfully, sometimes opportunistically. In this sense, it is indeed a 'time of monsters': a period in which old frameworks no longer command confidence, while new ones struggle to establish legitimacy. Yet moments like this are not only periods of risk. They are also moments of recalibration, when it becomes possible - necessary, even - to step back, take a longer view, and reassess what has been built and how it functions in practice.

Sustainability is at the centre of this turbulence. Over recent decades, it has moved from the margins into the mainstream of business, policy, and public debate. That success has brought influence, but it has also brought exposure. As sustainability has become more consequential, its weaknesses have become harder to ignore. The current pushback - the *shorting of sustainability*, as I describe it in this book - was not unexpected, even if its severity has surprised many. In truth, parts of it were avoidable, and most of us who work in this field have been, in different ways, complicit in its making. Too often we have been more comfortable refining narratives and frameworks than confronting the harder question of delivery, as well as issues of fairness and trust.

What sustainability needs now are not new definitions of the problem, but clearer accounts of action. This book offers an operational perspective, premised on a simple conviction: sustainability is not worth very much unless it is both implementable and implemented. That requires confronting trade-offs, operating under constraint, and accepting responsibility for outcomes that will rarely be neat or universally popular. It also requires letting go of a lingering self-image - as activists operating on the fringes - when sustainability has become an orthodoxy in the eyes of many. With that shift comes privilege, but also responsibility. The task now is not to demand attention, but to earn legitimacy.

*Remaking Sustainability* can be read as the final instalment of a loose trilogy, preceded by *The Social License* (2014) and *The Just Transition* (2024). I did not intend to write another book so soon after the last, but events have a way of accelerating things. Whether this really constitutes a trilogy is debatable, but some of the threads are continuous. This book draws on the social contract thinking of the first, and the systems perspective of the second, while turning more explicitly to the question of how sustainability operates when it is embedded in real organisations, markets, and institutions. In that sense, it feels both like an ending and a beginning. Sustainability, after all, is cyclical: periods of advance are followed by retrenchment, and progress is rarely linear.

There is much to be concerned about in the world today. But the future of sustainability should not be one of those concerns - provided we are willing to change how it is practiced. How we have done things in the past should not be how we act moving forwards. The chapters that follow are written for those who make decisions under pressure: leaders, practitioners, and institutions for whom sustainability is no longer optional, symbolic, or abstract. If the arguments here help clarify where sustainability must now sit, and what it demands of those who carry it forward, then this book will have served its purpose.

Eastbourne, UK                                                                     John Morrison
January 2026

# Acknowledgements

This was an ambitious book to write, and I owe a lot to all of those who helped me with ideas and reading early drafts. I would like to thank Alexandra Guaqueta, Benn Hogan, Daniel Esty, Dan Neale, Elaine Mitchel-Hill, Flynn Lebus, Georg Kell, George Foster, Georgie Erangey, Gerald Pachoud, Giulio Ferrini, Hiro Motoki, Ioannis Ioannou, Isabel Hilton, Jonathan Poole, Julia Batho, Lauren Smart, Liza Young, Luke Wilde, Lucy Amis, Mike Barry, Neill Wilkins, Phil Bennett, Rachel Cowburn-Walden, Rae Lindsay, Rob Cameron, Rita Clifton, Scott Jerbi, Shahila Perumalpillai, Susanne Stormer, Tom Smith, Vanessa Zimmerman, Vasuki Shastry, Vicky Bowman, Will Kernan, William Rook, and Wu Changhua. Beyond this to all my former colleagues at the Institute for Human Rights and Business, and all those other places where I have had the privilege of learning. Thanks to Leslie Morrison as always for all the proof reading. Thanks also to Stephen Partridge and all at Springer Nature for the opportunity and the trust.

**Competing Interests** The author has no competing interests to declare that are relevant to the content of this manuscript.

# Contents

# Acronyms

| | |
|---|---|
| AfDB | African Development Bank |
| AI | Artificial Intelligence |
| API | Application Programming Interface |
| BRSR | Business Responsibility and Sustainability Reporting |
| | CBAM |
| | Carbon Border Adjustment Mechanism |
| CDP | Carbon Disclosure Project |
| CEO | Chief Executive Officer |
| CFO | Chief Financial Officer |
| CHIPS | CHIPS and Science Act |
| COO | Chief Operating Officer |
| COP | Conference of the Parties |
| CPU | Central Processing Unit |
| CSO | Chief Sustainability Officer |
| CSDDD | Corporate Sustainability Due Diligence Directive |
| CSRD | Corporate Sustainability Reporting Directive |
| CTO | Chief Technology Officer |
| DESA | UN Department of Economic and Social Affairs |
| DRC | Democratic Republic of the Congo |
| DRR | Disaster Risk Reduction |
| EBA | Everything But Arms |
| EFRAG | European Financial Reporting Advisory Group |
| EPA | Environmental Protection Agency |

| | |
|---|---|
| ESG | Environmental, Social and Governance |
| ETS | Emissions Trading System |
| EU | European Union |
| EV | Electric Vehicle |
| FAIR | Fair Access to Insurance Requirements |
| G7 | Group of Seven |
| G20 | Group of Twenty |
| GATT | General Agreement on Tariffs and Trade |
| GCC | Gulf Cooperation Council |
| GCEW | Global Commission on the Economics of Water |
| GDP | Gross Domestic Product |
| GERD | Grand Ethiopian Renaissance Dam |
| GHG | Greenhouse Gas |
| GPIF | Government Pension Investment Fund |
| GRI | Global Reporting Initiative |
| GSP | Generalised System of Preferences |
| GW | Gigawatt |
| ICE | Internal Combustion Engine |
| IEA | International Energy Agency |
| IFC | International Finance Corporation |
| IIJA | Infrastructure Investment and Jobs Act |
| ILO | International Labour Organization |
| IRA | Inflation Reduction Act |
| ISO | International Organization for Standardization |
| ISSB | International Sustainability Standards Board |
| MDB | Multilateral Development Bank |
| MPT | Modern Portfolio Theory |
| NAFTA | North American Free Trade Agreement |
| NGO | Non-Governmental Organization |
| NZBA | Net-Zero Banking Alliance |
| OBBB | One Big Beautiful Bill Act |
| OECD | Organisation for Economic Co-operation and Development |
| PQC | Post-Quantum Cryptography |
| RMI | Rocky Mountain Institute |
| SDGs | Sustainable Development Goals |
| SME | Small and Medium-Sized Enterprise |
| TCFD | Task Force on Climate-related Financial Disclosures |
| TNFD | Taskforce on Nature-related Financial Disclosures |

| | |
|---|---|
| UN | United Nations |
| UNFCCC | United Nations Framework Convention on Climate Change |
| UNEP | United Nations Environment Programme |
| UNGPs | UN Guiding Principles on Business and Human Rights |
| UK | United Kingdom |
| US | United States |
| WEF | World Economic Forum |
| WTO | World Trade Organization |

# Part I

## Finding Bedrock

# 1

# Shorting Sustainability

At some point during the past few years, the idea of 'sustainability' moved from the fringes to the mainstream. Precisely when this happened is a matter of debate.[1] Climate change, in particular, has seeped into the public consciousness, in one form or another, almost everywhere.[2] Whilst sustainability is now a central concern, especially for the young, it is often framed and affected by a variety of local factors.[3] There is, however, much less consensus on the forms of action that must be taken and a lack of trust in how the choices are being made.

When Rachel Carson submitted an article about the indiscriminate and harmful effects of the pesticide DDT in the US to the Reader's Digest magazine, nearly 70 years ago, it was rejected.[4] DDT had revolutionised farming and medicine because it eliminated nearly all insects from the natural environment where it was applied, including malaria-carrying mosquitos. Its inventor – a Swiss chemist - had won the Nobel Prize for Medicine.[5] So instead, she wrote her book *Silent Spring*,[6] published in 1962. This work is often credited with having started modern environmentalism, but it remained at the margins. DDT was not banned in the US for another 10 years despite the scientific evidence, and internationally not for another 30 years after that.[7] When I began working in this


J. Morrison, *Remaking Sustainability*, https://doi.org/10.1007/978-3-032-23755-2_1

area in the 1980s, sustainability still felt marginal. So was it when Al Gore shocked the world with his surprise hit documentary film "*Inconvenient Truth*[8]" about climate change in 2006 that sustainability started to move centre stage? Or when the United Nations agreed its set of 17 ambitious Sustainable Development Goals (SDGs) in 2015?[9]

Wind forward to 2025 and it is strange to think that sustainability had become the established orthodoxy. By this I don't mean it was prioritised by most governments or companies in practice; clearly implementation has a long way to go. But rather that by the end of the first quarter of the twenty-first century, sustainability had become ubiquitous: regarded as a central issue in politics by both its proponents and opponents. This premise might be hard to stomach on both sides. Many environmentalists still see themselves as activists and not part of the established order, while those committed to the status quo – for reasons of money, power, or livelihood - resist alternatives.

This book starts from the current moment of pushback and accepts that significant mistakes have been made. Chief among them was underestimating how deeply sustainability is embedded in the functioning of the global economy and society itself. As sustainability moved from aspiration to orthodoxy, it was too often treated as a parallel agenda rather than an operational condition. *Remaking Sustainability* therefore means grounding it in the bedrock of how global systems actually function - in capital allocation, trade, technology, governance, and delivery. This book examines those systems directly, recognising that business is not an external actor but an intrinsic part of how planetary and developmental goals are realised. At bedrock, sustainability is no longer a claim or a narrative, but the *sustainability* of sustainability itself.


## 1.1   Sustainability as an Orthodoxy

2025 will be remembered as the year in which the new US administration and several European politicians explicitly turned away from climate goals and much else besides. The events of 2025 were widely characterised as being a 'backlash' against sustainability (or 'greenlash').[10] But you can't have a backlash unless you are pushing back against some perceived dogma. Whether we like it or not, sustainability has become an orthodoxy. And our refusal to embrace this, or to acknowledge the responsibilities that flow from that position of authority, is part of the challenge that now confronts us. I never imagined I would start this book in this way. It feels a strange thing to say that we are more powerful than we think we are. It still doesn't feel this way. But much of what I observe and the arguments I advance in this book do not make sense unless we start with the premise that much of the pushback against sustainability stems from the agenda's successes and not its impotence. If sustainability were not such a potent proposition, why would it be taking so much heat? Of the plethora of executive orders that came from the White House at the start of 2025, 70% of them were to reduce or prevent some potential environmental and/or social action.[11] In Europe, the June 2024 European Union parliamentary elections showed a 25% drop in green party seats and a sharp rise in representation for climate-sceptic parties.[12] Sustainability is now pervasive, regardless of which side of the argument you are on. Though of course, there should be differences of opinion, room for arguments and a range of sides – indeed that's part of the nuance missing from the current reductionist debate.

Two premises for my book sit in tension with each other. The first, is that certain dynamics are perhaps inevitable once concepts like sustainability mature into mainstream organising principles. The second, is the sense that the movement itself made choices that intensified or shaped the character of the pushback. In other words, things are worse than they needed to be and there are lessons to be learned. The backlash arose precisely because sustainability has become one of the most powerful organising ideas of our time. And to guide sustainability forward, we must expect greater humility, quiet self-confidence, and better leadership, from what has been loosely called the 'sustainability movement'. In fact, it is a moment for significant reform of the movement itself. Perhaps the mainstreaming of sustainability means we are no longer a movement at all but now implementers. It forces a scale up of action, a firmer operational ground.

## 1.2    A 'Time of Monsters'

The current messiness of it all perhaps should not be surprising. As Georg Kell and colleagues remind us in their article published soon after the 2025 pushback started:

> *In transitioning from one sustainability regime to another, leaders should not expect an orderly or predictable trajectory, but rather a complex and confusing liminal period, or what Italian philosopher Antonio Gramsci termed "a time of monsters.*[13]

I confess to be a sucker for this kind of invocation, and any use of the word 'liminal', but some kind of pushback was to be expected, and might - in some ways - be an opportunity. None of us should be surprised by the fact that there is a pushback. Sustainability itself has grown in a cyclical way, with retreats in the early 1990s and then again after the Financial Crisis of 2008–9, which ended much generic 'corporate social responsibility' (CSR).[14] These retreats were uncomfortable at the time but did serve a purpose and sustainability bounced back stronger each time. Yet the severity and form of the current pushback, in my opinion, are in significant part a result of the conduct, priorities, and internal discipline of the sustainability movement itself. Many of us have been negligent in not managing the sustainability agenda responsibly or effectively. It is for this reason that so much arbitrage has emerged, currently exploited by some businesses and politicians alike. There is money to be made, and political futures to be forged, on the false claim that the premises of the sustainability agenda are exaggerated or just 'fake news'. I have chosen the term 'shorting' not to infer that bets against sustainability always respond as would a financial market, although they can. Rather because it short-circuits the system, cutting away complexity and nuance for short-term gain, with potentially destructive results in the medium to long-term.

Allied to this is the perception that it is the sustainability movement and its orthodoxy that is pushing for increased public sacrifice as the global economy pursues a series of transitions towards rebalancing itself within planetary constraints.[15] Those exploiting this predicament, are milking hard dilemmas for their own ends. This includes the legitimate concern that it will be those with least to give that will be required to bear the largest load. Traditional working communities, least developed economies, and indigenous populations, very likely will feel the brunt of this change. But when workers are rightly worried about their livelihoods and their jobs, it becomes easy to cast those advocating for transition as callous, and seductive to paint a vision of the future that is a return to some halcyon non-existent past of full employment with decent wages, good family values, when petrol/gas was cheap, and when the trains ran on time.

Concern amongst many rural agricultural voters is not just with the effects of climate change and other environmental challenges, but over the impact that transitions might have and that the pain of these transitions will not be evenly shared. There is a perception – rightly or wrongly held – that sustainability places the interests of urban elites above those of rural,[16] poorer communities who must bear the effects of reforms in agriculture, the end of subsidies, higher taxes for farmers, as well as the installation of windfarms, solar panels, and new electrical transmission lines.[17] Such feelings have fuelled protests by farmers in India and Europe and lie behind how many Republicans in the US view, or portray, sustainability.[18] These anxieties are clearly exploited by many who wish to 'short' sustainability, but they have not been meaningfully addressed by environmentalists. The systems-thinking that sits behind a lot of sustainability policy is essential but it has tended to emphasize the global over the local. At the end of the day, the impacts of sustainability are felt locally. Yet those opposing climate action have been much more effective at using place-based thinking and articulating people's local needs than those advocating for it. This is one of the dichotomies that I will return to throughout this book.

## 1.3   A Failure to Deliver

You don't need to agree with the current pushback from those wishing to short sustainability to conclude that sustainability has some fundamental problems. Sustainability has failed to deliver much of what it promised. The United Nations reports that governments are only on course to meet

35% of the milestones agreed under the 2015–30 SDGs . The persistent challenges that remain in the 2025 SDG review included the 800 million people still living in extreme poverty, the 1 in 11 people facing hunger, over 1 billion people living in slums or informal settlements, and the number of forcibly displaced people had more than doubled since 2015.[19] After steady increases, official development assistance (ODA) fell by 7.1% in 2024, and significantly further in 2025.[20] Systemic disadvantages continued to harm women, persons with disabilities, and marginalized communities. Progress on some issues had even been reversed, including on obesity, press freedom, sustainable nitrogen management, extinction rates, and corruption.[21] The reasons given for being so far off-track included conflicts, climate change, rising inequality, and insufficient financing.[22] Debt repayments by low- and middle-income countries reached $1.4 trillion in 2023, while the annual SDG financing gap in developing countries stood at $4 trillion in 2025.[23] The UN underscored six transformative priorities for the remaining five years (2025–30), focusing on food systems, sustainable and universal energy access, digital connectivity, education reform, jobs and social protection, and climate and biodiversity action.[24]

The *Tony Blair Institute for Global Change* brought some controversial realism about climate action to the table in April 2025 when reflecting on the lack of progress.[25] They argued that the world is nowhere near the level of action required to meet Net Zero commitments by 2050. The central paradox is that whilst levels of awareness about the climate problem have continued to rise, the consensus around the action to be taken is diminishing. There are several critical strategic problems.[26] The lack of political momentum is feeding itself, as the public become more apprehensive, political voices raise fresh fears, feeding further apprehension. Promises of green jobs and cheaper energy have yet to materialise in many countries, and as China increasingly dominates on renewable energy, electric vehicles (EVs) and other essential investments, renewables can be framed as 'foreign' or 'unpatriotic' by other governments.[27] There is also a tragedy of the commons, those countries taking action can feel they are carrying the free-riders and inactions of others. Plenty of examples of races to the bottom, or vicious cycles.

The reality of climate transitions is also that most high-carbon assets have yet to close.[28] In my experience, most planned 'transitions' are still actually 'diversifications', with new energy needs being met through renewable energy or energy efficiencies, whilst legacy coal or gas-powered energy is kept in place. Even the UK Government, that closed its last coal-fired power station in 2024 (after 142 years of coal burning),[29] intervened to maintain the Scunthorpe steel blast furnaces in 2025. The reasons were justifiable (every single member of parliament voted for it in an emergency weekend convening of parliament) but it is a coal-powered resource, at least for the time being.[30] Meanwhile, oil and gas exploration is being ramped up everywhere again after a short hiatus. The pain of transition is largely still to come and with it the tensions around what is a 'just' transition and what is not.

This failure to deliver on most sustainability commitments yet reinforces the idea that they are not, in fact, as urgent or essential as they are claimed to be. Climate advocates will point to the radical transformation of China and its production of EVs, solar and wind.[31] But climate sceptics will point to the maintenance of coal and gas assets in the same country. Both realities are true at the same time, but each undermines the other. Delivery is arguably the only way through the current impasse, when governments and businesses start voting with their feet and investments.

## 1.4   Bursting the Bubble

The sages on the Brundtland Commission were not wrong in setting an intergenerational vision for sustainable development in 1987. Now nearly forty years later, we are upon the threshold of transgressing planetary boundaries with potential run-away effects that leave future generations with no way back. Few would deny the world faces environmental and social challenges, but would argue about what the priorities are, who sets them, and how policies are applied. It is here that the sustainability movement has made some significant mistakes, which have been co-opted by those wishing to short sustainability more generally. There is a 'sustainability bubble' of confusing acronyms, misleading and overstated claims, and performative behaviour which was not sufficiently criticised by environmentalists or business executives, and now are the 'hostages to fortune' for those shorting the system. The bubble should have been burst several years ago. Instead, it will be burst now but with more severe effect - bolstering and prolonging the current pushback. Here are a few examples of what I mean.

## The 'Notorious ESG'

Attacking 'Environmental, Social, Governance' (ESG) has become something of an obsession amongst Republican lawmakers in the US over recent years, more than in any other jurisdiction in the world. Since 2021 there have been over 480 state-level legislative proposals to block ESG investments, with over 50 laws enacted, according to the 'Anti-ESG Tracker' kept by Pleiades Strategy.[32] But ESG has also been increasingly attacked from within the sustainability movement itself. Vasuki Shastry is one of those who has written extensively about the "hype, hoopla, and hysteria" of the ESG industry.[33] In his 2023 book, 'The Notorious ESG' (surely still one of the best titles for any book in the sustainability field) he drew on his own experience in the finance sector to ask whether or not ESG was not just a "massive virtue-signalling operation" by so-called 'sustainability CEOs'.[34] Shastry finds that in trying to be all things to all people, ESG's current crisis is largely of its own making. At its core, ESG was developed as a tool for investors to make better decisions. He echoes the sentiments of Stuart Kirk, a former asset manager at HSBC, in wishing to separate 'ESG-inputs' from 'ESG-output'.[35] It is much less contentious to evaluate environmental, social and governance data when trying to calculate the potential risk-adjusted returns of an asset. In fact, 'ESG-inputs' make good strategic sense for any non-ideological investor. But 'ESG-output' is the whole issue of what is material to a business's actual financial performance, a much more contested space and one that is progressing slowly and carefully through initiatives such as the *International Sustainability Standards Board* (ISSB).[36] By mixing and confusing these two sustainability needs, ESG has done a disservice to both.

But the sustainability critique of ESG goes much wider. Many businesses have seen 'ESG' and 'sustainability' as synonymous and interchangeable, with many sustainability professionals rebranding themselves as ESG leaders. And so, in these companies every environmental or social policy, speech, or CEO comment was branded as 'ESG'. ESG became almost the entire business-sustainability interface even though ESG at its origins had a much narrower set of interests, those of investors. The trend reduced the whole complexity of sustainability policy and narratives into a set of measurements, compounding the undeniable reality that some aspects of sustainability are much more measurable and financially consequential than others. 'Carbon emissions' can be calculated in kilogrammes, and there is talk of a carbon price, whilst human rights much less so. Whilst it felt to many that bringing the 'E', 'S' and 'G' together into one acronym was breaking down silos, it has acted to reinforce them. ESG does little to assist with 'nexus issues' (a big focus of this book) and the reality that almost all the key business-sustainability strategic questions are a blend of two or more ESG issues, from across the different silos, in addition to other business imperatives. The bringing together the very different traditions of environmentalism, social justice and development, as well as good governance, into one ill-defined framework, with no methodological underpinnings, was unlikely to work.[37] It is an easy gift to all those wishing to dismiss sustainability as 'woke capitalism'.

Many leapt on the ESG bandwagon with many different motivations. For some environmentalists, ESG seemed to be a way of (at last) bringing business to heal, for investors it seemed a way to achieve a new form of asset class with increased returns, for business leaders and their companies to acquire new forms of legitimacy, and for governmental regulators as a means for better regulation. With such competing claims, broad-based ESG was bound to fail. This does not mean that there is no place for a more focused version of ESG in *Remaking Sustainability* as I will return to in Chap. 4. Investor needs have not disappeared. But the ESG bubble needed bursting, and in this regard, those shorting sustainability have done us all a favour.

## Climate Tunnel Vision

The world has successfully siloed its sustainability issues from each other. At the start, the Rio Earth Summit in 1992 provided a unity of vision,[38] but implementation came in three tracks: climate, desertification (water and land), and biodiversity – each with its own 'Conference of the Parties' or sequence of COPs. The extent to which climate has come to dominate all other considerations is reflected in the fact that the climate COP is the only COP many people have heard of, and that UNFCCC is already at COP30, whilst the others lag halfway behind.

It is true that climate is an existential issue but is it THE existential issue in the way many would have us believe. As far as the *Economist* Magazine is concerned, it is arguably the only aspect of sustainability that is presently material to business in a financial sense, the only bit of 'ESG' worth the sweat.[39] But the work of Johann Rockström and the *Stockholm Resilience Centre*[40] remind us of the systemic nature of the 'poly-crisis' we are facing. There are at least nine planetary boundaries that we transgress at our peril, and we have now over-stepped seven of them. Given the nexus between environmental issues, you don't solve the climate by focusing on climate alone.

I would go one step further; you don't solve environmental issues by focusing on the environment alone. The exclusion of most social impact considerations from the Climate COP process has been an eye opener for me – as a relatively recent newcomer with only four COPs (Glasgow – Dubai – Sharm El Sheik – Baku) under my belt. The Climate Justice movement has been successful in getting some voices to the table, in particular indigenous peoples. However, the social consequences of the climate action required have largely been ignored by decision-makers until recently (COP30 in Belem). A reference to a 'just transition' was in the preamble to the Paris Climate Agreement in 2015 but it was only in 2025 that a work programme between state parties was agreed.[41] Many shied away from introducing social complexity into science-based targets, fearing it would open the door to climate deniers. Yet the opposite has proven to be true. Not including issues affecting people twenty years ago and, the implications for working and low-income people, has contributed to the intensity of the current backlash. As with Frankenstein, we have helped in the creation of our own monster.

## Too Much Compartmentalisation

As I have already said, I think 'ESG' is one of the worst offenders here. There have been many others. How did everything environmental become about climate? How did everything about climate become about mitigation, and not also about adaptation and resilience? How did human rights become just about the *UN Guiding Principles on Business and Human Rights*, and how did these become mainly about human rights due diligence? I could go on, but you get the point: the 'tyranny of the silos' and the 'treachery of the lists'.[42] I fear we have forgotten what sustainability is really about, in the way that Gro Harlem Brundtland and her commission wrote about it in 1987, or how human rights were described by Eleanor Roosevelt and her commission in 1948.[43]

Many of us have given presentations about the 'alphabet soup' of sustainability. Showing lecture theatres that we know our CSDDD from our CSRD, our TCFD from our TNFDs, our ISOs from GRIs, and our ISSB from our EFRAG. Again, I could go on. I won't bother expanding these acronyms now as this is not the point here. Is it UNGPs or UNGP? Each of these standards has its place – but you know when a movement becomes so acronym heavy you are heading for trouble. Even 20 years ago, there was a publication called the 'Codes Book'[44] which tried to keep a map of all the corporate social responsibility standards that were emerging, I think its author just gave up trying to keep up. Even the term 'sustainability' has its limits, as I discuss in Chap. 19, but it gets you much further than the acronyms. There are now significant efforts to consolidate these standards underway, but it has taken us a very long time.

## Too Much Performing, Not Enough Performance

Two terms I will return to a lot in this book are 'greenwashing' and 'greenhushing'. Each has its own chapters (Chap. 17 and Chap. 18 respectively) when I get onto the 'how' the retelling of sustainability might happen in practice. The former speaks to the false and misleading claims businesses, and their CEOs, have all too often made when undertaking 'performative sustainability'. The latter refers to the lack of disclosures and communication about what is really going on. These are the 'evil twins' in a symbiotic dance. Greenwashing played a central part in creating the sustainability bubble, while greenhushing has contributed to the bubble's demise by obscuring the true nature of what we are up against and what needs to be done.

The fact is that businesses have been hushing for a long time. It has just become more pernicious and has also been given a name. In the UK, the modern slavery statements issued by companies over the last 10 years to comply with the law are a case in point.[45] With a notable few good exceptions, they have been an act of minimalism: the minimum to comply with law. And these businesses have a point. There is so little public or political awareness of how supply chains really work, or that the risk of forced labour exists within many complex business relationships. Honesty is unlikely to be rewarded. Unfortunately, the law has not developed far enough nor quickly enough to make transparency the norm, to make the violation not that the risk is present but rather your denials or inactions. The fact that hushing has had an added boost from Pennsylvania Avenue and that the European Union has drawn back the scope of its mandatory due diligence, will just make things worse.

## 1.5    A Social Licence for Sustainability

We need to question the legitimacy of the sustainability claims we make. By this I do not mean their scientific basis or even the imperative for us to live within planetary boundaries. I accede to these; in fact, I advocate for them. But what I do think we lack is social licence for the action that must be taken because of accepting these realities. Not only does this social licence not exist but we have only recently accepted the fact we even need one.[46] Many would deny this still, stating that scientific evidence alone, as well as doom-laden assertions of opinion leaders and celebrities, is sufficient to propel us forward. But if the current pushback is teaching us anything, it should be that these things are far from enough if we want populations to be willing to take the steps into the unknown; with the associated sacrifices required and the opportunities to be realised.

I always think about social licence in social contract terms.[47] Therefore, the legitimacy, trust and consent that will be required cannot be won directly, they are earned through managing and delivering on a second tier of considerations. As often stated, a 'social licence' is not a piece of paper, but its absence can become a very tangible issue resulting in opposition and even conflict.[48] First among these secondary considerations is that the benefits for the communities and individuals concerned must be clearly stated. Social licence as a form of social contract requires spelling out not just the potential beneficial outcomes but also the associated risks to those most affected by them. Attention should also be given to consent-based factors: recognising power relationships, knowledge, and participation in the key processes to define any community's sustainability journey. Finally, there are justice-based considerations that need to be baked in - transparency, accountability, risk mitigation and prevention, and (when required) effective remedies. These are all operational considerations. If 'sustainability' itself requires social licence, then these considerations need to be at the bedrock.

Creating a social licence for sustainability is the purpose of this book, and to do so in impact-led operational terms. Whilst it is not the explicit title of any of the chapters, it is in the DNA of *Remaking Sustainability*. There are three golden threads that are woven into this tapestry: good economic sense, engaging all stakeholders including the dissenters, and the need to act locally within a global context:

## Sustainability Needs to Make Economic Sense

There are clearly significant business opportunities within sustainability, particularly if business is willing to step up rather than step down during the current pushback and help to reshape markets.[49] But when undertaking research for this book, and in the interviews with politicians and senior business executives, a common refrain is that business customers, or consumers, are not willing to pay a 'sustainability price premium'.

Whilst there are some notable exceptions to this, as will come out later in the book, it is an uncomfortable reality that while doing the right thing does often cost more, the customer is unwilling to pay for it. For most people living in most countries, food and energy prices are crushingly high and there is little ability to pay more. This is also increasingly true for poorer segments of the population in industrialised countries as much as emerging markets. Although absolute poverty remains an issue for poor countries, wealth disparity is everywhere and increasing nearly everywhere.

But when discussing this affordability issue more deeply, there are several important nuances. First, what matters most is value not price. This brings in issues such as product quality, longevity, and effectiveness – and sits behind the trust between customer and seller.[50] It means that customers might be willing to pay a little more at point of purchase, if the value proposition is stronger. This is critical for understanding the growth in the circular economy trends that are emerging in fashion and household furniture and interiors, for example. It is also why some of the world's poorest will pay a little more for a detergent sachet from a trusted brand.[51] Sustainability and value need not be a zero-sum game; there is a vibrant array of viable sustainability solutions emerging from start-ups and entrepreneurs.[52] But it is also the case for better regulation. Market logic only gets you so far. Several of the larger transitions that need to be made require state-backed finance and legislation to level the playing field, redistribute resources accordingly, and create new incentives and disincentives for business.

## The Need to Engage the Confused and the Dissenters

*Remaking Sustainability* requires engagement with everyone, including those who are uncertain or openly opposed. As noted at the start of this chapter, books, films, and protests over the past two decades have succeeded in bringing sustainability - particularly climate change - into global consciousness, building on environmental work from the second half of the twentieth century. But we have now reached a critical juncture. Many people are no longer asking *whether* sustainability matters, but what it will mean for their own lives: what choices they will face, what costs they will bear, and what sacrifices will be expected of them? The sustainability movement has struggled to answer these questions clearly. In doing so, it has created a vacuum that has been filled by misinformation and by voices actively opposed to sustainability action. This opposition must be taken seriously. Many concerns are legitimate and rooted in long-standing mistrust, shaped by past behaviour of governments and businesses. For much of the last century, environmental movements shared these same scepticisms, as did social justice movements built on the experiences of workers, including mining communities and trade unions. There are important examples of workers developing credible climate transition narratives within their own communities, but these remain too limited and too rare.

One of the biggest challenges for operationalising sustainability is difficult discussions about trade-offs; recognising community concerns in the face of economic transitions, on the one hand, but not caving into NIMBYism and excessive planning restrictions, on the other.[53] Therefore, the method of engagement is critical, and a *Remade Sustainability* needs to be replete with the capabilities to reassure that there is some level of equity and fairness in how decisions will be made. This includes how business operationalises sustainability, as I will turn to in Chaps. 14–16, and in how sustainability is retold, in Chaps. 17–19.

## 'Think Global, Act Local'

The need to think globally but act locally has long been a mantra of green politics since the early 1970s. Ironically, or perhaps not ironically, many of the populists who are shorting sustainability at the moment are more the reverse - 'think local, act global' - in orientation, which is the antithesis of sustainability I would argue, as might they. Somehow, much of the contemporary sustainability movement has forgotten its roots. We do focus on impact assessments which are very project-based and identifying 'affected stakeholders', who might or might not be place-based, but this is not the same as organising and communicating locally. The sustainability professionals of today are largely city-based and well educated, but many have never milked a cow, killed a fish, or mended an engine. I don't mean this factiously, it matters. Time and time again in focus groups and opinion polls, sustainability is seen as a national or international agenda imposed on localities, not arising from within them – a sentiment particularly felt in rural areas as already stated.[54]

So, when *Remaking Sustainability*, there is a necessary tension between the global and local. We most definitely need good global thinking. By this I mean not just multilateralism and United Nations meetings, but systems-thinking that points out the interdependence and interrelatedness of all aspects of sustainability, to each other but also to wider bedrock issues. Systems-thinking means focusing in on nexus issues, identifying the bottlenecks and finding ways of exercising leverage effectively. I will come back to these issues throughout the book and more specifically in Chaps. 14–16.

But alongside this, we will need much stronger local relevance. Whilst there are many good case studies of sustainability in practice within local communities, such as regenerative agriculture, and small-scale circular economies, these are far too few and far between. Instead, we need a multitude of diverse approaches across every corner of the planet, all with local champions. Some approaches will work much better than others, and some will fail. There can be no 'cutting and pasting' of successful models but there can be inspiration, dialogue and – what a quantum physicist might call – 'entanglement' (a trailer for Chap. 13). Because, ultimately, the local is the global and the global is the local.

And one final thought on the social licence of sustainability. You will note I refer to the 'sustainability movement' at points during the book and even invoke the plural pronoun 'we' occasionally. I am not making any assumptions here, that there is such as singular movement or that you, or I, are legitimate members of it. There is excellent literature on social movements that suggests that the sustainability movement is not unique in facing some of its current travails, in particular the tension between institutionalisation and fragmentation.[55] I will not get into this here; the subject is worthy of several books in its own right. I use the term 'sustainability movement' loosely acknowledging its limitations.

## 1.6    Finding a Better Place to Stand

So, what replaces the sustainability "bubble" and helps restore its social licence? This book, *Remaking Sustainability*, argues that the answer lies in a more results-oriented approach: what I describe as *bedrock sustainability*. The central claim is simple. Sustainability impact matters most when it shapes real decisions, produces measurable outcomes, and affects people's lives in tangible ways - particularly through the actions of organisations, and especially businesses.

This book is written with a focus on two groups. The first is people the book is 'about', those who are already experiencing - or fear they soon will - the real consequences of sustainability failure or poorly designed sustainability action in their everyday lives: hunger, loss of housing or livelihoods, reduced autonomy, insecurity, or threats to personal safety. Sustainability is ultimately place-based, and "bedrock" is not an abstract idea. For that reason, people, more than systems or institutions, are the central object of this book.

The second group is those the book is 'for': those whose operational decisions most directly shape these outcomes. These decision-makers exist across government, business, trade unions, and civil society, but this book focuses primarily on business leadership. In particular, it speaks to executive-level decision-makers who influence strategy, capital allocation, technology choices, and market behaviour: Chief Executive Officers, Chief Financial Officers, Chief Technology Officers, Managing Directors, Country Managers, and others with direct operational authority. While Chief Sustainability Officers may be the ones most likely to pick up this book, it is written just as deliberately for those whose roles are not labelled "sustainability," but whose decisions determine whether sustainability succeeds or fails in practice. If the operational case for sustainability can be made convincingly, much of the broader debate begins to shift.

Before developing that case, Chap. 2 revisits how sustainability was first constructed and identifies the foundational principles that must be retained. Chapter 3 then returns to the question of *Remaking Sustainability*, setting out the "bedrock" areas on which a more operational approach can be built. The remainder of the book is structured in two parts. The first examines *what* remade sustainability means in practice across investment (Chaps. 4–7), value chains (Chaps. 8–10), and technology (Chaps. 11–13). The second part focuses on *how* sustainability can be delivered from within business, addressing leadership, governance, systems, and metrics (Chaps. 14–19), before concluding with final reflections in Chap. 20.

## Notes

1. Andrew Winston, *Sustainable Business Went Mainstream in 2021*, Harvard Business Review, 27 December 2021.
2. United Nations, *Peoples Climate Vote 2024*, UNDP, 27 June 2024.
3. For example, Pew Research Center, *How Republications view climate change and energy issues*, 1 March 2024.
4. NRDC, *The Story of Silent Spring*, 13 August 2015.
5. New York Times, *DDT wins the Nobel Prize*, 30 October 1948.
6. Rachel Carson, *Silent Spring*, 1962.
7. US Government, *DDT – A brief history and status*, Environmental Protection Agency, (website), November 2025.
8. Al Gore, *An Inconvenient Truth*, (film and book), 2006
9. United Nations, *Sustainable Development Goals*, 2015.
10. Erin Jones and Richard Youngs, *Confronting backlash against Europe's green transition*, Carnegie Endowment for International Peace, 11 September 2025.
11. UBS Editorial Team, US politics and policies, *Sustainable investing, The beginning of climate change pushback?* 7 May 2025.
12. Erin Jones and Richard Youngs, *Confronting backlash against Europe's green transition*, Carnegie Endowment for International Peace, 11 September 2025.
13. Georg Kell, Martin Reeves and Helena Fox, *What Should Companies Do Now?* Harvard Business Review, 22 April 2025.
14. Futerra, *Ride the Waves: Part One*, December 2025.
15. John Morrison, *The Just Transition: A systems-thinking approach to managing climate action*, 2024.
16. See for example: Stine Hesstvedt and Jo Saglie, *The urban-rural cleavage: Analysing more than 40 years of Norwegian survey data*, Electoral Studies, 96, August 2025; or Emily Pechar Diamond et al. *Rural Attitudes on*

*Climate Change: Lessons from National and Midwest Polling and Focus Groups*, Nicholas Institute for Environmental Policy Solutions, 2020; or Thora Tenbrink, *Survey reveals 'very rural' as least concerned about climate change*, Bangor University, 5 September 2023.

17. John Morrison, *The Just Transition: A systems-thinking approach to managing climate action*, 2024.
18. Pew Research Center, *How Republications view climate change and energy issues*, 1 March 2024.
19. Martina Igini, *None of 17 UN SDGs on Track to Be Achieved By 2030*, Earth.org, 24 June 2025.
20. OECD, *International aid falls in 2024 for the first time in six years, says OECD,* 15 April 2025.
21. Martina Igini, *None of 17 UN SDGs on Track to Be Achieved By 2030*, Earth.org, 24 June 2025.
22. Martina Igini, *None of 17 UN SDGs on Track to Be Achieved By 2030*, Earth.org, 24 June 2025.
23. United Nations, *Annual Sustainable Development Goals Report: 2025 edition*, UN Department of Economic and Social Affairs, 16 July 2025.
24. United Nations, *Annual Sustainable Development Goals Report: 2025 edition*, UN Department of Economic and Social Affairs, 16 July 2025.
25. Lindy Fursman, *Why we need to reset action on climate change*, Tony Blair Institute for Global Change, 29 April 2025.
26. Lindy Fursman, *Why we need to reset action on climate change*, Tony Blair Institute for Global Change, 29 April 2025.
27. Georg Kell, *Background Paper: Business Responsibility & Sustainability: New realities and conflicting signals*, Global Compact Network Germany, October 2025.
28. John Morrison, *The Just Transition: A systems-thinking approach to managing climate action*, 2024.
29. BBC News, *UK to finish with coal-power after 142 years*, 30 September 2024.
30. BBC News, *Minister says 'bright future' for steelmaking*, 6 November 2025.
31. Georg Kell, *Background Paper: Business Responsibility & Sustainability: New realities and conflicting signals*, Global Compact Network Germany, October 2025.
32. Pleiades Strategy, *Live Anti-ESG State Action Tracker*, (website), December 2025.
33. Vasuki Shastry, *The Notorious ESG*, 2023.

34. Vasuki Shastry, *The Notorious ESG*, 2023.

35. Stuart Kirk, *ESG is existentiality flawed and must be split into two*, Financial Times, 2 September 2022.

36. IFRS Foundation, *About the International Sustainability Standards Board*, 2025.

37. Kristen Talman, *How 'ESG' came to mean everything and nothing*, BBC Earth, 15 November 2023.

38. United Nations, *Conference on Environment and Development*, 1992.

39. The Economist, *ESG Investing: A broken system needs urgent repairs*, 21 July 2022.

40. Stockholm Resilience Centre, *Planetary Boundaries*, 2025.

41. John Morrison, *The Just Transition: A systems-thinking approach to managing climate action*, 2024.

42. John Morrison, *The Just Transition: A systems-thinking approach to managing climate action*, 2024.

43. United Nations, *Universal Declaration of Human Rights*, 10 December 1948.

44. Deborah Leipziger, *The Corporate Responsibility Code Book*, 2003.

45. UK Government, Section 54 of the *Modern Slavery Act*, 2015.

46. John Morrison, *The Just Transition: A systems-thinking approach to managing climate action*, 2024.

47. John Morrison, *The Social License: How to keep your organisation legitimate*, 2014.

48. John Morrison, *The Social License: How to keep your organisation legitimate*, 2014.

49. Cambridge Institute for Sustainability Leadership, *Competing in the age of disruption*, University of Cambridge, 7 April 2025.

50. Interviews with business leaders conducted when researching this book between July 2025 and January 2026.

51. Interviews with business leaders conducted when researching this book between July 2025 and January 2026.

52. John Elkington, *Green Swans: The coming boom in regenerative capitalism*, 2020.

53. John Morrison, *The Just Transition: A systems-thinking approach to managing climate action*, 2024.

54. Op cit. See for example: Stine Hesstvedt and Jo Saglie, *The urban-rural cleavage: Analysing more than 40 years of Norwegian survey data*, Electoral Studies, 96, August 2025; or Emily Pechar Diamond et al. *Rural Attitudes*

*on Climate Change: Lessons from National and Midwest Polling and Focus Groups*, Nicholas Institute for Environmental Policy Solutions, 2020; or Thora Tenbrink, *Survey reveals 'very rural' as least concerned about climate change*, Bangor University, 5 September 2023,

55. Thanking Lucy Amis for this observation. See, for example, the work of George Lundberg on social movements, and the frameworks and typologies developed by Alain Touraine, Ronald Inglehart, Jurgen Habermas, Alberto Melucci, Steve Buechler, or James Jasper.

# 2

# How Sustainability Was Made

When considering how humanity regards its planetary home, there are two images that possibly come to mind. The first is 'Earthrise', taken from Apollo 8 in 1968 as it orbited the Moon and the Earth rose above the Moon's horizon.[1] It has been described as "the most influential environmental photograph ever taken." Its message to all of us is clear. This is our home. And it is beautiful, precious and irreplaceable. A "marbled bowling ball" as Joni Mitchell put it. Technically, the Earth doesn't rise in the lunar sky as the Moon does in our sky, as it is tidally locked with one face of the Earth. It "rose" because the spacecraft was moving. The picture also conveys our uniqueness too, witnessing something only those able to explore in outer space could witness.

This second image is the 'Pale Blue Dot' taken from the Voyager 1 space probe in 1990,[2] from an unprecedented 6 billion kilometres from the Earth. The apparent size of the Earth is less than one pixel in diameter. We are unnoticeable in the picture, unless a red circle is drawn to mark the blue dot. Popular scientist of the time, and evermore, Carl Sagan, acknowledged the photo would have little scientific value. However, he still managed to persuade NASA to turn its camera to take one last photo given the uniqueness of the opportunity, an opportunity



J. Morrison, *Remaking Sustainability*, https://doi.org/10.1007/978-3-032-23755-2_2

which has not come again from such a distance. The dot could only be witnessed because of human technology, but the message it conveys is one of insignificance. If we decide to destroy ourselves, and many other lifeforms with us, will the universe even notice?

And so, we are both simultaneously unique and special, but also insignificant. This duality haunts the human psyche. It perhaps also explains the different ways people react to sustainability. It is both the most important thing for any government or business to manage, and the least important at the same time. Are we tending to the Garden of Eden or are we the 'fallen' who can only be redeemed if all earthly things are destroyed? It feels that our politics at the moment is swinging between these two extremes: neurosis or denial. Neither of these are great ways of managing our planet's future.

A better way is that offered by Johann Rockström and the Stockholm Resilience Centre in 2009,[3] that sets out nine planetary boundaries that we transgress at our peril. It is based on a systems approach, viewing all nine boundaries as interconnected and interdependent through our atmosphere, oceans, icesheets, forests and living species. Each of the environmental issues forms a wedge in a circle, creating a complete pie – with the boundaries representing its circumference. We do not yet understand the complexity of the systems that underpin the Holocene (our current planetary equilibrium in geological terms) yet the nine boundaries are the best estimates we have based on known science. Push these boundaries too much and we risk generating new feedback loops such as global warming, the desertification of our oceans and our land, or rapid declines in biodiversity.

## 2.1   The Nine Planetary Boundaries

The Earth has always been in flux. There have been several mass extinction events which have almost wiped-out life on the planet, the most recent being the rapid demise of nearly all dinosaurs when a large asteroid hit the coast of Mexico around 66 million years ago. So rapid change can also be 'natural', and some dismiss our current crisis as part of the normal cut and thrust of Darwinian evolution and survival – the law of the jungle. If all humans are to die, or if most humans are to die, so be it. If you doubt that some of the wealthiest people on the planet already think this way, then pay attention to all the bunkers and hideouts, currently being built in some very remote and inaccessible places.

For those of us who think humanity deserves a little better, Rockström's nine planetary boundary framework is more constructive.[4] Its thesis is that nearly all the planetary challenges we currently face are man-made and therefore we can still define our own destiny. We have reached the juncture where the Holocene is being replaced by a so-called 'Anthropocene' – an age in which human activity is the dominant influence on the environment, not asteroids, solar activity, or the slow coming and going of ice-ages. In geological terms, the Holocene – which is a mere 12,000 years old – must feel a little short changed.

And so, the Anthropocene's nine planetary boundaries over which we tread at our peril are:[5]

1. Climate Change

   The star of the show. Greenhouse gases act like an extra blanket around the planet, trapping heat that would otherwise escape to space. For millennia, carbon dioxide hovered around 280 parts per million. Today it soars past 420. Scientists proposed 350 ppm as the upper boundary - beyond which the risk of runaway feedback loops grows. Humanity crossed that line in the 1980s.

2. Novel Entities

   Perhaps the most enigmatic boundary is that of novel entities: synthetic chemicals, plastics, genetically modified organisms, and other innovations with planetary-scale consequences. Unlike carbon dioxide, these substances are myriad and are poorly monitored. Microplastics drift through the bloodstream of whales and babies alike. Endocrine disruptors meddle with hormones across species. In 2022, researchers concluded this boundary had been exceeded, placing us in a zone of unknown risk.

3. Stratospheric Ozone Depletion

   Here, the story starts to offer a rare note of hope. In the 1980s, scientists discovered a gaping hole in the ozone layer caused by chlorofluorocarbons (CFCs). International action followed swiftly: the

1987 Montreal Protocol phased out ozone-depleting substances.[6] Decades later, the ozone layer is healing. It remains the only planetary boundary we have successfully pulled back from transgressing.

4. Atmospheric Aerosol Loading

Tiny particles suspended in the air, such as soot, sulphates, or dust, alter rainfall, monsoons, and even the brightness of clouds. Their effects are complex, regional, and difficult to pin down. For now, the boundary has not been crossed and lies within the safe zone, though pressures mount. In India, aerosol pollution already reshapes monsoon patterns.[7] In cities, it chokes lungs and shortens lives.

5. Ocean Acidification

The oceans absorb a quarter of human carbon emissions, buffering climate change but at a cost: the water becomes more acidic. Since the Industrial Revolution, ocean acidity has increased by about 30–40%. Coral reefs, shellfish, and plankton struggle to build skeletons in such conditions. By 2025, scientists declared the ocean acidification boundary breached for the first time.[8] The sea, long a stabilizer, is losing its resilience.

6. Biogeochemical Flows

Life depends on nutrients, especially nitrogen and phosphorus. Modern agriculture has supercharged these cycles, with fertilizers seeping into rivers, lakes, and oceans. Dead zones (a condition called 'hypoxia' when oxygen levels drop too low to support life) now bloom in the Gulf of Mexico and the Baltic Sea.[9] Globally, humanity fixes more nitrogen than all natural processes combined. Both nitrogen and phosphorus boundaries have been transgressed.

7. Freshwater Change

Rivers, wetlands, and soil moisture form the veins of the planet. However, dams, irrigation, and deforestation have altered their flow. In 2022, researchers expanded the boundary to include "green water" - the soil moisture available to plants. The result: the freshwater boundary is exceeded. From the desiccated soils of the Sahel to shrinking aquifers in India, the warning signs multiply.

8. Land-System Change

Forests regulate climate, recycle water, and shelter biodiversity. But logging, farming, and urban expansion have shrunk their extent. The planetary boundary specifies safe thresholds for remaining forest cover in key biomes. Globally, we have crossed them, with tropical deforestation in the Amazon and Congo Basin driving the transgression.[10]

9. Biosphere Integrity

The living fabric of Earth - the millions of species and ecosystems - forms its most intricate safety net. Lose too many threads, and the net unravels. Scientists measure biosphere integrity in two ways: genetic diversity (species extinctions) and functional diversity (ecosystem roles). Both are outside safe limits. Indeed, some argue this boundary was crossed in the late nineteenth century, when industrial expansion began erasing habitats at unprecedented speed.[11]

It is really not great that as of the end of 2025, we have overshot seven of the nine environmental boundaries.[12] It would have been 8/9 if we had not been able to pull back on Ozone Depletion, which in itself must offer some hope.

The nine planetary boundaries framework has of course had its critics. For some boundaries - like climate change - thresholds have been well studied. For others, like novel entities, the numbers can seem more arbitrary. Earth systems often degrade gradually rather than flipping at neat tipping points. Was it misleading, critics asked, to present sharp boundaries where the science is a bit fuzzier. Another challenge is scale. The framework is global, yet many problems are regional. Water scarcity varies by basin; nutrient pollution strikes some rivers while sparing others. A global boundary might suggest safety even as local communities collapse. Conversely, global overuse might mask regional abundance.

However, I think the biggest limitation of the nine-planetary boundaries framework is that it ignores us – humanity - the 'wire in the blood'. Where are the politics and the justice? Who decides what counts as safe? Whose development must be curbed to stay within limits? Critics fear that universal boundaries could reinforce inequities, constraining poorer nations that contribute least to the problem. How was such a technocratic framework developed without democratic deliberation?

## 2.2   Raworth on Rockström

The boundaries framework can also overshadow the progress humanity has made over recent decades to respond to many basic development needs. This includes significant reductions in child and maternal mortality, increases in life expectancy in most countries, reductions in hunger and malnutrition, better primary education, access to clean water, and reductions in extreme poverty.[13] We must be able to hold in our minds two truths simultaneously about the world today. Yes - we have made some progress to improve the human condition. Yet there is also increasing evidence to suggest that this social progress might be stalled, or even reversed, because of our failure to do so sustainably, including by abiding by planetary constraints.

This brings us to the work of Kate Raworth and her 'Doughnut Economics'.[14] In her framework, she sees the nine Planetary Boundaries as the 'outer rim' of how humanity ought to constrain its footprint on the world. For her, this needs to be complemented by an 'inner rim' based on social values, as reflected in the United Nation's 17 Sustainable Development Goals (SDGs).[15] The SDGs cover a lot of ground, and try to cover both environmental and social sustainability priorities across issues such as: food security, health, education, income and work, peace and justice, political voice, social equity, gender equality, housing, networks, energy, and water.

The Doughnut has caught the popular imagination and does give us both inner and outer guardrails. Clearly a step in the right direction. By drawing on the SDGs, Raworth tackles the legitimacy question. The SDGs were adopted by nearly all member states of the United Nations in 2015, at the same time as the Paris Climate Agreement was signed. This consensus has held for ten years but is now under threat and is at risk of unravelling. The second Trump administration distanced itself from the consensus in March 2025:

> *Put simply, globalist endeavours like Agenda 2030 and the SDGs lost at the ballot box. Therefore, the United States rejects and denounces the 2030 Agenda for Sustainable Development and the Sustainable Development Goals, and it will no longer reaffirm them as a matter of course.*[16]

You don't have to be a Trump supporter to see the SDGs are in trouble. The fact that most of the milestones will not be reached by 2030 is frustrating. The past 30 years of multilateralism have brought significant progress. When I started my career in human rights and then sustainability in the 1990s, one billion more people lived in extreme poverty than is the case today. Whilst inequality within most nations has increased during this period, it has decreased between global regions – particularly with the economic rise of much of East and Southeast Asia. Globally, child mortality has more than halved, and the number of children trapped in child labour has also nearly halved. Significant progress has been made in combatting several major diseases: including polio, HIV/AIDs, and malaria, while several tropical diseases have been eradicated. Today millions more children are now in school, in particular girls, and virtually everyone on the planet now has access to electricity, with a large majority of people also having access to clean water and sanitation. Over this period, average global life expectancy has risen by over five years.

If you look back through human history and prehistory of the past few millennia, what humanity has achieved over the past 30 years is stunning. While this is no time for us to be self-congratulatory, it is worth taking a moment to reflect on the assessment of the Swedish statistician Hans Rosling, echoed in the words of former US President Barack Obama a decade ago.[17]

*If you had to choose any moment in history in which to be born, you would choose right now. The world has never been healthier, or wealthier, or better educated or in many ways more tolerant or less violent.*[18]

The dry retort nearly ten years later might be that many of us would indeed choose ten years ago as the better time to be alive. Perhaps we had reached 'peak optimism' and now that the social indicators, and not just the environment, are now flashing amber, if not red. There is no Sustainable Development Goal to 'not have a nuclear war', but if there were, then what grade would we be giving ourselves one quarter of the way through the twenty-first century? At the start of the millennium, the then UK Astronomer Royal, Lord Martin Rees, gave humanity a 50%

chance of surviving the twenty-first century.[19] I think we would still take those odds 25 years later.

## 2.3    Beyond Doughnuts and Wedges

The work of Rockstrom, Raworth and many others has been instrumental for many of us working in this space – theirs are the dashboards and frameworks essential for making progress. But they are not enough, especially when navigating the current sustainability backlash, or the many backlashes to come so long as humanity remains humanity. Perhaps there is one set of statistics that explains the current loss in faith more than any other. It is that whilst global inequality between nations has decreased in real terms, within 71% of countries (including all large countries), inequality within each nation has increased. If you were very rich thirty years ago you are likely to be even richer today. The richest 1% of the global population now own 20.6% of global wealth, up from 17.8% in 1980.[20]

Whilst increased national inequality is clearly on the rise, it is not true everywhere. There are some smaller countries in Latin America, the Caribbean, and Central Europe, where national inequality has decreased during this period with greater redistributions of national wealth.[21] So, increases in national inequality are not inevitable. At least in part, they are a matter of national choice.[22] For the world's very poorest, incomes have risen faster than for the entire population in two thirds of the countries that supply data. This is reflected in the progress made towards SDG1 – the eradication of all forms of poverty. But as the French economist Thomas Piketty reminds us, the real issue is not inequality of income, but inequality of wealth.[23] In most places, it is getting harder for young people to acquire the same assets or lifestyle as their parents. And even in countries that are breaking through from being 'least developed' to 'medium developed' economies - of which there are many - the patterns of ownership, of land and property are not really shifting. In most countries, if you are born poor the chances are you will end your life without significant assets to pass on to future generations. And even if you manage to, it will still be harder to catch up with those who already have the assets and have multiplied their wealth still further over the past 30 years.

Wealth inequality manifests itself in different ways in different places. For many emerging economies, things might well be better for many people in generations to come, despite the challenge of population growth and diminishing natural resources. But for the older economies, there is a perception of diminishing returns. Livelihoods are not what they were even a generation ago, and the prospects for future generations are increasingly worse. A significant part of this is relative, whilst more people need food banks and temporary housing, fewer people are starving in the way many did in the nineteenth century or even the early twentieth. But humanity does not measure its progress in absolute terms. The social contract tying many of our societies together is the belief that things gradually improve in most ways, generation on generation. If the opposite is now perceived to be the case in many post-industrial societies, even if it is a gradual decline, it is still a downward trajectory. Whilst the UK might still be the sixth or seventh largest economy in the world, and might remain such in 2050, it doesn't feel that way with aging infrastructure, poor productivity, and post-industrial areas in unremitting decline. It you travel around most European countries, it is clear to see where the inherited wealth is, and where it is not. Many people just do not believe things are getting better for them.

Perhaps a problem with Doughnut economics is that it fails to get to the essence of what drives humanity and therefore what drives economies. We must not forget our fickle nature, our jealousies, our fear of the unknown and change. Nationalists might call on us to put 'America First' or whatever other country you might live in, but our strongest bounds are sub-national and to family. Perhaps the current Vice President of the United States, J.D. Vance, is not wrong when he invokes his 'order of love' ('*ordo amoris*') as a true reflection of his politics – family first, then neighbours, then community and so on.[24] Not quite the parable of the good Samaritan, or the warm welcome given to strangers in many parts of the world in my experience, but it fits with the Vance vibe. The success of Trump's re-election is perhaps less 'America First' or 'Make America Great Again' but 'Me First', 'Family First', 'Make Me (and people like me) Great Again'. No one wants to feel impotent, when they still have electoral power to protect their livelihood and lifestyle in a world where there is less relative wealth available to the already rich countries, and even there it is squirreled away by the already rich. As Chap. 1 already explored, the rise in populism and anti-sustainability sentiment, makes short-term sense for some. But it, of course, makes very bad long-term sense for everyone without a spaceship and another spare planet to vacate to.

If we flip Kate Raworth's doughnut and so the social issues become the 'outer rim' instead of the inner: how many social boundaries have we transgressed over the past thirty years? And if we think about social boundaries not just in terms of development indicators but also the inherent values of trust, fairness, legitimacy, and consent, that form the basis of the social contracts that bind our societies together; perhaps we have overshot these as much as we have Johann Rockstrom's planetary boundaries. Sustainability lacks sufficient social licence.

## 2.4   The Devil That Loves the Detail

If sustainability is to move from aspiration to implementation, the question of scale becomes unavoidable. Planetary boundaries describe limits at the level of the entire Earth system, yet decisions about investment, production, and risk are made by individual organisations operating within competitive markets and legal constraints. This mismatch between global thresholds and organisational responsibility is not a technical footnote; it is one of the central reasons sustainability has struggled to translate into consistent business practice. Section 2.4 examines how this gap has been addressed in corporate governance, reporting, and regulation - and why, despite genuine progress, these approaches have so far fallen short of embedding planetary limits into everyday business decision-making.

Business has begun to embrace sustainability and commitments to carbon neutrality, deforestation-free supply chains, and circular economies have bloomed. Some even referenced planetary boundaries, adopting the language of safe operating space. Yet the fit has been uneasy. Planetary boundaries operate at the scale of the entire Biosphere, corporations at organizational scale. A boardroom can measure its emissions but cannot directly relate them to a global $CO_2$ threshold. How much of the nitrogen cycle belongs to a single fertilizer company? How much of the freshwater boundary does a beverage giant consume?

Allocation to the operations of specific companies has proved to be challenging. Without agreed methods, each company could claim its own "fair share." The result has risked greenwashing rather than accountability. Corporate governance itself poses hurdles. Boards are bound to fiduciary duties and short-term cycles of profit reporting. Planetary boundaries demand long-term, systemic responsibility. Unless encoded in law or markets, companies have little incentive to sacrifice margins for planetary health.

Measurement has been another barrier. While carbon accounting is advanced, metrics for biodiversity integrity or aerosol loading are beyond most firms. Reporting frameworks like the *Global Reporting Initiative* (GRI),[25] the *Sustainability Accounting Standards Board* (SASB),[26] and the *Task Force on Climate-related Financial Disclosures* (TCFD)[27] provide structure, but they do not map neatly onto the planetary boundaries model. In practice, companies have cherry-picked. A tech giant might commit to net-zero carbon but ignore the land-use impacts of data centres. An agribusiness might tout water stewardship while expanding fertilizer use. The nine planetary boundaries, intended as a holistic system, risk being fractured into a menu of convenient options.

Recognizing these limitations, businesses and regulators have turned to integrating frameworks. In Europe, the *Corporate Sustainability Reporting Directive* (CSRD)[28] introduced legally binding reporting standards, embracing "double materiality": impacts on both companies and society. The *International Sustainability Standards Board* (ISSB)[29] is seeking to harmonize the patchwork into a global baseline. Unless planetary boundaries are translated into binding regulations or market mechanisms (such as carbon pricing), companies face strong incentives not to voluntarily align with them. Corporate governance structures, driven by shareholder expectations and market competition, cannot easily prioritize planetary health over financial returns. Another barrier is the fragmented nature of global business. Planetary boundaries are holistic, interconnected thresholds, yet industries and corporations are highly specialised and regulated differently across jurisdictions. A chemical manufacturer in Europe, a palm oil company in Indonesia, and a tech giant in the United States all contribute to different boundaries in diverse ways, under different regulatory regimes.

Corporate governance frameworks are therefore ill-suited to address the systemic, cross-sectoral interactions that planetary boundaries emphasize. Even if one business adopts ambitious measures, the collective effect is negligible unless coordinated across industries and countries, something corporate governance mechanisms are not designed to achieve. Finally, the planetary boundaries model has no legal force. Corporate governance systems are ultimately shaped by laws, regulations, and enforcement mechanisms. Unless planetary boundaries are embedded into binding national or international legislation, corporate boards cannot be held accountable for respecting them. Voluntary initiatives, such as science-based targets, have attempted to bridge this gap, but participation remains uneven, and enforcement is weak. Corporate governance without external enforcement tends to reduce sustainability to reputational management rather than systemic change.

## 2.5   The Need to Remake Things

Sustainability has been built on rigorous science and a deepening understanding of the natural systems that sustain life on Earth. None of this should be abandoned. On the contrary, it remains essential. But science alone has never been sufficient to secure lasting change, and the current backlash demonstrates that the way sustainability has been positioned within our economic and political systems is no longer durable.

The problem is not the absence of knowledge, nor even the absence of intent. It is that sustainability has too often sat above, rather than within, the structures that govern how decisions are actually made. It has been treated as an additional objective, a moral overlay, or a specialist domain - important, but ultimately subordinate to the imperatives of growth, competitiveness, security, and short-term performance. As a result, sustainability has remained too marginal and too fragile. This fragility explains why it has been so easy to short: why political leaders and commercial actors can undermine or delay sustainability commitments at relatively low cost, and sometimes with immediate reward.

*Remaking Sustainability* therefore does not mean replacing science with pragmatism, or values with economics. It means embedding sustainability at the level of what this book describes as the *bedrock*: the operational foundations where trade-offs are confronted, capital is allocated, technologies are chosen, risks are priced, and accountability is enforced. At this level, sustainability must sit alongside other core imperatives - human dignity, economic viability, security, and prosperity - rather than competing with them from the margins.

To *Remake Sustainability* is to change the incentive structure that currently rewards delay, denial, and externalisation. It is to increase the cost of shorting the system, and to ensure that pushbacks against sustainability are no longer consequence-free. Some disruption is both inevitable and necessary; the bursting of the ESG bubble is one example. But as sustainability becomes more operational, more embedded, and more enforceable, the scope for opportunistic retreat should narrow rather than expand.

The task ahead is therefore not to invent new principles, but to reposition existing ones where they can no longer be easily ignored. How this can be done - by reshaping investment, value chains, technology choices, and organisational practice - is the focus of the next chapter, and of the book that follows.

## Notes

1. NASA, *Earthrise*, Image article, 25 June 2013.
2. Carl Sagan, *Pale Blue Dot*, 8 September 1997.
3. Stockholm Resilience Centre, *Planetary Boundaries*, 2025.
4. Stockholm Resilience Centre, *Planetary Boundaries*, 2025.
5. Stockholm Resilience Centre, *Planetary Boundaries*, 2025.
6. United Nations, *The Montreal Protocol on Substances That Deplete the Ozone Layer*, 16 September 1987. A Protocol to the 1985 *Vienna Convention for the Protection of the Ozone Layer.*

7. Arti Choudhary et al. *Spatiotemporal trends in sunshine hours over India during three decades from 1988 to 2018*, Scientific Reports, 15, 2025.

8. Potsdam Institute for Climate Impact Research, *Seven of nine planetary boundaries now breached – ocean acidification joins the danger zone*, 24 September 2025.

9. Enrico Gennari, *Ocean Dead Zones: The growing crisis beneath the waves*, Oceans Research, 15 May 2025.

10. Global Environment Facility, *Sustainable landscapes in the Amazon and the Congo Basin*, 2025.

11. Christopher Johnson, *Past and future decline and extinction of species*, The Royal Society, (website), December 2025.

12. Potsdam Institute for Climate Impact Research, *Planetary Health Check*, 2025.

13. Hannah Ritchie, *Not the end of the world*, 2024.

14. Kate Raworth, *Doughnut Economics*, 2017.

15. United Nations, *Sustainable Development Goals*, 2015.

16. Mark Segal, *US Rejects Sustainable Development Goals*, ESG Today, 7 March 2025.

17. Hans Rosling et al., *Factfulness: Ten Reasons We're Wrong About the World – and Why Things Are Better Than You Think*, 2018.

18. Liz Ford, *Obama: 'the world has never been healthier, wealthier or less violent'*, The Guardian, 25 September 2017.

19. Martin Rees, *Our Final Hour/Our Final Century*, 2003.

20. United Nations, *Inequality – Bridging the Divide*, October 2025.

21. United Nations, *Inequality – Bridging the Divide*, October 2025.

22. World Inequality Lab, *World Inequality Report*, UNDP, 2022.

23. Thomas Piketty, *Capital*, 2017.

24. Stephen Pope, *The Problem with JD Vance's theology of 'ordo amoris' – and its impact on policy*, America: The Jesuit Review, 13 February 2025.

25. GRI, *Global Reporting Initiative*, (website), November 2025.

26. SASB, *Sustainability Accounting Standards Board*, (website), November 2025.

27. IFRS, *Taskforce for Climate-related Financial Disclosures (TCFD)*, 2023.

28. European Commission, *Corporate responsibility reporting*, DG Finance, (website), 25 November 2025.

29. IFRS Foundation, *About the International Sustainability Standards Board*, 2025.

# 3

# How Sustainability Can Be Remade

If Chap. 1 describes the current challenge to sustainability, and Chap. 2 explains how we arrived here, then this chapter brings the argument down to ground level. If the backlash described in Chap. 1 reflects a crisis of legitimacy, then *Remaking Sustainability* must begin with how legitimacy is earned in practice: through competent decision-making under constraint. The question now is not *why* sustainability matters, nor even *whether* it has failed in important respects, but how it can be remade in practice. What does sustainability look like when it is no longer an aspiration, a framework, or a moral appeal, but an operational reality? *Remaking Sustainability* is changing how decisions are made when goals collide under real-world constraints. The tension between long-term planetary limits and short-term economic pressures is not something that can be resolved in theory. It must be managed in the everyday decisions of organisations - governments, businesses, trade unions, civil society bodies - where trade-offs are confronted rather than deferred. This chapter sets out the logic for doing so.

Although the analysis that follows applies broadly, this book focuses primarily on business. That choice is deliberate. Business is where sustainability claims are most severely tested as efficiency is expected and


J. Morrison, *Remaking Sustainability*, https://doi.org/10.1007/978-3-032-23755-2_3

financial performance must always be at the forefront of any decision matrix. Its purpose is neither moral nor charitable. It must convert activity into value and operate under competitive pressures. The best test of sustainability is when the operating environment is tough, and difficult decisions need to be made. The pressure to short sustainability might be considerable, when shareholders, customers, suppliers, and senior staff are all making different demands. Sustainability leadership is what business does during the times of challenge more than the times of plenty, and hence the current pushback is very revealing.

Throughout this book, I use the term *bedrock* to describe the level at which sustainability must now sit. Bedrock is where operational priorities meet strategic reality: where capital is allocated, technologies are chosen, supply chains configured, risks priced, and performance measured. Sustainability becomes durable only when it is embedded at this level, alongside other core imperatives such as profitability, security, resilience, and legitimacy. When sustainability sits above this layer - as an overlay, a reporting exercise, or a specialist function - it remains fragile. That fragility helps explain why sustainability has been so easy to short, and why the current backlash has been so effective.

In Chap. 1, I asked the reader to imagine a conversation between a Chief Sustainability Officer and a CEO, Chief Operating Officer,[1] or another functional leader. That conversation is the practical starting point for remaking sustainability. Bedrock is where sustainability must navigate both the enthusiasm of its advocates and the scepticism of its detractors. It is not about saving the world, nor about extracting maximum value at any cost. It is about operating competently in a world defined by constraint.

A natural question follows. Does remaking sustainability require incremental adjustment, or something closer to transformation? The honest answer is: it depends. For some organisations, sustainability will slot into existing change processes - around digitalisation, security of supply, market expansion, or workforce transition - as a horizontal concern that reshapes decisions already under way. For others, particularly those with weak internal alignment or siloed decision-making, the implications will feel more disruptive. In such cases, sustainability exposes deeper operational weaknesses rather than creating them.

What matters more than the label "sustainability" is the nature of the operational system itself. Organisations that already understand the importance of systems-thinking, place-based legitimacy, and resilience tend to find sustainability easier to integrate. The 'how' and the 'what' of operational sustainability are intimately connected. Those that rely on linear planning, narrow performance metrics, or short-term optimisation struggle. If, after reading this book, you are unsure where sustainability should sit in your organisation - or who would even listen - then the challenge is likely structural rather than conceptual.

Before going further, however, it is necessary to acknowledge a persistent presence in the room. Any discussion of operational sustainability, particularly in business, is haunted by an older argument about what corporations are for and whom they should serve. It is time to address that ghost directly.

## 3.1   Dealing with the Ghost of Friedman

In his legendary Op-Ed for the New York Times in 1970, the economist Milton Friedman set out the key tenets of his doctrine, that the 'business of business is business':

> *There is one and only one social responsibility of business - to use its resources and engage in activities designed to increase its profits so long as it stays within the rules of the game, which is to say, engages in open and free competition without deception or fraud.*[2]

The 'rules of the game' in Friedman's mind were those of free competition without corruption. 'Social responsibility' was explicitly not part of these rules, and Friedman criticised the environmental and social activities of businesses during his lifetime as a misuse of shareholders money. But fifty years later, Fortune Magazine exclaimed that Milton Friedman must be "turning in his grave" when the Business Roundtable broke from Friedman's shadow. Representing 200 of America's largest corporations, the Business Roundtable issued a new mission statement on "the purpose of a corporation" in 2019, stating the purpose was not just to respond to the needs of shareholders, but to lead their companies for the benefit of all stakeholders – customers, employees, suppliers, communities and share-holders. The Wall Street Journal leapt to Friedman's defence and accused the Business Roundtable of not "serving the interests of the shareholders who own the company." As Professor John Ruggie has written:

*This is not merely a theoretical issue. It matters for very practical reasons: it reinforces the deep divide in the American variant of capitalism between "private" and "social," which the Business Roundtable statement presumably sought to address and help bridge.*[3]

If indeed bridge-building was the intention, then many bridges have since been burned. The polarities of 1970 have returned, and the ghost of Friedman very much remains at the feast. The two main disagreements might be characterised as follows:

## Friedman Overstated the Rights of Shareholders

The main argument against Friedman remains that he overstates share-holder primacy for his own ideological reasons. Shareholders are entitled to a dividend at the discretion of the board, and at the annual general meeting they can vote on a pre-set slate of directors and on non-binding resolutions. If a shareholder owns a lot of shares in a single company, they might be able to demand a seat on the board or otherwise exert influence. And in case of bankruptcy or liquidation, shareholders are entitled to any residual assets left over after all secured obligations have been paid. But in no sense does any of this make them "owners" of the firm. After the process of incorporation, shareholders have no right of access to the assets of the corporation; they do not enter into any contract in its name. No liability can arise for them from the corporate activity. They do not run the corporation and do not own it.[4]

## Friedman Overstated the Power of the State

John Ruggie makes a second point. Friedman criticises corporate responsibility for being undemocratic and undermining the traditional role of government. He assumes all governments are as powerful and resourceful as the US Government was in the 1970s. But the reality of the past half century has been to remind us how fictitious this is. Multinational corporations can all too easily evade adequate enforcement in poorer countries where they might operate. International law has no direct binding effect on business, and there is no global regulator to hold them to account.[5]

## Friedman Had Never Run a Business During a Poly-crisis

My own critique of Friedman from the perspective of the second quarter of the twenty-first century is that the world of Friedman has now passed, if it ever existed. The interconnectedness of social and environmental issues into business realities is now so deep, so intrinsic, that to pretend shareholders are best served by ignoring them sounds abstract and academic. Friedman would find it hard to remain relevant in most of the boardrooms I know. Another Nobel-prize winning economist Herbert Simon, writing a decade before Friedman, might have surmised that to believe in the primacy of shareholder value above every other consideration is 'bounded rationality' of the highest order.[6]

I could go on but I won't. The purpose of my book is not to settle the ongoing arguments about the true purpose of the corporation, but only to point out that it is contested and that both the minimalist and maximalist arguments need particular scrutiny. As I have already stated in Chap. 1, expansionist ideas of what ESG should be - that every environmental and social issue should be material to a company's balance sheet - are as unhelpful as they are wrong. However, the same is true of the minimalists. To say, as Friedman did, that to include sustainability considerations in the operation of a business was somehow political, is - in itself - a political statement. When finding sustainability bedrock, it is important to be aware of this, and to ensure your business does not lie at one of the extremities. When *Remaking Sustainability*, it is wise to avoid ideology as much as possible and to look for something firmer to stand upon.

## 3.2    Operational Bottlenecks: Where Systems Break

Operational bottlenecks are the points at which complex systems come under stress and begin to fail.[7] They are rarely caused by a single factor. Instead, they emerge where economic efficiency, environmental limits, political tension, and social expectations collide. In a world of tightly coupled global systems, bottlenecks are not exceptions; they are structural features of how modern economies function.[8]

For much of the past three decades, businesses assumed that globalisation had solved the problem of scarcity. Inputs would flow, markets would clear, and disruptions would be temporary. That assumption no longer holds. Security of supply has re-emerged as a strategic concern precisely because many systems have been optimised for efficiency rather than resilience. Sustainability enters the picture not as an external constraint, but as a force multiplier: environmental degradation, climate volatility, and social instability all increase the frequency and severity of bottlenecks.[9]

### Security of Supply as a Systemic Risk

Security of supply is no longer confined to energy or defence. It now applies to food, data, labour, water, minerals, logistics, and infrastructure. What makes this shift significant is not just the number of exposed sectors, but the interconnectedness between them. A disruption in one domain quickly propagates into others. Extreme weather events affect agricultural yields, which in turn influence food prices, political stability, and migration. Energy shortages raise production costs across entire value chains. Regulatory responses to environmental harm reshape trade flows. Sustainability-related risks therefore materialise operationally as shortages, delays, price volatility, and reputational damage. Treating these as isolated "sustainability issues" misses their systemic character.

## Choke Points in Global Trade

Global trade depends on a surprisingly small number of physical and geopolitical nodes. The Suez Canal, the Strait of Hormuz, the Strait of Malacca, and the Panama Canal together carry a disproportionate share of global commerce. Disruption at any one of these points - through conflict, accident, or climate stress - has immediate global consequences. What matters operationally is not just the existence of these choke points, but the absence of viable substitutes. Rerouting around the Cape of Good Hope adds weeks to shipping times and significant cost.[10] Low water levels in the Panama Canal already constrain throughput. Attacks on shipping lanes or heightened geopolitical tension raise insurance premiums and reduce predictability. These are not hypothetical risks; they are now recurring features of the operating environment.

For individual businesses, exposure to such bottlenecks is rarely visible until disruption occurs. Sustainability strategies that ignore logistics, trade routes, and infrastructure resilience therefore fail at precisely the moment they are most needed.

## Food Systems Under Pressure

Food systems provide one of the clearest illustrations of how sustainability and operational risk converge. Global food security depends on a small number of regions, transport corridors, and input-intensive production systems. Conflict, climate shocks, and export controls can rapidly destabilise supply. The war in Ukraine exposed how dependent global grain markets are on the Black Sea region. Inland waterways in the United States, ports in Brazil, and rail links in Eastern Europe all represent critical nodes.[11] When any of these are disrupted, the consequences cascade: price spikes, political unrest, and humanitarian crises. Businesses operating across the food value chain - inputs, processing, logistics, retail - are unavoidably implicated.[12]

From an operational perspective, food security highlights a key point: sustainability failures often manifest first as affordability and access issues rather than environmental indicators. By the time ecological limits are visible, social and political consequences are already under way.

## Critical Minerals and Asymmetric Dependence

Critical minerals represent a different but equally instructive bottleneck. The energy transition depends on materials such as lithium, cobalt, nickel, niobium, and rare earth elements, yet processing capacity for many of these is highly concentrated. China's dominance in refining and processing creates asymmetric dependencies that are difficult to unwind quickly.[13] Unlike fossil fuels, where alternative suppliers can sometimes be mobilised, critical mineral supply chains take years or decades to develop. Export restrictions, geopolitical tension, or domestic policy shifts therefore carry disproportionate impact. For businesses reliant on electrification, digital infrastructure, or advanced manufacturing, this creates long-term exposure that cannot be hedged easily.

Recycling and circularity offer partial mitigation, but they too require time, investment, and regulatory alignment. In the meantime, critical minerals illustrate how sustainability transitions themselves generate new bottlenecks, rather than eliminating risk.

## The Operational Lesson of Bottlenecks

Across these examples, the pattern is consistent. Bottlenecks arise where systems are:

- tightly coupled,
- optimised for efficiency,
- dependent on concentrated nodes,
- and exposed to environmental or geopolitical stress.

Sustainability is not the cause of these bottlenecks, but it intensifies their consequences and shortens the time between shock and impact. For operational leaders, the implication is clear. Managing sustainability is inseparable from managing exposure to systemic risk. Resilience is built not by eliminating bottlenecks, but by anticipating them, diversifying dependencies, accepting redundancy, and aligning incentives across systems that no single organisation controls.

This is why sustainability must sit at bedrock. Bottlenecks cannot be managed through reporting frameworks or voluntary commitments alone. They demand operational decisions about sourcing, investment, technology, inventory, and collaboration - often at the expense of short-term efficiency. My version of operational sustainability does not resolve these trade-offs, but it contends that avoiding them is no longer an option.

## 3.3 Bedrock: The Sustainability of Sustainability

The central argument of this book is that sustainability itself must become sustainable. The severity of the current backlash is not an aberration; it is a symptom. It reveals that sustainability, as it has been practised, has not yet been sufficiently embedded in the structures that govern real-world decision-making. Where sustainability remains discretionary, symbolic, or weakly enforced, it invites arbitrage. It can be delayed, diluted, or abandoned at relatively low cost. That is what is now happening.

Chapters 1 and 2 showed how sustainability rose to prominence, and why the frameworks that carried it this far are no longer adequate on their own. This chapter has argued that the response is not retreat, nor the search for ever more comprehensive principles, but operational repositioning. Sustainability endures only when it is embedded at bedrock: where organisations allocate capital, manage risk, design systems, and absorb shocks. At this level, sustainability is no longer something that can be opted into or out of according to political mood or market cycle. It becomes part of how viability itself is judged.

A sustainability issue reaches bedrock when it can no longer be deferred, delegated, or externalised without undermining the stability of the system itself. At bedrock, trade-offs must be made explicit rather than obscured, costs must be carried rather than postponed, and responsibility for outcomes can no longer be displaced onto others or into the future. Sustainability ceases to be a matter of just values, targets, or narrative alignment and becomes also a question of governance, capital allocation, and operational judgement under constraint. Decisions taken at bedrock are rarely optimal, often uncomfortable, and always consequential. But it is only at this level that sustainability acquires legitimacy, because it is experienced not as aspiration, but as responsibility exercised in full view of its consequences.

Once sustainability reaches bedrock, it stops behaving like a discrete agenda and starts asserting itself across the systems that govern economic and social life. In the remainder of this book, I focus on a set of domains where sustainability has already crossed this threshold, not because ambition is highest there, but because deferral is no longer possible without destabilising the system itself. These are not thematic silos; they are the places where trade-offs, constraints, and responsibility now concentrate. The chapters ahead can be organised into several bedrock domains.

The first of these domains (Chaps. 4–7) is financial capital and risk. Sustainability reaches bedrock when climate, nature, and social risks begin to shape capital allocation, insurance availability, and the cost of finance, rather than sitting alongside them as disclosures or aspirations. At this point, sustainability is no longer something organisations *commit* to; it is something they are *priced for*. Decisions about investment horizons, asset valuation, and underwriting become sustainability decisions by default, even when the language used to describe them is financial rather than environmental or social.

The second domain (Chaps. 8–10) is value chains and trade. Sustainability becomes unavoidable when supply chains are no longer abstract networks optimised for cost, but contested systems shaped by geopolitics, labour conditions, resource scarcity, and environmental limits. At bedrock, responsibility cannot be pushed indefinitely upstream or downstream. Choices about sourcing, localisation, resilience, and diversification force explicit trade-offs between efficiency, security, and fairness, and expose the limits of voluntary standards or contractual distance.

The third domain (Chaps. 11–13) is technology and digital infrastructure. Sustainability reaches bedrock when technological change no longer promises simple solutions but instead amplifies existing constraints.

Digitalisation, automation, AI, and the arrival of quantum computing, reshape demand as much as they reduce it, introducing new pressures on energy systems, minerals, land, and skills. At this level, sustainability depends less on innovation itself than on governance: on how technologies are deployed, who benefits from them, and who bears their unintended consequences.

The next domain (Chaps. 14–16) is more internal than external. It is the governance, leadership, and operating models required for delivery to be effective. Sustainability becomes real when decisions migrate from specialist teams into core executive functions and boardrooms, where competing objectives must be reconciled under pressure. At bedrock, leadership is no longer about signalling commitment but about owning trade-offs, setting priorities, and accepting accountability for outcomes that will inevitably disappoint some stakeholders. Governance failures at this level are no longer reputational risks; they are systemic ones.

Finally, sustainability reaches bedrock in the domain of legitimacy and consent (Chaps. 17–19). It is the social licence of sustainability. When the impacts of transition are felt unevenly across communities, workers, and regions, sustainability can no longer rely on assumed agreement or moral authority. It must be experienced as fair, credible, and responsive in practice. This is where narrative and social licence intersect with delivery, and where failures of communication or engagement quickly translate into resistance, delay, or backlash.

Together, these domains explain why sustainability can no longer be treated as an add-on or a parallel agenda. They are the arenas in which sustainability has already become operational, whether acknowledged or not. The chapters that follow explore how these bedrock domains interact, where current approaches fall short, and what it takes to exercise responsibility within them when certainty is unavailable and trade-offs cannot be avoided.

## Notes

1. McKinsey and Company, *Why do Organisations have COOs?*, 5 December 2023.

2. Milton Friedman, *Capitalism and Freedom,* 1962.
3. John Ruggie, *Corporate Purpose in play: The role of ESG Investing*, Harvard Kennedy School, 1 January 2019.
4. Robé, 2012.
5. John Ruggie, *Corporate Purpose in play: The role of ESG Investing*, Harvard Kennedy School, 1 January 2019.
6. John Morrison, *The Just Transition: A systems-thinking approach to managing climate action*, October 2024.
7. Henry Farrell and Abraham Newman, *Choke Points*, Harvard Business Review, Jan-Feb 2020.
8. World Economic Forum, *In a polycrisis, how can businesses build the resilience to survive?* 5 June 2023.
9. Edgar Morin and Anne Brigitte Kern, *Terre-Patrie, 1993.*
10. Boston Consulting Group, *These Four Chokepoints are Threatening Global Trade*, 12 February 2024.
11. Rob Bailey and Laura Wellesley, *Choke Points and Vulnerabilities in Global Food Trade*, Chatham House, June 2017, updated May 2023.
12. Boston Consulting Group, *These Four Chokepoints are Threatening Global Trade*, 12 February 2024.
13. Michael Froman, *China, the United States, and a Critical Chokepoint on Minerals*, Council for Foreign Relations, 17 October 2025.

# Part II

## Bedrock in Investment

# 4

## Finance Already Flowing

When I am sea swimming, the story of King Canute often comes to mind: a ruler foolish enough to believe he could command the tide. It is a cautionary tale about hubris from the eleventh century. In its original form, however, the story may have meant the opposite. Canute, having his throne placed at the shoreline, demonstrated to his courtiers that even a king could not command the forces of nature. It was a lesson in limits, and in the danger of mistaking authority for control. Sometimes, for those in power, managing expectations requires making constraints visible.

I am used to watching waves and learning not to trust first impressions. Large swells can roll in, only for an undercurrent to pull you back out just as you think you have reached shore. On the beaches I know best, a steady lateral drift can move you hundreds of metres away from where you entered the water, while all the time the tide itself is either ebbing or flowing. Several forces act at once, often in different directions. From the waterline, it is rarely obvious which will prevail.

This feels like an apt description of sustainable finance in the mid-2020s. Headlines speak of retreat: banks leaving net-zero alliances, asset managers softening language, ESG becoming politically toxic in parts of the



J. Morrison, *Remaking Sustainability*, https://doi.org/10.1007/978-3-032-23755-2_4

United States. At the same time, capital continues to flow into renewable energy, electrification, grids, storage, climate technology, and transition infrastructure. Private equity activity remains strong. Disclosure standards are spreading globally. China is doubling down on industrial modernisation tied explicitly to sustainability outcomes. Multiple currents are at work simultaneously, and it is easy to mistake turbulence for reversal.

That lesson matters here. The recent retreat from some high-profile sustainability commitments by private financial institutions raises an obvious question. Are we witnessing an undertow following a period of exaggerated enthusiasm, or is the tide itself turning? And if so, who in this story believes they can command it? This chapter argues that, despite visible pullbacks and political noise, private finance is now structurally exposed to sustainability risks in ways that make a wholesale retreat unlikely if not impossible. Capital is not flowing because finance has become virtuous, nor because values have suddenly aligned. It is flowing because climate change, resource constraints, supply-chain fragility, and social instability increasingly threaten the viability of balance sheets, and markets themselves. Sustainability has begun to move from choreography to constraint.

This distinction matters. During the period when ESG rose rapidly to prominence, much of sustainable finance was performative: commitments, alliances, pledges, and disclosure frameworks multiplied faster than underlying incentives changed. That phase brought important progress. It built awareness, improved data, and expanded institutional capacity. But it also inflated expectations and blurred the line between intention and impact. As discussed in Chap. 1, this created a bubble that was always likely to burst. What we are seeing now is not the end of sustainable finance, but a shift in its centre of gravity. As sustainability moves closer to bedrock - where capital is allocated, risk is priced, and losses are realised - it becomes harder to treat as optional. Financial institutions may retreat from collective pledges, soften rhetoric, or rebrand ESG, but they cannot easily exit exposure to systemic risk. In this sense, finance is already flowing not because it wants to, but because it must.

This chapter is the first of four that examine the role of investment in remaking sustainability. Its purpose is not to defend ESG, nor to predict short-term market sentiment, but to assess whether finance has reached a point of structural entanglement with sustainability outcomes. To do so, the chapter looks in turn at private banks, asset managers and institutional investors, private equity, China, and emerging economies beyond China. The aim is not to catalogue every development, but to understand what these patterns reveal about sustainability bedrock.

The argument that follows is deliberately unsentimental. Banks are commercial organisations, not agents of social policy. Asset managers respond to incentives and client mandates. Private equity pursues opportunity where returns are competitive. Governments shape markets unevenly, and geopolitics matters. None of this is new. What *is* new is the extent to which environmental and social risks now manifest as financial risks across time horizons that investors can no longer ignore.

The key question, then, is not whether finance supports sustainability in principle, but how deeply sustainability is embedded in financial decision-making when trade-offs are real. Where sustainability aligns with profitability, momentum will continue. Where it does not, resistance remains strong. The critical issue for *Remaking Sustainability* is whether these tensions are being pushed to the margins - or absorbed at bedrock, where they shape how finance actually flows. The pages that follow explore this question in detail, beginning with the recent retrenchment by some major banks and what it does - and does not - tell us about the direction of sustainable finance.

## 4.1  Banks Rolling Back Their Pledges

There was a visible retreat from high-profile climate commitments by several major banks during 2025. In the United States, a number of leading institutions exited the *Net-Zero Banking Alliance* (NZBA), distancing themselves from collective pledges to align financed emissions with net-zero targets.[1] Similar moves followed in Europe, and by October 2025 the NZBA itself had closed.[2] These developments stand in stark contrast to the optimism surrounding the alliance's launch at COP26 in Glasgow in 2021, when banks pledged to align trillions of dollars in assets with the climate transition.[3]

At first glance, this retreat appears to confirm the narrative of a sustainability reversal. Political pressure, particularly in the US, has played a significant role. Threats of antitrust action against climate-related collaboration, alongside wider culture-war dynamics, made participation in alliances increasingly costly. At the same time, concerns about the impact of climate commitments on short-term growth and competitiveness resurfaced. In this sense, the exits were not irrational. Banks are commercial organisations operating under legal, regulatory, and political constraints, and they respond accordingly.

What matters, however, is not whether banks remain members of voluntary alliances, but whether climate risk has become embedded in the core mechanics of banking: credit policy, capital allocation, risk management, and supervisory expectations. On this deeper level, the picture looks markedly different. According to the *Rocky Mountain Institute* (RMI), banks today are *"structurally and culturally"* different from a decade ago.[4] Climate considerations are now embedded in regulatory stress tests, internal risk models, and governance processes. Banks have built specialist teams, invested heavily in data and modelling capabilities, updated lending policies, and developed transition plans that are scrutinised by supervisors and investors alike. Once climate risk enters these systems, it is far harder to remove quietly.

This institutionalisation has limits. Banks continue to finance fossil-fuel expansion, in part because such lending is capital-efficient under existing regulations. Large oil and gas companies offer strong balance sheets and predictable cash flows, allowing banks to extend credit without tying up significant amounts of their own capital.[5] By contrast, many low-carbon investments rely on project finance, which carries higher regulatory capital requirements and greater perceived risk. Ownership capital for renewables, grids, and emerging technologies is therefore more likely to come from private equity, asset managers, or pension funds than from banks themselves.

Recognising these constraints, civil society organisations have begun to recalibrate their engagement strategies. Rather than focusing on headline commitments or alliance membership, attention is shifting toward the mechanics of individual transactions: clean power, green steel, zero-carbon housing, methane abatement, and renewable fuels. As Kaitlin Crouch-Hess of RMI has put it, *"what we need now is less choreography and more closing of deals."*[6] This is an important adjustment. It reflects a growing understanding that sustainability progress in banking will be measured less by declarations of intent and more by the cumulative effect of thousands of financing decisions made under real constraints.

As one ethical investor put it to me when interviewed for this book: *"The story I'm reading is that banks made progress and when that progress started to have consequences for vested interests, the oil and gas lobby mobilised to push back, which resulted in a legally fraught context that killed off major initiatives. This compounded by the fact that the climate commitments were easy to make before they began to bite and commercial realities kicked in. In this case the banks are more like the swimmer dealing with multiple forces at the same time. They've been pushed up the beach by the wave of climate sustainability, been dragged back by vested interest undercurrents, while being subject to the rising and falling tides of the global economy."*[7]

Seen through this lens, the withdrawal from climate alliances looks less like a collapse and more like a thinning of the surface layer. The rhetoric has softened, and collective symbolism has receded, but the underlying exposure of banks to climate and transition risk remains. Sustainability may be easier to distance from in public statements than in loan books, stress tests, and regulatory dialogues. That is the bedrock distinction. Banks can step away from pledges, but they cannot step away from risk.

## 4.2  The High-Water Mark

Up until 2025, the direction of travel among investors - particularly in the United States - had been clear. Climate and sustainability disclosure expanded rapidly, moving from voluntary reporting into the core of financial analysis and regulatory expectation. According to the *Carbon Disclosure Project*, the number of companies reporting on climate-related issues grew from fewer than 5000 in 2014 to more than 22,000 by 2024.[8] In parallel, sustainability language became commonplace in regulatory filings. By the 2024 fiscal year, nearly half of US public companies referenced climate change in their annual reports, and more than half discussed sustainability in some form. This expansion reflected a deeper shift than rhetoric alone. Asset managers increasingly treated environmental, social, and governance (ESG) information as a component of market intelligence rather than moral positioning. The rapid growth of the ESG data industry - from a niche service to a multi-billion-dollar market - signalled that sustainability information was being absorbed into mainstream investment processes.[9] Today, almost all of the world's largest asset managers rely on ESG and climate datasets to inform portfolio construction, risk management, and stewardship.[10] Whatever the political noise, sustainability data has become embedded in how markets function.[11]

This distinction matters because much of the backlash against ESG has targeted its perceived ideological dimension, rather than its informational role.[12] At its most defensible, ESG is simply an attempt to improve how markets understand risk and opportunity in a changing world. At its most expansive, it has sometimes been presented as a proxy for social or environmental performance itself. As I discussed in Chap. 1, these two interpretations - ESG as input and ESG as outcome - have been repeatedly conflated, creating confusion and resistance on both sides of the debate.[13]

One way to clarify this is to distinguish between *financially relevant* and *sustainability-relevant* information.[14] Financial relevance is narrower: it asks which environmental or social factors are likely to affect cash flows, asset values, or cost of capital within a given investment horizon. Sustainability relevance is broader: it encompasses the full range of environmental and social impacts associated with economic activity, whether or not markets currently price them. These are not competing categories. They are concentric. Over longer time horizons, the boundary between them erodes, as environmental degradation, climate instability, and social stress increasingly feed back into financial performance. What is dismissed as "non-financial" today often becomes material tomorrow.[15]

This convergence is now being formalised through global reporting standards. In 2023, the *International Sustainability Standards Board* (ISSB) introduced IFRS S1 and S2, providing a common framework for disclosing material sustainability and climate-related risks.[16] These standards have been endorsed by major international bodies and adopted, or slated for adoption, across dozens of jurisdictions. While the United States has hesitated - most visibly through the *Securities and Exchange Commission*'s withdrawal of its defence of mandatory climate-risk disclosure - the global trajectory remains clear. Outside the US, sustainability disclosure is becoming part of the financial rulebook in 40 jurisdictions - among them Australia, Brazil, China, Kenya, and Turkey.[17]

This is why the notion of a simple retreat from ESG is misleading. Some US companies have begun to soften language or reduce visibility in response to political pressure, but this does not reverse the deeper integration of sustainability into risk assessment, valuation, and supervision. Disclosure regimes may fragment temporarily, and terminology may shift, but the underlying demand for information about climate and other systemic risks is unlikely to disappear.[18] Investors with medium- to long-term horizons cannot credibly assess value without it. Seen in this light, 2024–25 may come to represent the high-water mark of ESG as a broad, sometimes over-extended label, rather than the peak of sustainability integration into finance. Consolidation was inevitable. In 2021, the *World Economic Forum* identified more than 600 ESG ratings and rankings in use globally, allowing companies to cherry-pick metrics that flattered their performance.[19] That fragmentation weakened credibility and invited backlash. What follows is likely to be a narrower, more disciplined phase, focused less on signalling and more on decision-useful information.

At bedrock, this shift is significant. Financial institutions may argue about labels, mandates, and political boundaries, but they cannot avoid the gradual expansion of what counts as financially relevant risk. Over time, climate, resource constraints, and social stability move from the periphery of analysis to its core. When that happens, sustainability ceases to be an optional overlay and becomes part of how markets judge value itself.

## 4.3   Universal Ownership

Much of the contemporary debate about sustainable finance rests on a quiet but consequential shift in how capital is owned. To understand it, it is worth returning briefly to the foundations of investment theory. In the early 1950s, Harry Markowitz developed *Modern Portfolio Theory* (MPT), arguing that investors could optimise returns for a given level of risk through diversification. The insight transformed finance. But it also rested on an assumption that has since eroded: that individual investors were too small to influence the risk–return characteristics of the market as a whole.[20]

That assumption no longer holds. Today, large institutional investors – such as pension funds, sovereign wealth funds, insurers, and major asset managers - own substantial portions of entire markets. Their portfolios increasingly resemble the global economy itself. Jon Lukomnik and James Hawley describe these institutions as *universal owners*: investors whose long-term performance depends less on outperforming peers than on the health and stability of the overall system. For such investors, risks like climate change, biodiversity loss, and social instability cannot be diversified away. They show up everywhere.

This shift has profound implications. First, universal owners are structurally exposed to systemic risks that threaten aggregate returns. Second, their performance is driven primarily by *beta* - overall market performance - rather than *alpha*, or stock selection. Third, unlike the fragmented investors of the past, they possess the scale to influence market rules, norms, and expectations. This logic has given rise to what is often called *beta activism*: the idea that investors should seek to improve system-wide outcomes rather than merely reshuffle assets within it. Some of the most prominent advocates of this view have come from within the investment community itself. Hiro Mizuno, former Chief Investment Officer of Japan's *Government Pension Investment Fund*, has argued that because GPIF's portfolio mirrors the global economy, environmental damage or governance failures in one sector inevitably depress returns elsewhere.[21] From this perspective, stewardship aimed at improving systemic outcomes is not ideological, but fiduciary. Others, such as Steve Waygood – formerly of Aviva Investors - have framed this as *macro-stewardship*: engagement not just with companies, but with the rules and incentives that shape markets.[22]

In theory, the logic is compelling. In practice, it has proven difficult to translate into consistent action. Universal owners may recognise that unchecked fossil-fuel expansion, for example, threatens long-term portfolio value. But acting on that recognition through individual company engagement often runs into legal, political, and governance constraints. Directors are obliged to act in the interests of their own company, not an investor's wider portfolio. Forcing a firm to absorb costs today in order to generate diffuse benefits elsewhere remains contested terrain.

The recent history of shareholder activism in the United States illustrates these limits. High-profile interventions - such as Engine No.1's successful campaign to secure board seats at Exxon - demonstrated that investors could challenge strategic assumptions about climate risk.[23] Yet subsequent legal[24] and regulatory developments have shifted the balance back toward management. In 2025, the US *Securities and Exchange Commission* approved Exxon's move to automate proxy voting for retail shareholders, effectively defaulting votes in favour of management recommendations unless investors opt out.[25] Governance specialists argue that such mechanisms make it harder for activist resolutions on climate, governance, or pay to succeed. Other companies are expected to follow suit.[26]

These dynamics help explain why universal ownership has not delivered the scale of change some hoped for. As Tom Gosling has argued, the idea that institutional investors can unilaterally steer the global economy toward a specific temperature outcome - such as 1.5C with limited overshoot - was always optimistic.[27] The tools available to investors - engagement, voting, selective divestment - are generally too weak to overcome entrenched commercial incentives, especially where costs are concentrated and benefits diffuse. From this perspective, using universal ownership to internalise externalities across a portfolio may be attractive in theory but difficult to justify in practice.

This does not mean universal ownership is irrelevant. It means its leverage lies elsewhere. The greatest influence of large institutional investors is not at the level of individual corporate strategy, but in shaping the *rules of the game*. Universal owners are most effective when they push for regulatory standards that apply to all firms equally: robust disclosure regimes, carbon pricing, transition incentives, and prudential rules that reflect systemic risk. In these contexts, stewardship aligns more clearly with fiduciary duty, because it seeks to protect the entire market on which portfolio returns depend. The politicisation of ESG has made this role more visible. In the United States, some states have moved to penalise or blacklist institutions perceived as "woke," while others continue to demand stronger climate risk management. Shareholders clash over decarbonisation strategies, diversity policies, and executive pay. This turbulence is often portrayed as evidence of failure. It may be better understood as a sign that sustainability has become materially relevant enough to provoke conflict. Friction, in this sense, reflects salience.

At bedrock, the lesson of universal ownership is not that investors can solve sustainability, but that they can no longer ignore it. Systemic risk has entered the investment frame, even if the mechanisms for addressing it remain contested. Universal ownership has not delivered a neat solution, but it has made sustainability a question of long-term value preservation rather than ethical preference. That shift, however incomplete, is unlikely to be reversed.

## 4.4   Why Swim Away from a Good Deal

If parts of public-market sustainable finance have been chilled by political backlash, private markets tell a more revealing story. Capital continues to flow toward sustainability-linked investments not because of politics, but because the underlying economics increasingly make sense. According to *Boston Consulting Group*, private equity investment in climate-related sectors reached $73 billion in 2024, even as overall private equity fundraising declined.[28] Surveys of asset owners show a continued intention to increase allocations to climate-related strategies, particularly in mitigation, adaptation, and resilience. In other words, where returns are plausible and risk can be managed, capital has shown little inclination to retreat.[29]

One reason is technological maturity. More than half of low-carbon technologies are now cost-competitive with incumbent alternatives, with others close behind. This has shifted sustainability investment from speculative positioning toward operational deployment. For private equity, infrastructure investors, and growth capital, opportunities increasingly lie in assets that combine transition relevance with stable cash flows: electricity grids, energy storage, charging infrastructure, efficiency services, recycling systems, and industrial decarbonisation. These are not marginal bets. They are becoming part of mainstream capital allocation.

Private equity also illustrates an important bedrock distinction. Unlike public equity markets, where trading ownership rarely alters real-world outcomes, private capital operates closer to where decisions are made. Control over strategy, technology choice, and capital expenditure gives investors a more direct line of sight to impact. This does not guarantee positive outcomes, but it helps explain why sustainability-linked investment has remained resilient in private markets even as ESG rhetoric has cooled elsewhere.

China offers a further perspective on how capital follows structure rather than sentiment. In 2025, foreign investment into China rebounded to its highest level in four years, coinciding with preparations for the country's fifteenth *Five-Year Plan* (2026–2030).[30] The emphasis of this plan marks a shift from experimentation to scale: from technological breakthroughs to deployment, industrial upgrading, and ecosystem formation.[31] Sustainability is not treated as a parallel objective, but as integral to industrial competitiveness, resource efficiency, and energy security. Circularity, emissions reduction, food system resilience, and digital traceability are embedded within mainstream industrial policy rather than framed as separate agendas.[32]

This approach has clear implications for global capital. Investors respond to predictability, and policy coherence. China remains a high-emissions economy with unresolved social and environmental challenges, but it also offers a policy environment in which sustainability-linked investment is clearly aligned with long-term industrial strategy. In contrast to the United States, where signals have become fragmented, China is pushing its existing industrial base to become more efficient, automated, and lower carbon.[33] That clarity matters for investment decisions, regardless of political system.

Beyond China, however, the picture is markedly different. According to the International Energy Agency, only around 15% of global clean energy investment currently flows to emerging and developing economies outside China,[34] despite these regions requiring roughly half of the additional $5 trillion per year needed globally to reach net zero by mid-century.[35] Climate finance in the Global South remains dominated by debt, much of it at commercial rates, with relatively little equity and very limited funding for adaptation. This imbalance reflects not a lack of need, but a mismatch between risk, return, and institutional capacity.

This is the real sustainability finance gap. Private capital will not scale into emerging economies at the levels required without stronger risk-sharing mechanisms, blended finance, concessional capital, and credible project pipelines. Simply urging investors to "do more" ignores the constraints under which they operate. As political leaders such as Mia Mottley have argued, expecting countries already facing debt distress to shoulder the transition through additional borrowing is neither fair nor viable.[36] Without reforms to multilateral finance, currency-risk mitigation, and domestic institutional capacity, sustainability investment will remain unevenly distributed.[37] Across private equity, China, and emerging economies, the same logic applies. Capital does not flow because sustainability is fashionable. It flows where incentives are aligned, and returns are credible. Where these conditions are absent, investment stalls regardless of moral urgency. This is not a failure of finance so much as a reminder of how it works.

At bedrock, the lesson is clear. Sustainable finance advances most rapidly when sustainability is embedded in industrial strategy, market design, and risk allocation - rather than layered on as an expectation of virtue. Private capital is already responding to this reality in some contexts. The challenge ahead is extending those conditions to the places where investment is most urgently needed.

## 4.5   Remaking Sustainable Finance

Taken together, the evidence in this chapter points to a clear conclusion. Despite political backlash, and rhetorical retreat, private finance is now structurally entangled with sustainability outcomes. This is not because financial institutions have become more virtuous, nor because markets have suddenly aligned with social goals. It is because environmental, social, and geopolitical risks increasingly threaten the stability of portfolios, balance sheets, and economies themselves. Sustainability has moved from preference to exposure.

This shift places firm limits on how far finance can retreat. Banks may exit alliances, asset managers may soften language, and investors may debate mandates, but none can easily escape systemic risk. Climate volatility, resource constraints, supply-chain fragility, and social instability now affect asset values across time horizons that matter to long-term investors. In this sense, sustainable finance is no longer driven primarily by aspiration or reputation, but by risk management and value preservation. The bedrock has shifted.

At the same time, this chapter has shown that the tools of sustainable finance remain imperfect. Universal ownership has been oversold as a solution to systemic problems. Stewardship at the level of individual companies is constrained by law, incentives, and governance realities. Private equity can drive change where it has control, but only within markets that offer credible returns. Capital flows readily to jurisdictions with policy clarity and institutional capacity, and far more slowly to those without. None of these limitations are accidental. They reflect the underlying architecture of financial markets.

The most credible path forward lies not in expanding voluntary commitments, but in strengthening the rules of the game. Universal owners are most effective when advocating for market-wide standards that protect the value of the system as a whole: robust disclosure regimes, consistent transition incentives, credible carbon pricing, and prudential rules that reflect climate and nature-related risk. Private capital scales fastest where these guardrails exist, and stalls where they do not. Sustainability, in other words, advances when it is embedded in market design rather than appended as an expectation of virtue. This has important implications for the broader argument of the book. Finance is not leading sustainability, but neither is it simply obstructing it. It is responding to constraint – much as King Canute did centuries before. Where sustainability reshapes risk, return, and regulation, finance adapts. Where it does not, finance resists. *Remaking Sustainability* therefore requires engaging finance at bedrock: altering incentives, governance, and accountability so that sustainability considerations become inseparable from judgments of value.

The next chapter turns to insurance, where this logic is even starker. Unlike banks or asset managers, insurers cannot defer exposure indefinitely. When risks become uninsurable, markets do not merely reprice - they fail. If finance is already being pulled toward sustainability by systemic risk, insurance shows what happens when that pull becomes unavoidable.

## Notes


1. The Energy Mix, *Mark Carney's Net Zero Banking Alliance is done. Now what?* 16 October 2025.
2. Damien Gayle, *Banking industry's net zero alliance shuts down admit faltering climate commitments*, The Guardian, 3 October 2025.
3. The Energy Mix, *Mark Carney's Net Zero Banking Alliance is done. Now what?* 16 October 2025.
4. RMI, *Recalibrating the role of banks in the energy transition*, October 2025.
5. RMI, *Recalibrating the role of banks in the energy transition*, October 2025.
6. The Energy Mix, *Mark Carney's Net Zero Banking Alliance is done. Now what?* 16 October 2025.
7. Interview conducted in December 2025.
8. Florian Berg, *ESG might be more resilient than critics expect*, Financial Times, 4 October 2025.
9. Florian Berg, *ESG might be more resilient than critics expect*, Financial Times, 4 October 2025.
10. Florian Berg, *ESG might be more resilient than critics expect*, Financial Times, 4 October 2025.
11. Vasuki Shastry, *personal communication*, December 2025.
12. Blackrock, *Our fiduciary approach to sustainability and the low-carbon transition*, (website), 3 January 2026.
13. John Morrison, *The Just Transition: A systems-thinking approach to climate action*, 2024.
14. Quoted in Shastry op. cit., Stuart Kirk, '*ESG is existentiality flawed and must be split into two*', Financial Times, 2 September 2022.
15. Personal communication with Caroline Rees, *Shift*, April 2024.
16. IFRS Foundation, *About the International Sustainability Standards Board*, 2025.
17. IFRS Foundation, *About the International Sustainability Standards Board*, 2025.

18. Florian Berg, *ESG might be more resilient than critics expect*, Financial Times, 4 October 2025.

19. Quoted in Shastry op. cit., World Economic Forum, 'Here's why comparable ESG reporting is crucial for investors', 8 July 2021.

20. Global Association of Risk Professionals, *Is Modern Portfolio Theory obsolete?* 21 January 2022.

21. Said Business School, *Leading in extraordinary times with Hiro Mizuno*, University of Oxford, 21 April 2020.

22. Steve Waygood, *Macro Stewardship: An Introduction*, Aviva Investors, 21 September 2022.

23. The New York Times, *Exxon Mobil defeated by activist investor Engine No.1*, 9 June 2021.

24. The Guardian, *Texas court dismisses Exxon's lawsuit against climate activist shareholders*, 18 June 2024.

25. Jamie Smyth and Alexandra White, *SEC allows Exxon plan to limit shareholder activism*, Financial Times, 25 September 2025.

26. Jamie Smyth and Alexandra White, *SEC allows Exxon plan to limit shareholder activism*, Financial Times, 25 September 2025.

27. Tom Gosling, *Universal Owners and Climate Change*, Journal of Financial Regulation, 11(1), April 2025.

28. Boston Consulting Group, *Sustaining the Private Capital Opportunities in Climate*, 23 September 2025.

29. Boston Consulting Group, *Sustaining the Private Capital Opportunities in Climate*, 23 September 2025.

30. William Sandlund and Haohsiang Lo, *Foreign investors return to China's stock market*, 16 November 2025.

31. World Economic Forum, *How China's 15th Five-year plan signals a new phase in strategic adaptation*, 30 October 2025.

32. World Economic Forum, *How China's 15th Five-year plan signals a new phase in strategic adaptation*, 30 October 2025.

33. China Daily, *China's next five-year plan conducive to global well-being*, 4 November 2025.

34. International Energy Agency, *Financing Clean Energy Transitions in Emerging and Developing Economies, 2021*.

35. Junpei Guo, *How China's 15th five-year plan signals a new phase of strategic adaptation*, World Economic Forum, 30 October 2025.

36. https://www.climateworks.org/wp-content/uploads/2022/11/Using-the-Right-Mix-of-Financial-Instruments-to-Provide-and-Mobilize-Climate-Finance_iGSTFinance_Nov2022.pdf
37. https://climatenetwork.org/2023/12/13/new-path-to-transition-away-from-fossil-fuels-marred-by-lack-of-finance-and-loopholes/

# 5

# Underwriting the Future

Insurance occupies a distinctive place in the sustainability debate because it deals not in aspiration, but in probability. Unlike most other parts of the financial system, insurers cannot rely on narrative, or delay when risk intensifies. They must decide, explicitly and repeatedly, whether a risk is insurable, at what price, and under what conditions. When those decisions change, the consequences are immediate and visible. For much of the past century, insurance was built on a relatively stable set of assumptions. Risks were treated as largely independent, extreme events as rare, and experience was seen as a reliable guide to future loss. Climate change, environmental degradation, and social instability have now broken those assumptions. Losses are no longer random, extremes are no longer exceptional, and historical data is increasingly unreliable. What was once a technical challenge for actuaries has become a systemic issue for societies.

This makes insurance a critical test of whether sustainability has truly reached bedrock. Banks and asset managers can debate mandates, exit alliances, or soften language while remaining exposed to long-term risk. Insurers do not have that luxury. When risks become uninsurable, markets do not merely reprice - they fail. Homes cannot be mortgaged, businesses cannot operate, infrastructure cannot be financed, and communities


J. Morrison, *Remaking Sustainability*, https://doi.org/10.1007/978-3-032-23755-2_5

cannot recover. Insurance is therefore where sustainability stops being optional and becomes operationally unavoidable.

The signs of strain are already visible. In parts of California, Florida, Australia, and southern Europe, insurers have withdrawn from property markets or sharply restricted coverage. Premiums have risen faster than wages, deductibles have increased, and exclusions have multiplied. What is emerging are not isolated shocks, but patterns: areas where insurance is becoming unavailable or unaffordable for large segments of the population. These 'insurance deserts' are an early warning signal of deeper systemic stress. It is tempting to interpret these developments as failures of the insurance industry: evidence of short-termism, risk aversion, or regulatory gaming. That reading misses the point. Insurers are responding with bounded rationality to correlated risks that can no longer be pooled effectively. Climate-driven hazards such as heatwaves, floods, wildfires, and storms increasingly occur in clusters, compounding losses across regions and lines of business. When correlation rises, diversification breaks down. When diversification fails, insurance ceases to function as designed.

## 5.1   The Future Is Now

From this perspective, insurance deserts are not merely a sectoral issue. They are a signal that environmental and social risks are beginning to overwhelm existing economic arrangements. Sustainability debates often focus on long-term horizons: 2050 targets, transition pathways, future technologies. Insurance operates on much shorter timescales. Annual renewal cycles force risks to be confronted as they materialise. In doing so, insurance compresses the future into the present. This compression exposes a central tension. Societies continue to rely on insurance markets to absorb shocks that are increasingly predictable and increasingly severe. At the same time, the drivers of those shocks – such as land-use decisions, infrastructure design, emissions trajectories, and social vulnerability - remain largely outside the control of insurers themselves. The result is a growing mismatch between risk creation and risk bearing.

The remainder of this chapter examines how that mismatch is playing out, and what it tells us about the sustainability of sustainability itself. It begins by showing how systemic and correlated risks are undermining traditional insurance models, before turning to the emergence of insurance deserts and their social consequences. It then considers the limits of innovation within insurance, and why product design alone cannot resolve the problem. Finally, it argues that resilience, understood as a collective investment in reducing risk at source, must become the organising principle that reconnects insurance, finance, and sustainability.

If finance is being pulled toward sustainability by exposure to systemic risk, insurance shows what happens when that pull becomes unavoidable. It is here, at the point where risk can no longer be deferred or disguised, that the future is already being underwritten.

## 5.2    Extreme Weather Events

The 2025 California wildfires alone caused significant losses. Two major fires broke out in early January and burned for several days, forcing mass evacuation from the Palisades and Eaton districts of Los Angeles. While the final economic, insurance and reinsurance losses are yet to be finalised at time of writing, the total insured loss is estimated to be between $25 billion and $45 billion.[1] California's insurer of last resort, the *California Fair Access to Insurance Requirements* (FAIR) plan, was established in 1968 to provide coverage for properties deemed too risky by standard insurers. Between 2020 and 2024, the number of policies under the *FAIR Plan* more than doubled. However, the plan is now struggling to cover claims, leading to a proposed $1 billion bailout, funded through higher premiums and insurer contributions.[2]

Climate risks are also increasing elsewhere. In the UK, at least one in six people already lives with flood risk, heavy-rainfall extremes are increasing, and expected annual damages could rise by 27% by the 2050s.[3] Insurance claims from extreme weather are surging. The *Association of British Insurers* reported a record £585 million in home weather-damage payouts for 2024.[4] Policymakers in the UK tried to avert an insurance crisis by launching *Flood Re* in 2016, a joint reinsurance scheme between government and insurers designed to keep insurance affordable for households in high-risk areas. It was meant as a temporary bridge, until 2039, when stronger flood defences and better land-use are in place. But progress has been painfully slow. In January 2024, the UK *House of Commons Public Accounts Committee* reported that the government's £5.2 billion flood defence programme is 40% behind schedule and expected to protect just 200,000 properties by 2027 - far short of its original 336,000 homes target.[5]

Insured losses from natural catastrophes reached an estimated $100 billion in the first half of 2025, the second-highest half-year total on record, according to the insurer Aon. Yet global economic losses in the same period were far higher at $162 billion, revealing that a significant portion of the world's exposure remains uninsured.[6] Some of the other major insurance companies are beginning to raise sustainability concerns: for example Allianz, Aviva, AXA, and Zurich.[7] Insurance systems, particularly in high-income countries, are absorbing unprecedented losses; while vast regions of the Global South remain excluded from coverage altogether.[8] The industry's capacity to maintain affordability and availability - the foundations of its social contract - is eroding. The resulting crisis is both economic and systemic. It threatens the insurability of climate-exposed regions, distorts global capital flows, and undermines resilience planning. Without decisive reform, the industry risks becoming a casualty of the very risks it was designed to manage.

## 5.3    The Social Consequences of Insurance Deserts

The crisis is not solely about the frequency of events. Sustainability introduces compound and correlated risks - where multiple hazards interact, cascading through economic and social systems.[9] A single wildfire season may trigger housing shortages, mortgage defaults, and utility disruptions, amplifying insured and uninsured losses alike. For insurers, this breaks the principle of independent risk events, a cornerstone of actuarial science. When flood, drought, fire, and windstorm risks overlap within a single geography, diversification - the industry's primary defence - loses its potency. The insurance industry's business model also depends on predictability. Actuarial pricing requires stable, data-driven estimates of frequency and severity. Yet, weather patterns that have historically informed risk models are becoming increasingly unreliable. This undermines underwriting discipline and leads to mispriced risk. Over successive years, insurers have recorded cumulative underwriting losses exceeding $100 billion globally. Many have responded by reducing exposure in high-risk regions, limiting renewals, or exiting entire markets - giving rise to the phenomenon now widely referred to as insurance deserts.

Reinsurers took heavy losses before sharply tightening their terms in 2023, putting extra pressure on the ceding companies (the primary insurers). US property and casualty insurers incurred more than $20 billion in underwriting losses in both 2022 and 2023, according to rating agency *AM Best. State Farm*, the biggest US home insurer, suffered a net loss of more than $6 billion in both years.[10] As insurers retreat from exposed regions - such as wildfire-prone California or flood-affected Queensland - a feedback loop emerges. Reduced supply drives up premiums for remaining customers, pricing out lower-income households and small businesses. With fewer policyholders contributing to the risk pool, premiums rise further, and insurability declines. This "spiral of withdrawal" is not theoretical; it is already reshaping housing markets and credit access. In California, seven of the twelve largest homeowners' insurers placed limits on new policies even before the 2025 fire season began. Such actions, while financially rational, expose the systemic interdependence between insurance, finance, and social stability.

In the US and Europe, mature markets and deep reinsurance networks can absorb many of the current shocks, at least for the time being. In contrast, vast regions of Asia, Africa, and Latin America remain severely underinsured. In 2024, extreme weather events caused $320 billion in global damages, but only $140 billion was insured.[11] This means that more than half of global losses were borne by households, businesses, and governments without coverage. The consequences are profound: delayed recovery, persistent poverty, and dependence on volatile foreign aid. In low-income countries, post-disaster spending often exceeds investment in education or healthcare, perpetuating a cycle of vulnerability.[12] The sustainability crisis, therefore, is not merely a matter of profit margins - it is a question of global equity. Without affordable risk financing, developing economies cannot attract investment or maintain fiscal stability in the face of recurrent shocks. The contraction of traditional insurance markets has already created insurance deserts. This is not limited to developing countries; it now affects parts of California, Florida, and Australia too. The secondary impacts are severe: property values decline, mortgage markets falter, and public insurance programmes face mounting deficits.

## 5.4    Limitations of Existing Insurance Models

Insurance markets have always been cyclical. Periods of heavy losses are typically followed by rising premiums, tighter underwriting standards, and capital discipline, before competition gradually erodes margins again. This underwriting cycle is well understood within the industry and is often invoked to reassure observers that current pressures, while severe, remain manageable. From the San Francisco Earthquake in 1906 to Hurricane Katrina in 2005, or the attack on the World Trade Center in 2001, the industry had to cope with unexpectedly enormous losses.[13] The global property-casualty (non-life) insurance sector is known for recurring periods of instability. These underwriting cycles - characterized by significant swings in pricing and profitability - typically span five to eight years and are not closely tied to broader economic trends. They occur across different product lines and countries, though not always at the same time or pace. Historical data, such as long-term loss ratios in the US market, reveal clear multi-year fluctuations.[14]

There is truth in this perspective. Global reinsurance capital has continued to grow, innovation in modelling has improved risk pricing, and insurers have repeatedly adapted to new classes of risk over time. From this vantage point, recent loss years can be interpreted as an unusually sharp but familiar correction rather than a structural break. At their annual gathering in Monte Carlo in 2025 (no irony intended), reinsurers were discussing portfolio growth and acquisitions.[15] But not all speakers were entirely gun ho. 'Casualty insurance' remains a more vexing space: the category for all insurance that is not part of the main categories of life insurance, health insurance, or property insurance. It is within this category that many sustainability related issues arise, particularly when policies are combined with property insurance as they often are. The US casualty insurance market remains at high-risk given the unpredictability of legal precedents arising from loss-and-damage claims.

What distinguishes the current moment, however, is not the existence of losses, but their correlation and persistence. Climate-driven hazards - floods, wildfires, heatwaves, storms - are no longer independent events occurring sporadically across regions. They increasingly occur in clusters, across multiple geographies, and across multiple lines of business. When losses become correlated rather than diversifiable, the basic logic of insurance is undermined.[16] This is where historical analogy begins to fail. Past underwriting cycles assumed that adverse years would be offset by calmer ones, and that loss experience could be smoothed over time. Climate volatility weakens both assumptions. The distribution of losses is shifting, not oscillating. Extremes are becoming more frequent, baselines less reliable, and tail risks harder to bound. In such conditions, pricing adjustments alone are insufficient to restore equilibrium.

Industry responses reflect this tension. Premiums have risen sharply in exposed markets, deductibles have increased, exclusions have widened, and coverage has become more selective. In some cases, insurers have withdrawn altogether. These moves are often framed as temporary corrections, but their geographic persistence suggests something more structural. When withdrawal repeats year after year in the same regions, it signals not cyclical adjustment but declining insurability. Advanced modelling and simulation tools have improved insurers' ability to identify and price risk, but they have also accelerated this process of withdrawal. Better information does not reduce risk; it clarifies it. Where exposure is high and adaptation insufficient, improved models lead not to broader coverage, but to sharper exclusions. In this sense, technical sophistication compresses decision-making rather than softening outcomes. Reinsurers, for their part, continue to play a stabilising role, but their tolerance for accumulating correlated risk is finite. As global reinsurers rebalance portfolios, primary insurers face higher costs of capital and reduced capacity in precisely the markets where coverage is most needed. This dynamic reinforces the emergence of insurance deserts rather than reversing it.

What distinguishes the present period is therefore not the severity of losses alone, but the growing recognition that climate and social risks are no longer cyclical deviations from a stable mean. They are becoming structural features of the system itself. Insurance can adjust prices, terms, and participation, but it cannot indefinitely absorb risks that continue to intensify and converge. This recognition marks a turning point. It does not imply imminent collapse of insurance markets, but it does mean that the traditional expectation of recovery through cyclical adjustment is no longer sufficient. Where risk trajectories are worsening rather than fluctuating, the burden shifts away from insurance markets and toward the underlying systems that generate risk.

## Limits of Insurability

There is renewed interest in forms of insurance that can best protect workers from loss of income due to external factors such as extreme heat. Parametric insurance is not priced according to the risk profile of individual workers or consumers, but is triggered by external variables such as temperature, air quality or flooding. India exemplifies a context in which 80% of farmers operate without any private insurance, and farm workers, and all other low-paid workers, are generally uninsured. As the *Institute for Human Rights and Business* (IHRB)'s *Just Stories* programme has documented, extreme heat affects millions of workers every year. Parametric insurance initiatives in India, such as the *Self-Employed Women's Association* (SEWA)[17] in Gujarat or the informal and migrant workers protected by *Peoples Courage International*,[18] cover workers daily against heat stress, but are reliant on philanthropy as well as worker contributions. Can such schemes be fully commercially viable? Public-private finance approaches are being developed by organizations such as *The Blended Finance Company*[19] in Mumbai. But are they a sustainable solution to the people-centred impacts of climate change and other systemic challenges?

Parametric models should offer speed, transparency, and scalability, particularly in regions lacking detailed loss data. In the Global South, they offer a partial alternative to unreliable foreign aid, providing immediate liquidity after disasters. However, these innovations face limitations: they require robust data infrastructure, independent verification, and careful design to avoid "basis risk" (the mismatch between trigger and actual loss). Moreover, they cannot fully substitute for systemic investment in resilience. What distinguishes the current moment is not the severity of losses alone, but the growing recognition that climate and social risks are no longer cyclical deviations from the mean, but structural features of the system. Therefore, systemic responses are also required.

## 5.5  A Resilient Insurance System

When it comes to blowing the whistle on the risk of systemic insurance failure, it has largely been left to experts as no individual company is yet ready to sound the alarm publicly. In January 2025, the UK's *Institute and Faculty of Actuaries*, together with the *University of Exeter*, issued a report warning of 'planetary insolvency'.[20] The report warned of the same **tipping points** we covered in Chap. 2 of this book. The Greenland ice sheet, once it melts beyond a threshold, will continue to vanish for centuries, raising seas by metres. The Amazon, once degraded past a certain point, could flip from rainforest to savannah, releasing its stored carbon back into the atmosphere. Coral reefs, already bleaching at 1.1C of warming, could vanish altogether with cascading effects on fisheries and coastal protection. And so on. The Institute of Actuaries call this a *"risk of ruin."* Unlike ordinary risks, which can be diversified away, ruin means systemic failure. There is no portfolio rebalance if planetary insolvency materialises.[21] The authors of the UK's *Institute and Faculty of Actuaries* report[22] proposed several resilience principles to prevent systemic failure.

### Investing in Resilience

Better to invest in resilience itself. The US Department of Commerce estimates that every \$1 invested in disaster resilience yields \$13 in economic benefit. Yet, 88% of global disaster financing still goes toward post-disaster response. This imbalance is a fundamental cause of the insurance sustainability crisis. Without significant investment in disaster risk reduction (DRR) - from flood defences to resilient building standards - insurance becomes a reactive, rather than proactive, instrument. Partnerships such as the *Insurance Institute for Business & Home Safety Fortified Standards* in the US demonstrate how insurers, governments, and developers can align incentives for resilience.[23] By certifying buildings against wind, flood, or fire damage, these standards reduce losses and sustain insurability. Similar frameworks could be expanded globally, integrated into zoning, urban planning, and infrastructure finance. Advanced modelling - leveraging AI, geospatial data, and remote sensing - is transforming how risk is assessed. Tools like Aon's *Impact Forecasting tool*,[24] covering 12 perils across 90 territories, exemplify this shift. However, to achieve systemic resilience, these technologies must be shared beyond large insurers to local governments and small underwriters. Data transparency and interoperability will be crucial to closing protection gaps, a point I will return to in Chap. 11 on better data.

To make the business case, this requires high densities of policyholders in specific geographic regions. Admiral Insurance, for example, is the only major insurance company based in Wales, UK, and therefore can invest in resilience programmes, such as rewilding peatland in rural Wales.[25] These are known to retain water as well as carbon, and therefore decrease the likelihood of flooding. Similar thinking might be applied to the conditions facing the high density of migrant workers in Arabian Gulf States where climate risk and risk to workers often coincide.[26] But this cannot be left to the private sector alone. Governments have a pivotal role in maintaining insurability for high-risk populations. Public–private partnerships, such as the UK's *Flood Re*,[27] the US's *National Flood Insurance Program*,[28] and emerging models in Asia, can distribute systemic risks across broader pools, preventing market collapse. However, these programmes must evolve from subsidising risk to incentivising risk reduction through conditional coverage and resilience-linked pricing.

The insurance sector controls trillions in investment capital. Redirecting even a fraction toward climate-resilient infrastructure could have a transformative impact. Initiatives such as the Insurance Development Forum's *Infrastructure Resilience Development Fund*[29] exemplify how insurers can align underwriting and investment strategies, thus deploying capital not only to cover losses but to prevent them. New products will redefine the boundaries of what can be insured. Beyond property and casualty lines, insurers are entering climate-transition, carbon, and ecosystem insurance markets. These innovations, though complex, represent a strategic pivot by transforming insurance from a reactive mechanism into a proactive tool for sustainable development.

## Resilience as an Organising Principle

If insurance is to remain viable under conditions of escalating and correlated risk, resilience must shift from a peripheral concern to an organising principle of economic life. This does not mean eliminating risk, but reducing its severity, concentration, and amplification. Across jurisdictions and sectors, effective resilience strategies tend to converge around five core principles.

1. *Risk must be reduced at source, not merely redistributed.*

    Insurance can pool losses, but it cannot compensate indefinitely for decisions that continue to amplify exposure. Land-use planning, building standards, infrastructure design, and ecosystem protection are therefore not ancillary to insurance markets; they are prerequisites for insurability. Where risk continues to be created faster than it is reduced, insurance withdraws.

2. *Resilience requires investment ahead of loss.*

    *Ex post* compensation is politically visible but economically inefficient. Flood defences, heat adaptation, fire management, and early-warning systems consistently deliver returns that far exceed their costs, yet they remain underfunded because benefits are diffuse and long-term. Insurance signals where preventive investment is overdue by pricing, or refusing to price, risk.

3. *Risk must be shared explicitly and fairly.*

    As climate and social risks intensify, purely private insurance becomes insufficient. Public–private risk-sharing arrangements are increasingly unavoidable, particularly for catastrophic and systemic risks. The key challenge is not whether the state should be involved, but how responsibilities are allocated transparently between households, firms, insurers, and governments.

4. *Resilience depends on data, but cannot be driven by data alone.*

   Advances in modelling, remote sensing, and artificial intelligence improve risk visibility and pricing accuracy, but they do not substitute for political and social choices. Better data clarifies trade-offs; it does not resolve them. Without accompanying decisions about acceptable risk and collective investment, information alone accelerates withdrawal rather than stability.

5. *Resilience is inseparable from legitimacy.*

   Risk-based pricing exposes inequality. Those least able to absorb loss are often the most exposed, and rapid premium increases or coverage withdrawal can erode trust in both markets and institutions. Durable resilience therefore requires social consent: clear communication of risks, credible pathways for adaptation, and mechanisms to prevent resilience from becoming a privilege of wealth.

Taken together, these principles clarify why resilience cannot be delivered by insurance markets alone. They also explain why sustainability becomes operational at the point where societies decide which risks to tolerate, which to reduce, and which to share. When resilience is treated as infrastructure rather than emergency response, insurance remains viable. When it is not, withdrawal becomes inevitable. If the insurance sector once looked to financial cycles or regulatory shifts to plan its future, it must now look to the planetary boundaries and social requirements discussed in Chap. 2. The industry's long-term viability will depend on keeping climate and ecological risks within insurable boundaries. This makes sustainability one of the industry's key strategic constraints and opportunities. Insurers that embed sustainability into their modelling, products, investments, and partnerships will be better positioned to navigate a world of compounding risks. Those that fail to adapt will find themselves unable to price risk accurately, unable to secure capital, and ultimately unable to fulfil their societal mandate.

In this sense, sustainability is not just an add-on to insurance; it is becoming an organising principle even if many in the industry have yet to recognise this. As planetary risk intensifies, sustainability will increasingly determine not just the affordability of insurance, but its continued existence and purpose. Insurance shows where unmanaged risk becomes intolerable, industrial strategy - the next chapter - determines whether that risk is reduced at source.

## Notes

1. https://axaxl.com/fast-fast-forward/articles/los-angeles-wildfires-the-reinsurance-claims-picture
2. Josh Recamara, *Insurance industry could be making the climate crisis worse*, Insurance Business, 19 February 2025.
3. Meilan Yan and Qiuhua Liang, *Climate Change is becoming an insurance crisis*, The Conversation, 31 October 2025.
4. Lee Harris, *Investors Hitting 'limit for insuring against UK floods, warns Flood Re chief*, The Financial Times, 21 July 2025.
5. UK House of Commons, *Resilience to Flooding*, Seventh report of the Session 2023–24, Committee of Public Accounts, 17 January 2024.
6. World Economic Forum, *Natural disasters have cost us $162 billion this year. Insurance covered most of it*, 8 August 2025.
7. Damian Carrington, *Climate crisis on track to destroy capitalism, warns top insurer*, The Guardian, 3 April 2025.
8. Christoph Möhr et al., *Mind the climate-related protection gap – reinsurance pricing and underwriting considerations*, Financial Stability Institute, March 2025.
9. Bank of England, *PRA Climate Change Adaptation Report 2025*, 30 January 2025.
10. Ian Smith and Kenza Byran, *The uninsurable world: how the insurance industry fell behind on climate change*, The Financial Times, 2 June 2024.
11. World Economic Forum, *From safety net to resilience-builder: how the insurance industry is stepping up*, 27 August 2025.
12. World Economic Forum, *From safety net to resilience-builder: how the insurance industry is stepping up*, 27 August 2025.
13. Sean Djalilvand, *The Silent Guardian*, 2025.
14. Iqbal Owadally et al., *The insurance industry as a complex social system: competition, cycles, and crises*, Journal of Artificial Societies and Social Simulation 21(4)2, October 2018.

15. The Voice of Insurance Podcast, *The State of Reinsurance 2025*, 30 September 2025.
16. Helle Bank Jorgensen and Agnes K Y Tai, *Rethinking climate risk and insurance can help boards boost company value and resilience*, World Economic Forum, 13 October 2025.
17. https://jpia.princeton.edu/news/heat-linked-parametric-insurance-system-offers-climate-change-lifeline-indian-women-informal
18. https://www.peoplescourageinternational.org/pdfs/AQI%20REPORT-FINAL.pdf
19. https://avpn.asia/organisation/the-blended-finance-company/
20. Institute and Faculty of Actuaries, *Planetary Solvency - finding our balance with nature.* January 2025.
21. Institute and Faculty of Actuaries, *Planetary Solvency - finding our balance with nature.* January 2025.
22. Institute and Faculty of Actuaries, *Planetary Solvency - finding our balance with nature.* January 2025.
23. Insurance Institute for Business and Home Safety, *Construction Standards*, (website), December 2025.
24. Aon, *Impact Forecasting*, Elements 15, 2021.
25. https://businessnewswales.com/admiral-becomes-largest-contributor-to-wwt-climate-resilience-fund/
26. See for example, *Closing the Gulf's Green Investment Gap: Insurance is the Missing ESG Enforcer*, forthcoming, Gulf Sustain, Institute for Human Rights and Business (IHRB).
27. Flood Re, UK. https://www.floodre.co.uk/
28. US Government, *Flood Insurance*, FEMA, (website), December 2025.
29. Insurance Development Forum, *Launch of Infrastructure Resilience Development Fund*, 16 October 2025.

# 6

# Modern Industrial Strategies

*"Erst kommt das Fressen, dann kommt die Moral"*[1]

We are approaching the centenary of Berthold Brecht's *Threepenny Opera* first published in 1928.[2] The quote literally translates as a reminder, should any be needed, that our animalistic need to eat comes before any sense of morality or ethics. The sustainability movement has always been torn on this issue. On the one hand, many fear that economic growth is closely linked to increases in production, consumption and resource use and has detrimental effects on the natural environment and human health. Yet, we also know growth is highly correlated with indicators for human well-being, such as life expectancy, education and a full stomach.[3] Arguments about growth and sustainability are real but increasingly unproductive. The question confronting governments today is no longer whether growth should continue, but how economic activity will be organised in a world of constraint.

Industrial strategy has returned not because ideology has shifted, but because conditions have. Climate risk, energy insecurity, supply-chain fragility, geopolitical competition, and technological transformation have converged to expose the limits of *laissez-faire* coordination. Markets

© The Author(s), under exclusive license to Springer Nature Switzerland AG 2026
J. Morrison, *Remaking Sustainability*, https://doi.org/10.1007/978-3-032-23755-2_6

remain essential, but they no longer reliably deliver outcomes aligned with national security, economic resilience, or sustainability on their own. In this context, industrial policy is not a departure from economic orthodoxy so much as a response to its blind spots. This matters for sustainability because industrial strategy is where abstract commitments are translated into material outcomes. Emissions targets, transition pathways, and disclosure set direction, but they do not build factories, retrain workers, or secure supply chains. Those tasks require deliberate choices about production, infrastructure, skills, and technology. Industrial strategy is therefore the point at which sustainability stops being framed as a constraint on growth and becomes a condition of competitiveness.

The re-emergence of industrial policy is visible across political systems and regions. During 2021–24, the United States mobilised hundreds of billions of dollars through the *Infrastructure Investment and Jobs Act* (IIJA), *Inflation Reduction Act,* and the *CHIPS and Science Act* to accelerate clean energy, advanced manufacturing, and domestic supply chains. Some of these investments were stalled or repurposed under the Trump Presidency during 2025, but many of the non-energy related investments remain and are being leveraged.[4] The European Union has combined climate ambition with industrial instruments through the *Green Deal Industrial Plan*, state aid reform, and carbon border measures.[5] China continues to integrate sustainability objectives into long-term industrial planning, embedding energy efficiency, circularity, and technological upgrading within its core development strategy. Even traditionally market-led economies in the Gulf and Southeast Asia are deploying industrial policy to manage economic diversification.

Seen through this lens, the familiar opposition between "green growth" and "degrowth" obscures more than it reveals. What matters is not the aggregate size of the economy, but its composition and productivity. Industrial strategy reshapes *what* economies produce, *how* they produce it, and *where* value is created. Sustainability enters this picture not as a moral imperative, but as a driver of efficiency, security, and long-term competitiveness. Energy systems that are cleaner are also less volatile. Supply chains that are more circular are often more resilient. Technologies that reduce resource intensity frequently lower costs over time. This does not mean that all industrial strategies are benign, or that sustainability goals will automatically prevail. Industrial policy can entrench incumbents, misallocate capital, or exacerbate inequality if poorly designed. Nor does it eliminate trade-offs. Choices about which sectors to support, which regions to prioritise, and which technologies to scale are inherently political. But these choices are being made regardless. The absence of strategy is itself a strategy - one that leaves outcomes to chance and external shocks.[6]

The relevance of this chapter follows directly from the argument developed in Chaps. 4 and 5. Finance is already being pulled toward sustainability by systemic risk, and insurance is withdrawing where that risk becomes intolerable. Industrial strategy is how states respond when those pressures move beyond the capacity of markets to manage them alone. It is the mechanism through which governments attempt to reduce risk at source rather than merely reprice its consequences. This chapter examines how modern industrial strategies are being used to remake sustainability in practice. It begins by situating the return of industrial policy within today's geopolitical and economic context, before turning to the design principles that distinguish effective strategies from rhetorical ones. It then explores the role of clusters, hubs, and economic zones in concentrating capability and accelerating deployment, and concludes by assessing what this shift means for the future of sustainability as an organising principle of economic life.

Industrial strategy does not guarantee success. It cannot eliminate uncertainty, nor resolve all tensions between growth, equity, and environmental limits. But it does change the terms of the debate. Sustainability ceases to be something that must be justified against economic priorities and becomes something through which those priorities are pursued. When that happens, sustainability has moved decisively from the margins to bedrock.

## 6.1   The Return of Industrial Policy

As insurance shows the cost of unmanaged risk, industrial policy shows how states now choose to manage it directly. It can be understood as being the strategic use of tools such as targeted subsidies, tax incentives, and regulations to reshape economic structures and stimulate growth in key sectors. Such an approach has long been rejected by neoliberal ortho-doxy, which argues that minimal government intervention produces the best outcomes.[7] Yet, as confidence in purely market-based solutions wanes, many countries are once again embracing industrial policy to pro-mote broader prosperity.[8] This is welcomed by economists such as Dani Rodrik, Joseph Stiglitz, and Mariana Mazzucato.[9] The latter emphasizes that industrial strategy should prioritize the collective good. When exe-cuted correctly, she contends, a *"mission-oriented"* approach, whereby governments mobilize resources and coordinate with businesses pursuing common goals, can *"maximize long-term public value and shared prosperity."*[10]

## Industrial Policies Everywhere

Many policymakers across the political spectrum now look for frame-works to address issues such as national security, inequality, and climate change in a way that integrate economic and political factors.[11] This kind of thinking never went away in China, now into its 15th five-year plan since the revolution. It is interesting just how current this is becoming elsewhere.[12] Western governments will stress that they still believe in free markets, but the rise in protectionism (and increased tariffs), even between otherwise friendly states, suggests classic ideas about neo-liberalism are on the decline, with or without sustainability.

Governments are increasingly using industrial policy to rebuild domes-tic production and reduce dependence on foreign suppliers, especially after the pandemic and geopolitical disruptions.[13] Companies that align their investments with government priorities can secure funding, lower costs, or ease market access. Companies may benefit from new local sup-ply chain ecosystems and stable access to inputs (such as cheaper energy). In such contexts, businesses that rely heavily on global supply chains may face higher costs or trade frictions as policies favour local sourcing. Many modern industrial policies target innovation-intensive sectors such as green technology, AI, biotechnology, and digital infrastructure.[14] The policies bring direct public funding for R&D, infrastructure, and work-force training in partnership with universities and 'industrial hubs' to co-develop technologies and expand into future growth areas.[15] State-backed financial incentives continue to grow: whether this be to attract greater foreign investment, or to incentivise exports through export credit loans and guarantees.

There is also a knock-on effect across borders. When one country adopts aggressive industrial policy others often respond to stay competitive.[16] Companies operating internationally may need to navigate competing subsidy regimes and different compliance requirements. It can also trigger global subsidy races, raising the stakes for where businesses choose to locate operations. While industrial policy creates opportunities, it can also introduce uncertainty. Shifts in national political leadership or international trade rules can alter policy direction or reverse support measures, affecting long-term planning. Companies must therefore monitor policy trends closely and build flexibility into their strategies.

## Green Industrial Strategy

Sustainability policies are increasingly integral to national industrial strategy.[17] In the European Union, *The Green Deal Industrial Plan*[18] aims to make Europe the hub for net-zero technologies, reinforcing climate neutrality by 2050. An analysis by the OECD[19] of G20 and OECD leading markets shows that green industrial policy is now 15% of total industrial expenditure and increasing, with $1.29 trillion of public spending for the development and deployment of low-carbon technologies.

From an Asian perspective, scarcity has long been treated less as an episodic shock and more as a structural condition. China, Japan, and South Korea industrialized under conditions of limited domestic resource endowments, shaping policy traditions that emphasize long-term planning, strategic reserves, and infrastructure-led resilience. China's modern approach to resource security - covering energy, water, food, and minerals - is embedded in successive Five-Year Plans, which explicitly link ecological limits, industrial policy, and national security.[20] This contrasts with the more market-reactive approaches historically dominant in many

Western economies. The five-year plans and *Made in China* 2025 initiatives invest heavily in renewable energy, battery technology, and electric mobility.[21] Similar water–mineral–energy trade-offs are now being actively managed within China's own borders. Lithium extraction in Qinghai and Sichuan, rare earth processing in Inner Mongolia, and nickel refining in Indonesia-linked value chains have forced Chinese regulators and firms to integrate water-use efficiency, recycling, and processing standards earlier in project lifecycles.

While not without environmental controversy, these cases illustrate how scarcity increasingly shapes industrial design rather than simply constraining it after the fact.[22] Even within the members of the Gulf Cooperation Council (GCC), the home of economies grown almost exclusively from wealth derived from oil and gas, the need to diversify investment has led to green energy targets that are increasingly ambitious.[23] In all these cases, sustainability isn't just a side effect, it's a strategic driver.

Meanwhile, the situation in the US seemed to reverse in January 2025 with President Donald Trump's first executive order "*14148*"[24] directing that all agencies immediately pause disbursement of funds appropriated under the *Inflation Reduction Act* (IRA) and the *Infrastructure Investment and Jobs Act* (IIJA). The administration took multiple actions to freeze or claw back funds previously earmarked under the IRA. For example, during 2025 the *Environmental Protection Agency* (EPA) terminated or froze about $20 billion in grants under the IRA's greenhouse-gas reduction fund.[25] But the IRA is a law passed by the US Congress. Many of its provisions are statutory, not solely dependent on executive discretion. The *One Big Beautiful Bill* (OBBB) Act does revoke some of this, but other IRA programmes remain active or are still being implemented.[26] Freezing disbursements doesn't always mean full cancellation. In some cases, the administration has said it will honour contracts that were already made. But several legal and market uncertainties remain. Some companies are having to fight expensive legal battles to protect renewable investments. At the time of writing, it seems that Equinor's 800 MW windfarm off the New York coast might be proceeding,[27] in part due to the intervention of the Norwegian prime minister. The 2.4GW Southcoast Wind project a little further north faces an uncertain future, however.[28]

Under the new *One Big Beautiful Bill* (OBBB) law, tax credits for wind and solar projects phase out sooner than originally planned.[29] To qualify, these projects must either be completed by the end of 2027 or have begun construction. This compressed timeline will likely force developers to accelerate their project schedules or risk losing critical tax credits. By contrast, the OBBB largely preserves tax credits into the next decade for newer clean energy technologies, like battery storage and carbon capture.[30] Nevertheless, the OBBB Act is expected to have a significant impact on the US renewable energy industry.[31] Developers, manufacturers, investors, tax equity and financing parties, and other industry stakeholders are all revisiting their strategies, often scaling back, or delaying US-focused investments.

Clearly the current confusion is not conducive to investing in sustainability within the United States - deliberately so. Businesses and investors face uncertainty which may delay investment, but it is not a full reversal. It is not just Democrat states that have heavily invested in green energy. Texas now leads the US in both wind-powered electricity generation and utility-scale solar capacity.[32] The foreign investment in US cleantech sectors has also been notable, rising from \$4.5 billion in Q4 2022 to \$13.5 billion in the second quarter of 2024, and domestic investment in the same sectors doubled from \$2.5 billion to over \$5.5 billion over the same time period.[33] Batteries received over 68% of this investment, making this the leading cleantech investment sector in the US by far. Asian countries have been the biggest investors in US cleantech, with over 80% of foreign cleantech investment coming from South Korea, Japan and China. Most of these green infrastructure investments will remain and will continue to grow.

So, around the world, national and sub-national industrial policy can be a fickle friend of sustainability, but in most cases a friend, nevertheless. What then is the architecture of a green industrial policy?

## 6.2   The Anatomy of Green Industrial Policy

Modern industrial strategy is no longer about picking winners in the abstract, nor about protecting declining sectors from inevitable change. It is about organising economic activity under constraint: constraints of energy, materials, labour, security, legitimacy, and time. Across countries and political systems, effective industrial strategies are converging around a shared set of design principles, even where their institutional forms differ.

The UK is an example of a country that has come slowly to the conclusion that industrial policy is necessary and overrides party politics. Particularly through times of international turbulence, governments are uniquely placed, not just to set strategic direction, but also to pool and share risk, which is one of the conclusions I also reached in the previous chapter on insurance (Chap. 5). There are countless historic examples of state-intervention into markets for clear economic or social purpose: for example from the birth of Silicon Valley in the US, to the aftermath of the 2008–9 Financial Crisis, and the response to the COVID epidemic.[34] "Too big to fail" was often used as the political excuse to protect or even nationalise: major banks, steel manufacturers, rail companies, and other critical industry players. It is not necessarily a slight. It is rather a reflection of national self-interest. The UK is an interesting example. Its free-market instincts means that the arguments for industrial strategy have had to be hard won.[35] Or, to put it even more bluntly:

> *The UK has a patchy record in industrial strategy. Perhaps it is a downside to being the first to industrialise: having no other country to emulate, the UK gained a habit of fumbling forward, rather than planning. Long after being overtaken by both Germany and the US, with their more consciously developed approaches, the UK never managed to create and stick to an industrial strategy for more than a few years at a time.*[36]

Nevertheless, successive UK governments - from the political right as well as the left - have gradually returned to some form of industrial strategy.[37] During 2025, the new UK Government published both its *Trade Strategy*[38] and its *Modern Industrial Strategy*,[39] both with a five-year gaze. This shortly after intervening to save the UK steel industry through re-nationalising key strategic assets. In many ways it matters less whether the government comes from the left or right, as many elements had been seeded by previous governments. There are also some challenges of 'now', including the overriding governmental imperative of achieving economic growth whilst also cutting 'red tape' by 25%. Drawing on the UK's own experiences,[40] as well as those within the European Union,[41] there are perhaps seven key elements to industrial strategy relevant to how sustainability can now be integrated.

## General Design Principles for Sustainability in Modern Industrial Strategy

In many ways these principles relate to modern industrial strategy in general but are prerequisites for any strategy to deliver sustainability outcomes effectively.

1. *Strategic focus.*

   Successful industrial strategies are selective rather than comprehensive. They concentrate resources on a limited number of technologies, sectors, or capabilities that are systemically important; because they unlock productivity gains, reduce exposure to external risk, or enable wider decarbonisation. Attempts to spread support thinly across the economy tend to dilute impact and undermine credibility. Focus does not eliminate political contestation, but it clarifies priorities and trade-offs.

2. *Alignment across policy domains.*

   Industrial strategy fails when incentives pull in opposing directions: when planning rules obstruct infrastructure delivery, skills systems lag technological ambition, or trade policy undermines domestic capability. Modern strategies therefore place increasing emphasis on coherence—between energy policy, innovation funding, procurement, competition policy, and regional development. Sustainability enters here not as an add-on, but as a unifying constraint that shapes decisions across silos.

3. *Risk-sharing rather than risk avoidance.*

Many of the investments required for sustainability transitions involve high upfront capital costs, long payback periods, and uncertain demand. Left entirely to markets, these risks slow deployment. Effective industrial strategies therefore use public capital, guarantees, or co-investment to absorb early-stage risk and crowd in private finance. Crucially, this does not imply permanent subsidy. The objective is to accelerate learning, scale, and cost reduction until markets can function independently.

4. *Place-based delivery.*

Industrial transformation does not happen evenly across space. It concentrates in specific regions where skills, infrastructure, institutions, and social licence intersect. Modern industrial strategies recognise this by supporting clusters, hubs, and ecosystems rather than isolated projects. Place-based approaches also matter politically. They connect abstract transition goals to tangible employment, regeneration, and identity, helping to rebuild trust in economic change.

5. *Institutional capability.*

Industrial policy is only as effective as the institutions that design and implement it. This includes technical expertise within government, credible delivery bodies, transparent governance, and mechanisms for learning and adjustment. Weak institutions turn strategy into rhetoric. Strong institutions allow experimentation, course correction, and accountability over time. In a world of uncertainty, the capacity to adapt matters as much as initial design.

6. *Discipline and conditionality.*

Public support without conditions risks entrenching inefficiency or rent seeking. Effective strategies attach clear expectations to support – on performance, learning, localisation, or environmental outcomes – and withdraw assistance where those conditions are not met. Discipline is what distinguishes industrial strategy from open-ended subsidy, and what maintains political legitimacy over time.

7. *Effective temporal sequencing.*

Some interventions are transitional, designed to unlock early momentum or protect vulnerable groups. Others must endure for decades, such as investment in grids, skills, and research infrastructure. Confusing these time horizons leads to frustration and backlash. Clear sequencing allows governments to explain why some forms of support are temporary, while others are foundational.

Taken together, these principles illustrate how sustainability becomes operational within industrial strategy. Environmental limits, energy security, and social resilience are not treated as external constraints on economic policy, but as parameters within which competitiveness is pursued. This does not eliminate trade-offs, nor guarantee success. But it does reposition sustainability from aspiration to architecture. Industrial strategy, in this sense, is not about the state replacing markets. It is about shaping the conditions under which markets operate, so that private investment, innovation, and employment align more closely with long-term societal objectives. When these design principles are absent, sustainability remains fragile. When they are present, it becomes embedded at bedrock.

## 6.3  Concentrating Capability: Hubs, Clusters, and Zones

A defining feature of modern industrial strategy is its focus on concentration rather than dispersion (principle 4 in the list above). Economic transformation rarely occurs evenly across sectors or regions. It happens where capital, skills, infrastructure, institutions, and legitimacy intersect. The UK *Institute for Government's* 2020 report on industrial strategy calls for a highly focused approach to avoid spreading the jam too thinly and for the strategy to be *"lumpy, but with carefully chosen lumps"*.[42] What a wonderful use of the language. And so inspired by plain English! Let's unpack a little what kind of *"lumps"* we might be talking about. I have already covered the business sectors themselves, as well as the renewable energy and other technologies that might relate to them. There are also what we might call the "structural lumps": hubs, clusters, and economic zones. Sometimes the lines between each of these can be blurry ('blurry lumps' - you heard it here first), with some initiatives using several or none of these terms.

Clusters, hubs, and zones are not policy buzzwords; they are mechanisms for concentrating capability and accelerating learning under conditions of constraint. This logic reflects how innovation and production scale. Firms benefit from proximity to specialised suppliers, research institutions, skilled labour, and shared infrastructure.[43] Knowledge spills over more easily. Risks are pooled. Bottlenecks are identified and resolved faster. For sustainability transitions - where technologies are evolving, costs are falling, and coordination failures are common - these advantages are decisive.

'Clusters' typically form around existing industrial strengths: advanced manufacturing regions, energy-intensive industries, ports, or research universities. 'Hubs' provide shared assets that individual firms cannot justify alone, such as test facilities, pilot plants, grid connections, or hydrogen networks. 'Zones' and other forms of economic ecosystems extend beyond production to include finance, trade and tax incentives, infrastructure, shared logistics, training, regulation, and community engagement. Together, they reduce uncertainty and lower the cost of entry for new participants.

Governments increasingly use these structures to target support without attempting to micromanage outcomes. Rather than subsidising individual firms indefinitely, policy focuses on enabling conditions: infrastructure investment, skills pipelines, planning reform, procurement commitments, and early demand signals. This approach allows competition and experimentation to continue within a framework that accelerates deployment. Crucially, concentration is not about picking corporate winners. It is about selecting *places and capabilities* where spillovers are most likely to occur. This distinction matters politically. Supporting ecosystems rather than individual firms reduces perceptions of favouritism and makes industrial strategy easier to defend. However, bail outs and subsidies to individual companies still occur when governments perceive them to be 'too big' or 'too strategic' to fail. Sometimes this requires bringing assets back into public control or ownership. Either way, sustainability objectives are better served through anchoring transitions in real communities rather than abstract markets.

Clusters and hubs also play a vital role in managing social licence. Industrial change generates disruption as well as opportunity. Place-based strategies make those trade-offs visible and negotiable. Workers can see pathways for reskilling. Local authorities can plan infrastructure and housing. Communities can assess impacts on land, water, and identity. Without this grounding, industrial strategy risks repeating the mistakes of past transitions, where benefits were diffuse and costs concentrated. 'Special Economic Zones' (SEZs) are a case in point, sometimes regarded as carve outs from social and environmental accountability with little local benefit, the estimated 5000 SEZs worldwide now need to be retooled to be effective localised sustainability.[44]

Here are some examples of hubs, clusters, and zones explicitly referencing sustainability. These are mainly UK and Chinese examples I am aware of, but many more can be found.

Hubs (including accelerators):

- *Carbon13 accelerator* in Cambridge, UK;[45]
- European Institute of Innovation and Technology's *Climate-KIC's accelerators*;[46]
- Manchester-based *GC Angels accelerator, UK*;[47]
- *Henry Royce Institute, UK*;[48]
- *Edinburgh Climate Change Institute* at the University of Edinburgh, UK;[49]
- Bristol's *Future Space, UK* hosts both robotics and green-tech accelerators within its innovation hub.[50]

Clusters:

- *West Midlands Growth Company's* automotive cluster accelerates the shift to electric vehicles through shared supply chains (UK);[51]
- *Net Zero Teesside's* industrial cluster uses shared carbon capture and hydrogen infrastructure to cut emissions for multiple industries (UK);[52]
- Humber offshore wind clusters, around Hull and Grimsby (UK).[53]

Economic Zones:

- The *Hefei Economic & Technology Development Zone* in Anhui, China, for example, uses AI to track energy production and consumption in real time, improving efficiency and reducing waste.[54]
- The *Tianjin Economic-Technological Development Area* in Binhai, China, uses a carbon-tracking app to give residents "sustainability points".[55]
- The *Suzhou Industrial Park* in Jiangsu, China, with its 'ESG toolkits' to tenant companies, with regulatory guidance and emissions-tracking services.[56]
- *Masdar City* in the UAE hosts a clean-tech accelerator.[57]
- *Zona Franca* in Barcelona, Spain, operates an *Industry 4.0* incubator focused on circular manufacturing.[58]
- The *Coyol Free Zone* in Costa Rica trains workers for life sciences and smart manufacturing.[59]
- The *Tanger Med* in Morocco runs an in-zone technical high school supporting logistics and green industrial skills.[60]

But there are limits. Concentrations do not emerge on command, and poorly designed initiatives can devolve into branding exercises or real-estate plays. Local economic ecosystems require time, institutional capacity, and sustained coordination. They also risk reinforcing regional inequality if investment flows only to already-advantaged areas.[61] These tensions must be managed explicitly through complementary regional and social policy.

Nevertheless, the direction of travel is clear. As sustainability constraints tighten, industrial strategy increasingly relies on spatial concentration to deliver speed, scale, and legitimacy. Clusters, hubs, and zones are how abstract ambitions are translated into productive capacity. They are not optional embellishments, but core instruments of delivery. In the context of this book's argument, they illustrate how sustainability becomes operational. By shaping where investment flows, how skills are developed, and which technologies scale first, place-based industrial strategies embed sustainability at bedrock, where economic change happens.

## 6.4   Remade Industrial Strategy

Modern industrial strategy marks a decisive shift in how sustainability is pursued. Rather than treating environmental limits as external constraints on economic policy, governments are increasingly embedding them within the infrastructure of competitiveness itself. Industrial strategy becomes the means through which sustainability is translated into production, employment, and national capability.[62] This shift reflects a recognition that markets alone cannot deliver the pace or coordination required under conditions of tightening constraint.[63] Climate risk, supply insecurity, and geopolitical fragmentation have moved beyond the margins of economic planning. They now shape core questions about energy systems, materials, food, housing, and transport. Industrial strategy is the response when these pressures exceed the capacity of price signals and voluntary coordination to manage them.

At bedrock, industrial strategy operates by reshaping incentives rather than prescribing outcomes. Public investment, procurement, standards, and regulation are used to steer private capital toward activities that strengthen resilience, reduce exposure to systemic risk, and build long-term productive capacity.[64] Where this alignment succeeds, sustainability ceases to be experienced as a cost and becomes part of how competitiveness is achieved. Where it fails, transitions stall, and political resistance hardens.

This does not eliminate trade-offs. Choices about which sectors to support, which regions to prioritise, and which technologies to scale inevitably create winners and losers. Nor does industrial strategy guarantee success. Poor design, weak institutions, or capture by incumbents can undermine its effectiveness. But the absence of strategy does not avoid these risks; it merely allows them to be resolved implicitly, through market volatility, crisis response, and social disruption. *Verschlimmbessserung*, as the Germans might put it today one hundred years after Brecht: why would you make things worse in an attempt to make things better?

What distinguishes contemporary industrial strategy is its integration of sustainability into core economic functions.[65] Energy policy becomes industrial policy. Skills policy becomes transition policy. Infrastructure investment becomes climate adaptation. These linkages are not rhetorical; they are operational. They determine whether economies can absorb shocks, maintain social licence, and adapt over time. In this sense, industrial strategy functions as sustainability infrastructure. It provides the durable platforms - physical, institutional, and social - on which transitions can proceed without constant renegotiation. It shortens feedback loops between ambition and outcome, and between risk creation and risk reduction. It also makes visible the choices that sustainability requires, allowing them to be contested democratically rather than deferred indefinitely.

The argument of this chapter is not that industrial strategy replaces markets, nor that sustainability can be engineered from above. It is that sustainability becomes viable only when embedded in the structures that govern production and investment. Industrial strategy is one such structure. When designed with discipline and legitimacy, it allows sustainability to move from aspiration to architecture. The next chapter turns from national strategy in more mature economies to the role of green investment in emerging markets.

## Notes


1. Berthold Brecht, *Die Dreigroschenoper (Threepenny Opera)*, 1928.
2. Berthold Brecht, *Die Dreigroschenoper (Threepenny Opera)*, 1928.
3. European Environment Agency, *Growth without economic growth*, 2021.
4. Wall Street Journal, *How Trump will decline which Chips Act companies will give up equity*, 21 August 2025.
5. European Commission, *The Green Deal Industrial Plan*, 1 February 2023.
6. Torsten Bell, *Great Britain? How to get our future back*, 2024.
7. Milton Friedman, *A Friedman Doctrine: The social responsibility of business is to increase profits*, The New York Times, 13 September 1970.
8. Project Syndicate, *Industrial Policy is back*, 28 September 2023.
9. Dani Rodrik, *Green Industrial Policy*, Oxford Review of Economic Policy 30(3), 2014.
10. Mariana Mazzucato, *Mission Economy: A Moonshot Guide to Changing Capitalism*, 2021.

11. Mircea Popa, *Is industrial policy back in fashion? Text-as-data evidence from UK policy documents*, Cambridge University Press, 2024.

12. Valentine Millot and Lukasz Rawdanowicz, *The return of industrial policies*, Economic Policy Paper No.34, OECD, 2024.

13. Valentine Millot and Lukasz Rawdanowicz, *The return of industrial policies*, Economic Policy Paper No.34, OECD, 2024.

14. Ezra Klein and Derek Thompson, *Abundance: How we build a better future*, 2025.

15. Torsten Bell, *Great Britain? How to get our future back*, 2024.

16. Valentine Millot and Lukasz Rawdanowicz, *The return of industrial policies*, Economic Policy Paper No.34, OECD, 2024.

17. World Economic Forum, UNITO, and Cambridge Industrial Innovation Policy, *The New Era of Industrial Policies: Tackling grand challenges through public-private collaboration*, January 2024.

18. European Commission, *The Green Deal Industrial Plan*, 1 February 2023.

19. OECD, *Green industrial policies*, (website), December 2025.

20. Wu Changhua, *personal communication*, January 2026.

21. Bonnie Chan, *How China is helping power the world's green transition*, World Economic Forum, 17 January 2025.

22. Wu Changhua, *personal communication*, January 2026.

23. Jean El Achkar and Salem Alhajraf, *GCC Net Zero Scenarios: Choosing the future we want*, London School of Economics, 1 September 2025.

24. US Government, *Initial Rescissions of Harmful Executive Orders and Actions*, The White House, 20 January 2025.

25. US Government, *EPA Administrator Lee Zeldin Cancels 400+ Grants in 4th Round of Cuts with DOGE, Saving Americans More than $1.7B*, Environmental Protection Agency, 10 March 2025.

26. Latham and Watkins LLP, *One Big Beautiful Bill: New law disrupts clean energy investment*, 8 July 2025.

27. Upstream, *Equinor's Empire Wind winds court battle: this time Trump was on its team*, 27 October 2025.

28. EnergyWatch, *Court ruled in Trump's favor: Approvals for off-shore wind farms can be revoked*, 5 November 2025.

29. Latham and Watkins LLP, *One Big Beautiful Bill: new law disrupts clean energy investment*, 8 July 2025.

30. Latham and Watkins LLP, *One Big Beautiful Bill: new law disrupts clean energy investment*, 8 July 2025.

31. Sidley Austin LLP, *The "One Big Beautiful Bill Act"- Navigating the new energy landscape*, 15 July 2025.

32. Texas Development Corporation, *Texas leads US renewable energy growth*, 30 April 2025.

33. E3G, *The US Inflation Reduction Act: Impacts on cleantech, trade and investment*, 23 September 2025.

34. Torsten Bell, *Great Britain? How to get our future back*, 2024.

35. David Willetts, *How to do industrial strategy: a guide for practitioners*, Resolution Foundation, 7 April 2025.

36. Giles Wilkes, *How to design a successful industrial strategy*, Institute for Government, December 2020.

37. David Willetts, *How to do industrial strategy: a guide for practitioners*, Resolution Foundation, 7 April 2025.

38. UK Government, *Trade Strategy* (Department for Business and Trade), 2025.

39. UK Government, *Modern Industrial Strategy* (Downing Street, Treasury and Department for Business and Trade) and new *Trade Strategy* (Department for Business and Trade), 2025.

40. See Giles Wilkes, *How to design a successful industrial strategy*, Institute for Government, December 2020; and David Willetts, *How to do industrial strategy: a guide for practitioners*, Resolution Foundation, 7 April 2025.

41. Sander Tordoir and Elisbetta Cornago, *How to build and fund better EU Green Industrial Policy*, Centre for European Reform, 19 February 2025.

42. Giles Wilkes, *How to design a successful industrial strategy*, Institute for Government, December 2020.

43. Ezra Klein and Derek Thompson, *Abdundance: How we build a better future*, 2025.

44. World Investment Forum, *Special Economic Zones as engines for the Sustainable Development Goals*, October 2021.

45. Carbon 13, *Carbon 13's Impact Report 2023–2024*, 20 November 2025.

46. European Institute of Innovation and Technology (EIT), *Climate-KIC*, (website), December 2025.

47. GC Angels, *Connecting Angels, Funding Innovation*, (website), December 2025.

48. Henry Royce Institute, (website), December 2025.

49. Edinburgh Climate Change Institute, Department of Geosciences, University of Edinburgh, (website), December 2025.

50. Future Space, Bristol, (website), December 2025.

51. West Midlands Growth Company, Invest in the West Midlands: Automotive, (website), December 2025.
52. Net Zero Teesside, *NZT Power*, (website), December 2025.
53. *Industrial Decarbonisation Research and Innovation Centre, Humber Industrial Cluster, (website), December 2025.*
54. Invest in China, *Hefei Economic and Technological Development Area*, 26 July 2018.
55. Tianjin Economic-Technological Development Area (TEDA), (website), December 2025.
56. World Economic Forum, *Suzhou Industrial Park – Integrated drivers of competitiveness to boost global value chain participation*, Case 15, (website), December 2025.
57. Masdar City, (website), December 2025.
58. Zona Franca Industrial Estate, (website), December 2025.
59. Coyol Free Zone, (website), December 2025.
60. Groupe Tanger Med, (website), December 2025.
61. Interview conducted with CEO of a Net-Zero Hub in the UK, October 2025.
62. UK Government, *Modern Industrial Strategy* (Downing Street, Treasury and Department for Business and Trade), 2025.
63. Torsten Bell, *Great Britain? How to get our future back*, 2024.
64. John Doerr, *Speed and Scale*, 2021.
65. Torsten Bell, *Great Britain? How to get our future back*, 2024.

# 7

# Emerging Green Economies

Emerging economies sit at the centre of the future sustainability transition, not by moral appeal alone, but by arithmetic. Emerging economies account for nearly 90% of global youth under age 30, providing both a workforce and a vast consumer base. Africa's population alone is expected to reach 2.5 billion by 2050, with its working-age population nearly doubling.[1] This demographic dividend, if coupled with education and digital infrastructure, can drive unprecedented productivity growth. Over the next two decades, the majority of global population growth, urbanisation, infrastructure build-out, and energy demand will occur outside the OECD.[2] Decisions taken in these economies will determine whether sustainability remains a marginal adjustment to existing systems or becomes a structural transformation of how growth itself is delivered. This reality reframes the role of emerging economies. They are no longer passive recipients of sustainability standards set elsewhere, nor simply sites of low-cost production or abundant resources.[3]

This chapter examines how these dynamics are playing out in practice. It does not ask whether emerging economies should pursue sustainability, but how they are doing so under conditions of constraint, and with what risks? Critical factors are governmental capacity as well as access to key



J. Morrison, *Remaking Sustainability*, https://doi.org/10.1007/978-3-032-23755-2_7

requirements: access to markets, finance, insurance, technology, and geopolitical alignment. The sections that follow treat specific initiatives and country cases not as models to be replicated,[4] but as stress tests of whether sustainability can be reconciled with rapid development in a more volatile world.

## 7.1    Markets of the Future

Emerging economies are not starting from zero. Many are experimenting with industrial strategies that integrate sustainability more directly into development pathways: renewable energy linked to industrial zones, manufacturing aligned with export standards, and infrastructure designed with climate resilience in mind. These approaches are uneven and politically contested, but they reflect a growing recognition that high-carbon, resource-intensive development paths now carry rising economic and strategic risk.

What distinguishes emerging economies is not simply vulnerability, but exposure. Their growth trajectories are more sensitive to external shocks: commodity price volatility, climate impacts, trade measures, and capital flows. As Chaps. 4–6 have shown, sustainability is increasingly enforced through these channels, whether intentionally or not. Access to markets, finance, insurance, and technology is progressively conditioned by environmental and social performance. For emerging economies, this turns sustainability from a long-term aspiration into an immediate strategic constraint. This creates a narrowing window for choice. Countries that align industrialisation with sustainability constraints can attract investment, stabilise growth, and build resilience. Those that do not risk lock-in to development paths that are increasingly penalised by global markets and physical risk alike. The difference is not commitment alone, but state capacity: the ability to coordinate investment, manage trade-offs, and maintain social licence under pressure.

Simultaneously, sustainability standards, once shaped mainly by global north investors, are being localized. India's *Business Responsibility and Sustainability Reporting* (BRSR) framework,[5] for example, aligns global international norms with national priorities, requiring listed companies to disclose progress on emissions, water use, and social inclusion. China's new green taxonomy[6] has influenced similar systems in Southeast Asia, while Latin American[7] and Arabian Gulf[8] stock exchanges now integrate ESG indices tied to issues ranging from biodiversity to social inclusion.

Perhaps the most striking transformation is the rise of homegrown companies seeking to proactively engage in sustainability. A 2024 survey by PwC found that 68% of large firms in Asia, 54% in Africa, and 61% in Latin America now publish annual sustainability reports - up from less than 20% a decade earlier.[9] Over the past 10 years, companies headquartered in emerging economies have moved from followers to innovators in green technology, social entrepreneurship, and circular manufacturing. For example, in 2025 Chinese carmaker BYD[10] became the world's largest electric vehicle producer, outpacing Tesla in EV sales by leveraging economies of scale and state-backed research.[11] Infosys (in India)[12] achieved carbon neutrality ahead of most global peers, proving that digital firms from emerging markets can lead on emissions reductions. Olam International[13] (Singapore-based, operating across Africa) has pioneered sustainable cocoa and coffee supply chains through farmer training, traceability systems, and fair pricing. The Brazilian mining company Vale has been involved in the failure of two recent disasters in Brazil as tailing dams have collapsed, but the company is now active across 30 markets with significant investments in green steel production.[14]

## 7.2    Fragile Foundations

Large-scale nature-based initiatives are often presented as an attractive solution to the sustainability challenges facing emerging economies. They promise multiple benefits at once: climate mitigation and adaptation, biodiversity protection, rural employment, and social stability. The appeal is understandable. Where fiscal space is limited and development needs are urgent, projects that appear to align environmental restoration with livelihoods and security are politically compelling.

## The Great Green Wall: A Stress Test for Green Ambition

Few initiatives capture the intersection of environmental urgency and economic opportunity in emerging economies as vividly as the *Great Green Wall*. Spanning 11 countries across Africa's Sahel region - from Senegal in the west to Djibouti in the east - this ambitious project seeks to restore 100 million hectares of degraded land, sequester 250 million tons of carbon, and create 10 million 'green jobs' by 2030.[15] As of 2024, roughly 20 million hectares of land have been restored, about 15% of the total ambition.[16] The *Great Green Wall* illustrates both the necessity and the limits of this approach. Progress has been uneven. While restoration activities have advanced in some places, delivery has been constrained by weak institutions, fragmented governance, and persistent insecurity. In areas affected by conflict or political instability, implementation has stalled or reversed. These challenges are not incidental. They go to the heart of whether large-scale environmental programmes can be sustained where state capacity is limited and authority contested.

This exposes a central risk of relying too heavily on nature-based solutions. Environmental restoration cannot substitute for governance. Projects that depend on long-term coordination, land tenure clarity, and community trust are especially vulnerable where these conditions are absent. In such contexts, ecological gains are easily undermined by renewed exploitation, displacement, or violence. Security dynamics further complicate delivery. Parts of the Sahel face overlapping pressures from climate stress and armed conflict.[17] Where violence disrupts access and erodes trust, environmental initiatives struggle to take root. This is not simply a failure of project design, but a reflection of the broader political economy in which sustainability interventions operate. Recent events in Mali, Burkina Faso, Niger, and Chad are all testament to this,[18] as well as the extreme deterioration in Sudan driven by external interference as well as internal factors.[19] Sustainability can almost seem an abstract luxury at such moments, but that would be a misreading of what many people in these countries want, and how Africa itself wishes to be perceived.

International support has helped sustain momentum for the *Great Green Wall*, but it has also introduced new fragilities. Funding is often fragmented across donors with differing priorities and time horizons. Monitoring and verification requirements can overwhelm local capacity. Expectations of private-sector participation frequently exceed what risk conditions allow. The result is a patchwork of initiatives that struggle to cohere into durable systems of land management and livelihood support. The lesson is not that nature-based solutions are misguided, but that they are insufficient on their own. Without parallel investment in governance, security, and institutional capacity, their impact remains limited and reversible. In the absence of state capacity, sustainability programmes become exposed to the very risks they seek to mitigate.

This matters beyond the Sahel. As climate impacts intensify, similar pressures are emerging across other parts of Africa, South Asia, and Latin America. Environmental degradation can interact with governance and social stress to create feedback loops that are difficult to interrupt. Nature-based solutions can play a role, but only as part of a wider strategy that addresses the underlying political and institutional foundations of sustainability. In the context of this chapter, the *Great Green Wall* functions less as a model to be replicated than as a stress test. It shows how sustainability initiatives falter when they are asked to compensate for absent state capacity.

## Africa's Next Phase

Whilst the stresses facing many African nations are undeniable, there are also now clear opportunities linked to the global sustainability agenda. From Morocco's battery manufacturing investments to Kenya's electric bus fleets and South Africa's EV assembly plants, the continent's emerging economies are aligning growth ambitions with sustainability imperatives. The question is no longer whether Africa can industrialize, but how it can industrialize sustainably.[20] Africa accounts for less than 4% of global carbon emissions yet bears a disproportionate burden of climate risk. At the same time, it possesses the resources and demographics that could define the next era of sustainable growth. The continent is home to

30% of the world's mineral reserves, including cobalt, lithium, manganese, and rare earths; essential for electric vehicles (EVs), renewable technologies, and battery storage systems.[21]

Morocco seeks to leverage its proximity to Europe and has attracted billions in green investment. In 2024, Chinese manufacturer Gotion High-Tech announced a $6.4 billion gigafactory to produce EV batteries in Morocco's *Tangier Tech City*. Expected to create 25,000 jobs, this follows Morocco's aspiration to be a 'regional anchor' in the global clean-energy supply chain.[22] Over 40% of Morocco's electricity already comes from renewable sources, including the *Noor Ouarzazate Solar Complex*, one of the largest in the world. Further south, Zambia and the Democratic Republic of Congo (DRC) are collaborating on a joint initiative to establish a regional battery production hub. The partnership, supported by the African Development Bank and the United Nations Economic Commission for Africa, aims to move both countries up the value chain from raw mineral exporters to processors and manufacturers. Together, Zambia and the DRC supply over 70% of the world's cobalt and significant shares of copper and manganese.[23] By developing refining, assembly, and recycling capacities, they could capture a much larger portion of the $400 billion global battery value chain.[24]

However, infrastructure and governance gaps remain significant. Reliable electricity, cross-border transport corridors, and transparent regulatory regimes are prerequisites for success. If achieved, the model could become a blueprint for regionalized green industrialization, demonstrating how neighbouring states can pool comparative advantages to participate competitively in the global sustainability economy.

China's engagement is central to Africa's green transformation. As the world's largest producer of EVs and solar panels, China is exporting affordable clean technologies to markets previously priced out of the energy transition. This has made it possible for African consumers and small businesses to adopt sustainable technologies at scale. South Africa remains the continent's automotive powerhouse, producing over 600,000 vehicles annually.[25] Although the transition to EVs has been slower than in Asia or Europe, momentum is growing. Chinese automakers such as BYD, Chery, and Haval have opened local assembly plants, while domestic companies like Enviro Automotive are importing and distributing affordable EVs for urban markets. South African government policy is catching up: the *Electric Vehicles White Paper* in 2024 set a goal for 20% of new vehicles sold by 2030 to be electric.[26] The strategy focuses on fiscal incentives, charging infrastructure, and domestic battery manufacturing. Elsewhere, Kenya's BasiGo and Moja EVs are electrifying public transport.[27] BasiGo, in partnership with BYD, plans to deliver 1000 electric buses across East Africa by 2026, while Moja EV Kenya began deploying Chinese-made Neta V taxis and expanded into assembly during 2025.[28] These ventures show how local innovation and global technology can converge to deliver sustainable mobility solutions.

Critics warn, however, that unchecked imports risk undermining local industry. If African countries merely become markets for Chinese products, the continent could repeat the extractive patterns of the past. Policymakers are therefore seeking balanced partnerships that include technology transfer, local content requirements, and skills development. Much depends on how much African governments can leverage competition between investors to demand fairer terms of trade and stronger investment in domestic value addition.

## 7.3  Bangladesh: Can Governance Guide Growth?

Many of us remember the 2014 Rana Plaza factory collapse in Dhaka, killing over 1100 workers, mainly women.[29] The business and human rights community learned many things from the disaster: how corruption can maintain unsafe buildings and working conditions, and how workers who feel they have no voice can be coerced back into an unsafe building and to their deaths. Yet the progress the country has made over the past 12 years, whilst confronting political uncertainty and systemic corruption, shows that emerging economies can be highly resilient and greater accountability should be no impediment to economic growth.[30] In barely five decades the country has moved from extreme poverty to lower-middle-income status, achieving average annual GDP growth of more than 6% between 2010 and 2023.[31] Its rise has been powered by a dynamic export sector, large inflows of remittances from Bangladeshi workers abroad, and significant amounts of investment. Yet the next phase of development, anchored in sustainability and governance reform, will determine whether Bangladesh can translate growth into long-term resilience. Many things are still uncertain, and the challenges facing its current caretaker government are many.

Bangladesh's transformation rests on a few pillars. Textiles and garments, account for more than 80% of exports, employing four million workers, mostly women.[32] Remittances from over 10 million migrant workers provide foreign-exchange stability. Agricultural modernization has doubled rice production since 2000 and improved food security. Social progress, with near-universal primary-school enrolment and life expectancy, now exceeds 72 years.[33] This combination has made Bangladesh a template for inclusive industrialization even if direct comparisons are very difficult.[34] The model also reveals vulnerabilities: dependence on a single export sector, limited diversification, and political corruption.

Bangladesh is also among the countries in the world most exposed to climate risk according to the World Bank.[35] Rising sea levels threaten to displace millions, and floods and cyclones routinely damage infrastructure and crops. Recognizing these threats early, the government has developed an integrated response. Bangladesh's *Delta Plan 2100* aims to make the delta region climate-resilient through river management, coastal embankments, and renewable-energy expansion.[36] The country has also launched a *Climate Fiscal Framework* that allocates over 7% of the national budget to adaptation projects, the first such mechanism in South Asia.[37] International partnerships are reinforcing this agenda. The Green Climate Fund and the World Bank's *Resilience and Sustainability Facility* are providing low-interest financing for green infrastructure. For global businesses operating in Bangladesh's manufacturing hubs, these investments reduce supply-chain risk and signal an emerging commitment to sustainability.

Despite economic progress, Bangladesh faces persistent governance challenges. Allegations of corruption, weak financial oversight, and politicized statistics have eroded investor confidence. A government-commissioned white paper in 2025 acknowledged that official GDP figures had been overstated and that approximately 3–4% of annual output had been lost to illicit financial outflows.[38] The 2025 interim administration led by Nobel laureate Muhammad Yunus pledged reforms to restore transparency - establishing an independent statistical commission, restructuring state banks, and strengthening the anti-corruption framework. For international partners, these efforts are more than political housekeeping: they are essential to maintaining the credibility of a rapidly integrating economy. Strong institutions are now viewed as a prerequisite for sustainable investment and sustainability alike.

The textile industry, long criticized for labour and environmental violations, has begun to reposition itself. More than 270 Bangladeshi garment factories have earned LEED certification from the US Green Building Council, the highest number of any country worldwide.[39] Major buyers such as H&M and Nike now require traceability on water use and emissions, pushing suppliers toward cleaner production technologies. The government's *Renewable Energy Policy* targets 40% clean-energy generation by 2041, supported by solar parks, rooftop projects, and the expansion of off-grid mini-systems. The *Sustainable Finance Policy* of Bangladesh Bank directs commercial banks to allocate at least 10% of portfolios to green projects.[40] Local entrepreneurs are responding with initiatives ranging from solar-irrigation schemes to eco-textiles that appeal to global buyers seeking lower-carbon supply chains.

Bangladesh illustrates how an emerging economy can pivot from cost-based competitiveness to sustainability-led growth. Its future success will depend less on cheap labour and more on credible governance, innovation, and climate resilience; foundations that will increasingly define the new global sustainability agenda for business.

## 7.4   Ethiopia: Can Leapfrogging Deliver Sustainability?

Ethiopia is an unlikely but powerful symbol of how emerging economies can leapfrog traditional development pathways by aligning industrialization with sustainability. Once associated primarily with agriculture and aid dependency, the country is now repositioning itself as a regional leader in renewable energy and electric mobility.[41] Ethiopia's policy experiment, anchored in an outright ban on internal combustion engine (ICE) vehicle imports and massive investments in hydropower, offers an instructive glimpse into how sustainability can underpin long-term competitiveness even in resource-constrained settings.[42]

Ethiopia historically had one of the lowest vehicle ownership ratios in Africa: barely seven vehicles per 1000 people as recently as 2016.[43] That scarcity reflected low-income levels, restrictive import duties, and chronic foreign exchange shortages. Yet within less than a decade, the government turned that limitation into opportunity. In 2023, Ethiopia became the first country in the world to ban the import of all ICE vehicles, positioning electric mobility as the default for national transport. Supported by tax exemptions and import duty waivers for electric vehicles (EVs), the transition has been rapid. By mid-2025, officials estimated over 115,000 EVs were on Ethiopian roads, accounting for roughly 8% of all registered cars.[44] The transport ministry wants to increase the number to 500,000 by 2030.[45]

Although data reliability remains a challenge, even conservative estimates suggest the country has achieved one of the highest EV adoption rates in Africa. The majority of EVs are concentrated in Addis Ababa, where short commutes and high electricity access have created a receptive market. The success of Ethiopia's electrification drive depends on its abundant renewable resources. Hydropower already provides over 90% of national electricity, and the *Grand Ethiopian Renaissance Dam* (GERD) - Africa's largest - will add more than 5000 MW of capacity once fully operational. The dam is not uncontroversial given its potential impact on countries downstream, in particular Egypt. Ethiopia's renewable generation potential exceeds domestic demand, offering a chance to anchor industrial growth in clean energy.[46]

However, challenges persist. Nationwide, only 55% of Ethiopians currently have access to electricity, and grid reliability remains uneven. The expansion of charging infrastructure is also limited: fewer than 100 public charging stations operate, and these are mainly in and around the capital.[47] Nevertheless, local entrepreneurs are stepping in. Start-ups supported by the UNIDO and the World Bank's *Energy Access Project* are piloting solar-powered charging hubs and battery-swap stations that could decentralize the EV ecosystem. Beyond electrification, Ethiopia aims to create an EV manufacturing base. The government's *Industrial Parks Development Corporation* offers tax holidays and export incentives to attract investors assembling vehicles domestically.[48] Chinese and Turkish firms have established small-scale assembly operations, while the state-owned Ethiopian Electric Power Corporation is exploring partnerships for battery recycling and local component production.[49]

The approach mirrors broader industrial policy: leveraging sustainable sectors to accelerate industrialization. The Ministry of Transport and Logistics projects that by 2032 Ethiopia will host 400,000 EVs and thousands of local assembly jobs. If achieved, that would make Ethiopia a continental reference point for green mobility.[50] The transition to electric mobility delivers multiple benefits. Import substitution reduces pressure on scarce foreign exchange reserves by cutting fuel imports. Electrification lowers transport costs, which in turn improves agricultural value chains and logistics. For businesses, reliable access to renewable energy reduces operational volatility caused by oil price swings.

Socially, the shift stimulates new forms of employment: from electrical maintenance and battery recycling to digital mobility services. However, equitable access remains an issue. Without affordable financing, EV ownership risks remaining concentrated among urban elites. Expanding microcredit and pay-as-you-go models, like those used for solar energy, will be critical to democratizing benefits. For international businesses, Ethiopia's story is more than a local anomaly. It represents the possibility of sustainability-driven leapfrogging - a model in which green policy ambition catalyses industrial innovation, even in low-income contexts. As global businesses reassess supply chains and seek credible sustainability partners, Ethiopia and similar economies are emerging as laboratories of practical transition strategies.

## 7.5 Remaking Capacity and Market Access

The experience of emerging economies makes clear that sustainability is no longer spreading primarily through persuasion or example. It is increasingly enforced through access to markets, finance, insurance, technology, and geopolitical alignment. For countries seeking rapid development, sustainability has become less a question of intent than of the conditions under which growth remains possible. The application of sustainability levers often remains uneven and indirect. Trade standards, supply-chain requirements, export finance conditions, and risk pricing transmit sustainability constraints without a single governing authority. Yet the result is a fragmented but powerful system of incentives and penalties that rewards alignment and punishes deviation. Emerging economies feel these pressures earlier and more sharply because their growth trajectories are more exposed to external shocks and conditionality.

The case studies in this chapter illustrate the stakes. Where governance capacity allows states to coordinate investment, manage trade-offs, and maintain social licence, sustainability can be integrated into development pathways. Where that capacity is weak, sustainability initiatives remain fragile, vulnerable to reversal, or confined to enclaves. The difference is not ambition, but institutional strength under pressure.

This has implications for how sustainability should be understood globally. The transition is not unfolding as a linear diffusion of best practice from advanced economies to the rest of the world. It is being shaped through contestation over standards, access, and power. The ability to leap-frog the costs and risks associated with the high-carbon and often deteriorating legacy infrastructure of older economies is clearly an opportunity. Emerging economies are not merely adapting to rules set elsewhere; they are negotiating, resisting, and reshaping them in pursuit of growth, employment, and stability. At the same time, the window for strategic choice is narrowing. As sustainability constraints become embedded in trade regimes, financial systems, and insurance markets, late adjustment will become more costly. Lock-in to high-risk development paths reduces room for manoeuvre and increases exposure to both physical and economic shocks. Sustainability, in this sense, becomes a filter through which development options are progressively screened. The central lesson of this chapter is therefore unsentimental. Sustainability in emerging economies will advance where it is enforced by material incentives and supported by state capacity. Where it relies on goodwill alone, it will falter. This does not make the transition fair, nor does it resolve the deep inequalities in who bears its costs. But it does describe how it is unfolding.

The four chapters in the investment bedrock section of this book (Chaps. 4–7) have aimed to show how sustainability moves from aspiration to exposure: finance begins to price sustainability risk (Chap. 4), insurance withdraws cover as environment-related losses become uninsurable (Chap. 5), industrial strategy reshapes what can be produced and where within sustainability constraints (Chap. 6), and emerging economies confront the unequal distribution of sustainability adjustment costs (Chap. 7). Together, these chapters establish that sustainability is no longer driven by alignment or intent but is now at the bedrock of investment: who is exposed to risk, who loses access, and who is forced to adapt first. It is in the interest of these governments, companies, and populations to ensure that better governance and sustainability standards are baked into what comes next.

The upcoming chapters in the next section turn to value chains and where these dynamics become operational at the enterprise level. It is through supply-chain standards, procurement decisions, and production requirements that sustainability constraints are translated into daily economic practice. If developed and emerging economies are negotiating the terms of sustainability, value chains are where those terms are ultimately applied within business.

## Notes


1. United Nations, *Africa's Fast-Growing Population*, Department of Economic and Social Affairs, 2024.
2. S&P Global, *Emerging Markets: A decisive decade*, 16 October 2024.
3. Ed Conway, *Material World: a substantial story of our past and future*, 2023.
4. Stefan Dercon, *Gambling on development: Why some countries win and others lose*, 2023.
5. Securities and Exchange Board (SEBI), *Business Responsibility and Sustainability Reporting* (BRSR), 2023.

6. People's Bank of China (PBOC), National Financial Regulatory Administration and the China Securities Regulatory Commission, *Green Finance Endorsed Project Catalogue*, August 2025.
7. MSCI, *EM Latin America ESG Leaders Select 5% Issuer Capped Index*, November 2025.
8. Ecodrisil, *GCC's unified ESG metrics: A bold step towards sustainable capital markets*, 4 August 2025.
9. PwC, *Global Sustainability Reporting Survey 2025*, 25 September 2025.
10. Wang Chuanfu, *The Innovator behind BYD's Global Success*, EV Magazine, 4 September 2024.
11. The Guardian, *China's BYD overtakes Tesla as world's biggest electric car seller*, 2 January 2026.
12. Infosys, (website), December 2025.
13. Olam International, (website), December 2025.
14. Vale, (website), December 2025.
15. United Nations, *Great Green Wall Initiative*, Convention to Combat Desertification, 2024.
16. Great Green Wall, (website), December 2025.
17. United Nations, *Great Green Wall Initiative*, Convention to Combat Desertification, 2024.
18. Center for Preventative Action, Violent Extremism in the Sahel, 4 September 2025.
19. Bronwen Maddox and Ahmed Solimen, *Independent thinking: Sudan – the internal and external forced tearing it apart*, Chatham House, 21 November 2025.
20. Mugwe Manga, *The Energy Future of Africa: A journey through Africa's green revolution and how it can change the world*, 2022.
21. Ed Conway, *Material World: a substantial story of our past and future*, 2023.
22. Investor Monitor, *Deal of the week: Gotion High Tech's $6.4bn battery plant in Morocco*, 16 June 2023.
23. Ed Conway, *Material World: a substantial story of our past and future*, 2023.
24. McKinsey Battery Insights, 2024.
25. NAAMSA, *Numbers up across the board for new energy vehicles in South Africa*, 2024.
26. South African Government, *Electric Vehicles White Paper*, 2024.
27. Mugwe Manga, *The Energy Future of Africa: A journey through Africa's green revolution and how it can change the world*, 2022.

28. EVXL, *Chinese Automakers Target Africa with Affordable EVS and Hybrids*, 27 June 2025.

29. United Nations, *The Rana Plaza disaster ten years on: What has changed?* International Labour Organisation, April 2023.

30. Stefan Dercon, *Gambling on development: Why some countries win and others lose*, 2023.

31. World Bank Group, *Data: GDP Growth – Bangladesh, (website)*, December 2025.

32. Stefan Dercon, *Gambling on development: Why some countries win and others lose*, 2023.

33. Stefan Dercon, *Gambling on development: Why some countries win and others lose*, 2023.

34. Stefan Dercon, *Gambling on development: Why some countries win and others lose*, 2023.

35. World Bank Group, *Climate Risk Country Profile: Bangladesh*, 2024.

36. Government of Bangladesh, *Bangladesh Delta Plan 2100*, General Economics Division, October 2018.

37. Government of Bangladesh, *Climate Fiscal Framework 2020*, Ministry of Finance, 2020.

38. Anti-Corruption Evidence et al., *Briefing on illicit financial flow risks from Bangladesh*, December 2024.

39. Bangladesh Textile Journal, *Bangladesh garment sector adds record number of LEED-certified green factories in 2025*, 30 December 2025.

40. Green Finance Platform, *Sustainable Finance Policy: Bangladesh Bank*, 2020.

41. Stefan Dercon, *Gambling on development: Why some countries win and others lose*, 2023.

42. Energy for Growth Hub, *Ethiopia's EV Pivot: How one of Africa's least motorized countries became its most electrified*, 23 June 2025.

43. Fred Harter, *Powering up: how Ethiopia is becoming an unlikely leader in the electric vehicle revolution*, The Guardian, 12 September 2025.

44. China Daily, *Chinese EV makers invest in Africa to boost green economy*, 1 September 2025.

45. Fred Harter, *Powering up: how Ethiopia is becoming an unlikely leader in the electric vehicle revolution*, The Guardian, 12 September 2025.

46. Farouk Chothia and Yemane Nagish, *Ethiopia outfoxes Egypt over the Nile's waters with its mighty dam*, BBC News, 7 September 2025.

47. Fred Harter, *Powering up: how Ethiopia is becoming an unlikely leader in the electric vehicle revolution*, The Guardian, 12 September 2025.
48. DEVEX, *Industrial Parks Development Corporation*, Ethiopia, 2014.
49. Ethiopian Electric Power, (website), December 2025.
50. Energy for Growth Hub, *Ethiopia's EV Pivot: How one of Africa's least motorized countries became its most electrified*, 23 June 2025.

# Part III

## Bedrock in Value Chains

# 8

# Security of Supply

Tennis fans might have noticed that the Wimbledon Cup is topped with a small silver pineapple. As expensive as the silver gilt might have been in the nineteenth century when the trophy was made, it is a replica of something far more valuable at the time. Until commercial production began in Hawaii in the early 1900s, pineapples were a rare and extremely expensive commodity in much of Europe.[1] In the seventeenth and eighteenth centuries, the English aristocracy would impress each other by attempting to grow pineapples in coal-heated glasshouses, often with disastrous results. Valued then at around $15,000 each in today's money, a pineapple was far too expensive to eat. Rather it would sit in the centre of a dinner table until rotten.[2] Pineapples sometimes had their own security guards and were rented just for the evening to impress dinner guests. The 1807 Proceedings of the Old Bailey, London's main criminal court, show several cases of pineapple theft, including that of a Mr Godding who was sentenced to seven years transportation to Australia for stealing seven pineapples.[3]

Today, security of supply is where sustainability stops being a policy debate and becomes a physical constraint. When water, energy, materials, food, and ecosystems are unreliable, no amount of finance, regulation, or



J. Morrison, *Remaking Sustainability*, https://doi.org/10.1007/978-3-032-23755-2_8

political intent can compensate. Production stalls, prices spike, and social stability erodes. Under sustainability conditions, scarcity is no longer an exception to be managed episodically, but a structural feature of economic life that must be designed around. This chapter examines how sustainability reshapes security of supply, not as a question of efficiency or optimisation, but as a matter of systemic resilience and exposure.

## 8.1    The Geopolitics of Scarcity

The World Economic Forum's *Global Risks Report* ranks "natural resource crises" among the most severe global threats over the next decade.[4] Climate change compounds these risks by amplifying droughts, floods, and extreme weather events: disrupting supply chains and damaging infrastructure. At the same time, the energy transition - while essential for climate goals - creates new dependencies on critical minerals and technologies concentrated in a few countries. This convergence of ecological and geopolitical pressures is reshaping how nations and corporations think about resilience.

Supply security cannot be understood in isolation. Water shortages can trigger food crises; energy instability can halt industrial production; ecosystem degradation can undermine entire economic sectors. The World Bank's *Integrated Food Security Framework*[5] and the International Energy Agency's *Critical Minerals Outlook*[6] both stress that resource interconnections, often invisible in traditional planning, must be integrated into future policy design. For example, producing one ton of lithium carbonate for electric vehicle batteries can require half a million litres of water, largely drawn from already-stressed aquifers in South America.[7] Similarly, water scarcity threatens the operation of power plants and manufacturing facilities, while energy is required for water treatment and agricultural irrigation. To give another very topical example, large data centres can consume up to 18 million litres of water *per day*, equivalent to the use of a town populated by 10,000 to 50,000 people.[8] Water can be reused in closed systems, but much is still lost to evaporation.

Such circular dependency means that failure in one domain can cascade across others. The result is not a series of isolated shortages, but a systemic risk to supply. This can have implications for security of supply for essential resources such as fresh water, energy, critical minerals, and food.

## 8.2  Water Security

Water security lies at the heart of many other supply systems. It is indispensable for food production, energy generation, industry, and human health. It wasn't until 2010 that the right to water and adequate sanitation became a human right.[9] However progress has been made. Between 2015 and 2024, about a billion more people have gained access to safe clean drinking water worldwide, increasing global coverage to 74%.[10]

Yet, global demand for freshwater is increasing far faster than sustainable supply. The gap between water demand and supply could reach 40% by 2030.[11] This is not simply a regional challenge, but a systemic global crisis shaped by population growth, urbanization, economic expansion, and the intensifying effects of climate change. The *Global Commission on the Economics of Water* (GCEW) has warned that humanity now faces a fundamentally destabilized hydrological cycle.[12] Decades of mismanagement, over-extraction of aquifers, river diversion, deforestation, and pollution, have eroded the natural systems that regulate water availability. More than half of the world's population already experiences water scarcity for at least part of the year, and nearly three billion people live in areas where total water storage is declining.

This crisis threatens multiple facets of sustainability. Ecologically, depleted rivers and wetlands disrupt biodiversity and carbon cycles. Economically, water scarcity undermines agriculture, industry, and energy production. Socially, it deepens inequality, as poorer communities are least able to afford or access reliable supplies. In short, water scarcity is a 'first-order' risk: a driver of wider environmental, social, and political instability. Traditional assessments have underestimated the volume of water required to sustain human welfare. The 2024 GCEW report found that while 50–100 litres per person per day are needed for basic hygiene, achieving adequate nutrition, sanitation, and livelihood security requires closer to 4000 litres per person per day.[13] Much of this is "embedded" water - used to produce food, clothing, and consumer goods. This means that international trade effectively transfers water from one region to another. For most countries, local water resources alone cannot meet this full requirement. As a result, global supply chains depend on 'virtual water trade', where countries import water-intensive products rather than the water itself. This interdependence makes water a global common good, yet governance remains largely national or local.

Resilient water systems, therefore, demand adaptive governance. This includes basin-scale management that reflects ecological boundaries rather than political ones; investment in storage, desalination, and reuse; and ecosystem-based solutions such as wetland restoration and reforestation to enhance natural regulation. In many cases, 'green' infrastructure provides more cost-effective protection than 'grey' engineering approaches like dams or levees. Water scarcity is as much a governance challenge as a technical one. The risk of water-related conflict between regions or nations rises as supplies tighten. Shared river basins such as the Nile, Mekong, and Indus already experience tensions over allocation. For example, The India-Pakistan water treaty, officially the Indus Waters Treaty,[14] was signed in 1960 to govern the Indus River system. It divided the six rivers of the Indus basin, giving Pakistan control over the three western rivers (Indus, Jhelum, and Chenab) and India control over the three eastern rivers (Ravi, Beas, and Sutlej). While it has largely survived for decades, recent geopolitical events, particularly the temporary suspension of the treaty by India following an attack in April 2025, have heightened tensions. Other recent flashpoints have been water sharing arrangements between Mexico and the US, Ethiopia and Sudan, India and China, and following the Russian invasion of Ukraine.

Still, frameworks such as the UN Watercourses Convention[15] show that shared management can yield peace dividends and long-term security. At the community level, equitable access to water strengthens social stability and gender equality. Women, who often bear primary responsibility for water collection in developing regions, are disproportionately affected by shortages. Integrating gender and inclusion into water governance is thus a critical component of social sustainability. The challenge moving forward is to maintain progress towards community resilience at a time when the demands for water are ever increasing, including from business, as are the environmental impacts.

## 8.3   Energy Security

Energy security has always been central to economic and political stability, but sustainability fundamentally alters its meaning. Historically, energy security focused on access, affordability, and geopolitical control of fuels.[16] Under sustainability constraints, it becomes a question of whether energy systems can deliver reliability and scale while reducing emissions, exposure, and systemic fragility at the same time. The transition away from fossil fuels does not eliminate security risks; it reshapes them. Electrification increases dependence on grids, storage, and critical materials. Renewable energy reduces fuel import exposure, but introduces new vulnerabilities related to intermittency, spatial concentration, and infrastructure resilience. As a result, energy security is no longer about securing barrels or cargoes alone, but about managing complex, interdependent systems.[17]

This complexity is already visible. Electricity demand is rising rapidly due to electrification of transport, heating, and industry, while grids in many countries remain underinvested and poorly adapted to variable generation.[18] Extreme weather events – such as heatwaves, storms, and droughts - are simultaneously increasing demand and disrupting supply. Where systems lack redundancy or flexibility, reliability deteriorates quickly. Concentration remains a central risk. While renewables diversify energy sources, supply chains for key components – such as solar modules, wind turbines, batteries, and power electronics - are highly concentrated geographically. This creates new dependencies that mirror, rather than replace, earlier fossil-fuel vulnerabilities. Energy security under sustainability therefore requires attention not only to generation, but to manufacturing capacity and materials access.

Storage and flexibility have become decisive. Without sufficient storage, demand response, and grid interconnection, renewable-heavy systems remain brittle.[19] These assets are capital-intensive, slow to permit, and politically contentious.[20] Where they lag generation build-out, systems experience curtailment, price volatility, and reliability concerns that undermine public and political support for the transition. Energy security is also increasingly shaped by cross-border interdependence. Power interconnectors, shared gas and hydrogen infrastructure, and regional balancing markets improve efficiency but transmit shocks. In tightly coupled systems, failures propagate faster. Sustainability therefore raises a fundamental trade-off: greater integration improves decarbonisation efficiency but increases exposure to cascading risk. Crucially, energy security can no longer be treated as separate from climate risk. Heat reduces thermal plant efficiency, drought constrains hydro and cooling water availability, and extreme events damage transmission and distribution assets. These impacts are no longer future scenarios; they are current operating conditions. Energy systems designed for historical climate baselines are increasingly misaligned with physical reality.

The implication is clear. Energy security under sustainability constraint cannot be delivered through fuel substitution alone. It requires sustained investment in grids, storage, resilience, and system coordination. Where this investment is delayed, security risks intensify, costs rise, and political resistance hardens. Where it proceeds, sustainability becomes embedded not as an aspiration, but as a condition of reliable supply.

In the context of this chapter, energy illustrates how security of supply becomes a physical limit rather than a policy preference. Without reliable, resilient energy systems, neither industrial strategy nor trade enforcement can function. Energy security is therefore not a parallel objective to sustainability, but one of the primary mechanisms through which sustainability is delivered.

## 8.4   Critical Minerals

The global shift towards renewable energy, electric vehicles (EVs), and digitalization has unleashed an unprecedented demand for a new class of strategic commodities - critical minerals.[21] These include lithium, cobalt, nickel, copper, graphite, niobium, and rare earth elements, all essential for batteries, wind turbines, grid infrastructure, and electronics. As nations decarbonize or chase technologies such as AI, minerals have become the new oil: indispensable, geopolitically sensitive, and increasingly contested. The projections of the IEA,[22] the World Bank[23] and others suggest that compared to 2022 annual production levels the world might see are:[24]

- A 58% increase in aluminium (bauxite) by 2030, rising to 64% by 2050.[25]
- A 260% increase in cobalt, rising to anywhere between 6–40 times current production by 2050.[26]
- A 160% increase in copper by 2030, rising to 200% by 2050.[27]
- A 400% increase in graphite by 2030, rising to 460% by 2050.[28]
- A rise of over 500% of lithium by 2030, rising to between 13–40 times current production by 2050.[29]
- A 160% increase of nickel by 2030% perhaps declining to a 70% increase by 2050.[30]
- A slow steady increase in zinc to represent about 200% of current production by 2050.[31]

In my last book on *The Just Transition*, I looked specifically at copper.[32] It is an interesting case study, as human interest in the commodity is not by any means new. In fact, a whole stage in our cultural development is named after it: the Bronze Age which is essentially the 'copper age' with a little tin added. It is estimated that about 700 million metric tons of copper have been picked out of rivers and then dug from the ground through the whole of human history.[33] Current global production as about 25 million metric tons a year and if this is to steadily increase to around 50 million metric tons annually by 2035, then by 2041 we will have dug an additional 700 million tons from the ground - matching the amount dug in the whole of human history up until 2024. In other words, at these predicted rates we would produce as much copper in the next 17 years as we have in the previous 10,000.

As well as copper, the other two commodities to see the greatest absolute increases in demand will be aluminium and zinc, both out-stripping total historical production before we reach 2050. So copper, aluminium and zinc will eventually become the coal and iron of the future, although it will be a very long time - if ever - for them to replace them in absolute terms in the weight mined. However, the greatest relative increases will come from global demand for cobalt, graphite and lithium. Starting from a much lower base, their production rates will need to increase by at least fivefold in most cases.[34] Niobium is also a metal we are likely to hear much more about over the coming years. Currently mined in modest amounts in Brazil, China, and Canada, its superconductor properties make it a key asset for quantum computing (the focus of Chap. 13). Access to niobium is one factor below the surface of the US-Canada tensions witnessed at the start of 2026, and Donald Trump's territorial ambitions in Greenland.

There are plenty of bottlenecks in critical mineral supply chains. The markets are characterized by extreme geographic concentration, long lead times for new projects, and volatile price cycles. The refining and processing of most critical minerals are dominated by a handful of countries. For lithium, cobalt, nickel, graphite, and rare earths, the top three refining nations control an average of 86% of global supply. A level of concentration which is exceeding that of any other major commodity class. China is the dominant player across most mineral value chains, while Indonesia leads in nickel, and the Democratic Republic of the Congo (DRC) supplies roughly 70% of the world's cobalt.[35]

This concentration poses significant geopolitical risks. Export restrictions, trade disputes, or domestic disruptions in any major producer could trigger cascading shortages and price shocks across global industries. Indeed, recent years have seen a proliferation of export controls: China restricted exports of gallium, germanium, and rare earths in 2024–25, while the DRC suspended cobalt exports to stabilize prices. More than half of key energy-related minerals are now subject to some form of export restriction. Conversely, supply expansions in China, Indonesia, and the DRC temporarily pushed prices down after sharp surges in 2021–22. This volatility deters long-term investment. While overall spending on critical minerals mining rose by 14% in 2023, growth slowed to just 5% in 2024 as prices softened.[36]

So, the global mining industry does not always align with the longer-term needs for greater supply. At the time of writing, exploration funding has plateaued, particularly for nickel and cobalt, while start-up investment has declined. In Copper, the merger of Anglo American and Teck

Resources will make it one of the 'big five' copper producers,[37] and further industry consolidation is possible. Yet a consolidated industry will still be vulnerable. In 2024, 7% of global copper supply was disrupted by floods or droughts,[38] a situation that will only worsen as extreme weather patterns become more common.

The mismatch between short-term market signals and long-term energy transition goals threatens future supply adequacy. Even in optimistic scenarios, copper faces a projected 30% shortfall by 2035 due to declining ore grades, high capital costs, and limited discoveries.[39] Lithium, though well-supplied in the near term, is also expected to enter deficit by the 2030s.[40]

## 8.5  Food Security

Food security is often framed as a humanitarian or development issue,[41] but under sustainability constraints it becomes a question of systemic resilience. Modern food systems are highly productive, but they are also tightly coupled to energy, water, fertilisers, transport, and trade. This interdependence delivers efficiency in stable conditions, but fragility under stress. Climate impacts are already disrupting production through heat stress, drought, flooding, and shifting growing seasons. These effects are uneven, but they propagate quickly through global markets. When major producing regions experience simultaneous shocks, price volatility increases and buffers erode. Food insecurity in this context is less about absolute scarcity than about exposure to cascading disruption. Water stress is a central driver. Much of global food production depends on irrigated agriculture in water-stressed basins. As shown above, declining water availability directly constrains yields and increases competition between food, energy, and urban demand. Where groundwater depletion or river stress accelerates, food production becomes increasingly brittle, regardless of market demand.

Energy dependence further amplifies vulnerability. Modern agriculture relies heavily on fossil fuels for mechanisation, fertiliser production, processing, and transport. As energy systems transition, food systems inherit new risks: higher input costs, fertiliser volatility, and exposure to supply-chain disruption. These pressures are structural, not cyclical, and they disproportionately affect import-dependent countries. Trade has historically acted as a stabiliser, allowing surplus regions to offset local shocks. Under sustainability constraints, this role becomes more contested. Export restrictions, strategic stockpiling, and carbon-related trade measures reduce the reliability of global food flows. Food security is therefore increasingly shaped by access to trade, logistics capacity, and compliance with emerging sustainability standards.

Dietary change and waste reduction are often presented as solutions, and they matter over time. But they do not remove the immediate structural vulnerabilities of production systems. Nor do they resolve political sensitivity around food prices, which remains one of the fastest triggers of social unrest.[42] Governments therefore face strong incentives to prioritise domestic stability, even at the expense of global efficiency. The implication is that food security can no longer be treated as a downstream outcome of agricultural productivity alone. It is shaped by upstream constraints in water, energy, fertilisers, and trade, and by the resilience of infrastructure and institutions that connect them. Where these systems fail, food insecurity emerges rapidly and unevenly.[43]

In the context of this chapter, food illustrates how security of supply extends beyond materials and energy to the most politically sensitive domain of all. Sustainability constraints do not simply reshape how food is produced; they determine who bears risk when systems are stressed. Food security therefore reinforces the central argument of this section: under sustainability conditions, supply security becomes a matter of systemic design rather than market balance.

## 8.6   Remaking Sustainable Supply

Ecosystem services - the benefits that flow from functioning natural systems - are the ultimate foundation of all supply chains. Forests regulate rainfall and climate; wetlands filter water; soils store carbon and sustain crop production; oceans moderate temperatures and supply protein. Collectively, these systems form the planet's natural capital, the underlying infrastructure on which every business sector depends. Yet these systems are deteriorating faster than at any point in modern history, as I discussed in Chap. 2. The United Nations Environment Programme's *Global Resources Outlook (2024)* warns that current extraction and land-use patterns are pushing ecosystems beyond safe ecological limits.[44] The WWF's Living Planet Index shows a 73% decline in global biodiversity since 1970, while more than three-quarters of terrestrial ecosystems have been significantly altered.[45] For companies, this degradation is no longer an abstract environmental issue - it is a direct and escalating threat to operational continuity, supply availability, and long-term profitability.

If energy, minerals, and food are the visible pillars of the global economy, ecosystems are the invisible scaffolding holding those pillars in place. Their decline creates systemic risks. Water scarcity disrupts manufacturing and agriculture; soil degradation reduces yields and increases dependence on costly inputs; climate-driven natural disasters destroy infrastructure and interrupt logistics; collapsing fisheries undermine global protein supply chains. For businesses, these impacts translate into higher input costs, volatile markets, lost production days, stranded assets, and rising insurance premiums. Historically, natural systems have been treated as externalities - free inputs into production. But, as the *Dasgupta Review on the Economics of Biodiversity* (2021) argues, this represents a profound institutional failure: the value of ecosystem services - estimated at \$125–150 trillion per year - far exceeds global GDP and yet remains largely invisible on corporate balance sheets.[46] As a result, firms systematically underinvest in the very systems that underpin their long-term operating environment.

The consequences are increasingly material. Deforestation alters rainfall patterns and water availability, directly affecting hydropower, agriculture, and beverage industries. Soil erosion and loss of pollinators reduce productivity across entire agricultural value chains. Ocean acidification undermines fisheries and aquaculture, with implications for global food systems and coastal economies. When ecosystems fail, the cost of replacing their functions through engineered solutions, such as flood defences, desalination plants, or artificial pollination, can be immense, and often technically unfeasible. In short, ecosystem degradation is a business-continuity risk, not a distant ecological concern.

Recognising these systemic threats, governments and investors are increasingly integrating nature into economic and regulatory frameworks. The *Kunming–Montreal Global Biodiversity Framework* (GBF), adopted in 2022, commits countries to halt and reverse biodiversity loss by 2030, with the "30 by 30" target requiring at least 30% of land and sea to be effectively conserved.[47] This is not simply environmental policy - it signals an intention to realign capital flows, set risk disclosure expectations, and operational standards. Businesses will face growing requirements to demonstrate how their operations and supply chains depend on, impact, and restore natural capital. The rise of nature-related financial disclosure frameworks (such as the Taskforce on Nature-related Financial Disclosures, TNFD) underscores a shift toward mandatory reporting on biodiversity and ecosystem dependencies.[48]

Taken together, the analyses above point to five overarching principles that will define both secure and sustainable supply systems - and determine competitive advantage for businesses in the decades ahead.

## Principles for Sustainable Supply Systems

1. *Resilience over efficiency.*

   Traditional supply chains optimised for cost and speed are brittle in the face of climate and ecological shocks. Businesses will need diversified sourcing, redundancy, circular material flows, and adaptive planning to remain viable.

2. *Integration of natural capital.*

   Companies must account for the ecological foundations of their operations - soil, water, biodiversity, and climate stability. Incorporating natural capital accounting, ecosystem-service valuation, and nature-positive strategies into governance and reporting is becoming essential for investor confidence and regulatory compliance.

3. *Equity and inclusion.*

   Resource insecurity disproportionately impacts vulnerable communities, including many in the labour forces and supply bases of global companies. Fair access, participation, and benefit-sharing are becoming preconditions for stable, reputable, and legally secure operations.

4. *Transparency and data.*

As supply chains become more exposed to environmental stress, real-time monitoring, digital traceability, and satellite and AI-based early-warning systems will become core operational tools. Sustainability data will increasingly inform risk management, procurement, and investment decisions.

5. *International cooperation and rules-based management.*

No business can insulate itself from global resource interdependence. Coordinated policies on trade, investment, and ecosystem protection are essential to stabilise markets. Fragmented national approaches raise the risk of conflict, supply disruption, and regulatory uncertainty – all of which are direct threats to corporate planning.

Security of supply under sustainability conditions does not fail gradually. It fails abruptly, unevenly, and politically. When water systems run dry, energy grids falter, materials bottleneck, or food prices spike, the consequences are immediate and difficult to reverse. These are not market corrections that can be smoothed over time, but physical limits that expose the fragility of economic systems built for a more stable world.

The cases in this chapter demonstrate a common pattern. Efficiency without resilience amplifies risk. Concentration without redundancy accelerates failure. Systems designed around historical baselines become liabilities when conditions change. Under sustainability constraints, supply security therefore becomes less about optimisation and more about whether systems can absorb shock without cascading collapse. This shift has profound implications. Scarcity becomes normal rather than exceptional. Trade-offs between cost, resilience, and equity move from the margins of policy into its centre. Governments, businesses, and communities are forced to decide not only how resources are allocated, but who bears risk when systems are stressed. These choices cannot be deferred indefinitely, because physical systems impose their own timelines.

Security of supply thus functions as a form of enforcement. It translates sustainability from targets and standards into lived consequences, shaping behaviour through exposure rather than persuasion. Where systems are redesigned for resilience, sustainability becomes embedded. Where they are not, scarcity and instability do the embedding instead.

The next chapter turns to trade, where these physical constraints are formalised into rules, conditions, and exclusions. If security of supply reveals the limits of the system, trade determines who gains access within those limits.

## Notes

1. Wimbledon, *Why is there a pineapple on the Wimbledon trophy?* 15 July 2018.
2. Bethen Bell, *The rise, fall, and rise of the status pineapple*, 2 August 2020.
3. Bethen Bell, *The rise, fall, and rise of the status pineapple*, 2 August 2020.
4. World Economic Forum, *Global Risks Report*, 2023.
5. World Bank, *Integrated Food Security Framework*, 2024.
6. International Energy Agency, *Critical Minerals Outlook*, 2025.
7. Marco Tedesco, *The Paradox of Lithium*, Columbia Climate School, Columbia University, 18 January 2023.
8. Miguel Yanez-Barnuevo, *Data Centers and Water Consumption*, Environmental and Energy Study Institute, June 2025.
9. United Nations, *The human right to water and sanitation*, Resolution adopted by the General Assembly on 28 July 2010: 64/292.
10. United Nations, Sustainable Development Goal 6.1, 2025.
11. World Economic Forum, *Global Risks Report*, 2023.
12. Global Commission on the Economics of Water, *The economics of water*, October, 2024.
13. Global Commission on the Economics of Water, *The economics of water*, October, 2024.
14. United Nations, *Indus Waters Treaty*, 1960.
15. United Nations, *Convention on the Law of Non-Navigational Uses of International Watercourses*, 1997.
16. International Energy Agency, *Sustainable Development Scenario*, 2018.
17. International Energy Agency, *Sustainable Development Scenario*, 2018.
18. European Commission, *Clean Energy Package*, Directorate General for Energy, 2019.
19. US Federal Energy Regulatory Commission (FERC), *Order 842*, 2018.
20. International Energy Agency, *Energy and AI*, 10 April 2025.
21. Ed Conway, *Material World: A substantial story of our past and future*, 2023.

22. International Energy Agency, *Growth in demand for selected minerals*, 2023.
23. World Bank, Projected annual mineral demand compared with 2018, 2022.
24. These figures were first used in my previous book: John Morrison, *The Just Transition: a systems-thinking approach to managing climate action*, 2024.
25. International Aluminium Institute, *Why the aluminium industry must be at COP28*, 2023.
26. Benchmark Minerals, *Forecasts to 2050*, 2023.
27. McKinsey, *Global Materials Perspective*, 2025.
28. Benchmark Minerals, *Forecasts to 2050*, 2023.
29. Benchmark Minerals, *Forecasts to 2050*, 2023.
30. International Energy Agency, *Growth in demand for selected minerals*, 2023.
31. World Bank, *Projected annual mineral demand*, 2022.
32. John Morrison, *The Just Transition: a systems-thinking approach to managing climate action*, 2024.
33. US Geological Survey. *How much copper has been found*, March 2025.
34. World Bank, *Projected annual mineral demand compared with 2018*, 2022.
35. Ed Conway, *Material World: A substantial story of our past and future*, 2023.
36. International Energy Agency, *Growth in demand for selected minerals*, 2023.
37. Global Finance, *Anglo American-Teck forming copper producing giant*, 27 October 2025.
38. International Energy Agency, *Critical Minerals Outlook*, 2025.
39. International Energy Agency, *Critical Minerals Outlook*, 2025.
40. International Energy Agency, *Critical Minerals Outlook*, 2025.
41. United Nations, World Food Summit, 1996.
42. The Economist, *Costly good and energy are fostering global unrest*, 23 June 2022.
43. John Morrison, *The Just Transition: a systems-thinking approach to managing climate action*, 2024.
44. UNEP, *Global Resources Outlook 2024*, 1 March 2024.
45. WWF, *Living Planet Report 2024*, 10 October 2024.
46. UK Government, *Dasgupta Review on the Economics of Biodiversity*, 2 February 2021.

47. United Nations, *Kumming-Montreal Global Diversity Framework*, Convention on Biological Diversity, COP 15, 10 January 2024.
48. TNFD, *Taskforce on Nature-related Financial Disclosures*, (website), December 2025.

# 9

# Sustainable Trade

*This year, I want to challenge you to join me in taking our relationship to a still higher level. I propose that you, the business leaders gathered in Davos, and we, the United Nations, initiate a global compact of shared values and principles, which will give a human face to the global market.*[1]
(Kofi Annan, Davos, 31 January 1999)

The last year of the last millennium witnessed an upsurge in anti-globalisation sentiment. The rules of trade were broadly seen to benefit big business to the detriment of poor countries and poor people. Even by mid-1999 it was clear that the World Trade Organisation (WTO) meeting planned for Seattle was going to be met with a *"massive mobilisation against globalisation"*.[2] Developing economies were particularly concerned about issues such as market access for textiles, arbitrary use of anti-dumping measures, and overuse of *Trade Related aspects of Intellectual Property Rights* (TRIPS). It was not long before Kofi Annan's Davos speech had been converted into the United Nations Global Compact by John Ruggie and Georg Kell, an initiative that continues a quarter of a century later.[3]

Wind forward to today, and the WTO fights to remain relevant. The 'global south' now has a much louder voice, with India and China using their increased leverage and the US threatening to leave. A range of reforms are needed, such as new rules for digital trade; resolving the stalemate on agricultural negotiations: limiting misuse of farm support programmes and ensuring food-security needs are addressed as well as greater efficiency; and setting clearer criteria for developing-country status. The WTO itself seems much keener on sustainability than it did in its early years.[4] The push for environmental reform has grown from the start, and became a key tenant under Pascal Lamy's tenure as Director General in the first decade of the century.[5] While no specific WTO agreement focuses solely on the environment, rules allow members to adopt trade-related environmental measures, provided they meet conditions that prevent misuse for protectionist purposes.[6] In 2020, the *Trade and Environmental Sustainability Structured Discussions* started at the WTO to advance the agenda. The current Director-General, Dr. Ngozi Okonjo-Iweala, has prioritised sustainability, as seen under the *2023 Fisheries Agreement*, for example.[7] According to OECD analysis, while the total number of regional trade agreements signed each year has declined, the number of environmental provisions per agreement has increased steadily.[8] These provisions now cover issues ranging from environmental goods and services to sustainable agriculture, biodiversity protection, and fossil fuel subsidy reform.

This chapter explores the extent and ways in which trade flows are aligned with sustainability outcomes, as part of global value chains, and more effective way of doing so. Trade is where sustainability moves from aspiration to enforcement. When market access depends on carbon intensity, deforestation risk, or labour standards, sustainability becomes a condition of participation rather than a matter of choice. Done well, trade policy can be one of the ultimate leverage points for advancing the sustainability agenda. For its part, trade too can ill afford to ignore sustainability.

## 9.1    Sustainability in Trade Policy

Outside of the WTO, some of the first bilateral trade agreements to include environmental and labour rights clauses were those negotiated by the US government at the turn of the millennium. The *North American Free Trade Agreement* (NAFTA) of 1994 was the first U.S. trade agreement to include detailed sustainability provisions and the *US-Jordan Free Trade Agreement* of 2001 set a precedent for subsequent agreements that followed. The *United States-Mexico-Canada Agreement*, which replaced NAFTA under the first Trump administration, contained the strongest and most enforceable sustainability obligations of any US trade agreement to date. These provisions included commitments to combat illegal fishing and wildlife trafficking, promote sustainable fishing, and address issues like air quality and marine litter, as well as labour standards.

The European Union (EU) incorporates *Trade and Sustainable Development* chapters in its free trade agreements. These chapters require partner countries (and the EU) to implement international labour conventions and environmental agreements. These include the International Labour Organization (ILO) core conventions; the *Paris Agreement* on climate change; and to sustainably trade natural resources (timber, fish), fight illegal trade in threatened species, promote circular economy and deforestation-free supply chains. There are also commitments to monitoring and raising of complaints under the "Single Entry Point" mechanism for any breaches.

Investor-state dispute settlement mechanisms linked to bilateral treaties also pose challenges. Companies affected by sustainability policies sometimes seek compensation for project cancellation through international arbitration. For example, Canada's TC Energy Corporation sought $15 billion in damages from the United States for cancelling the Keystone XL pipeline, although this was dismissed by the tribunal in July 2024.[9] Such cases highlight tensions that can arise between sustainability regulations and investor rights.

Other countries are using national tariffs to discourage environmentally harmful products while incentivising green alternatives. The United Kingdom's *Global Tariff* regime, for example, removes duties on goods that support environmental conservation: such as thermostats, heat pumps, and energy-efficient lighting.[10] Similarly, the proposed *Agreement on Climate Change, Trade, and Sustainability*, led by Costa Rica, New Zealand, Norway, and others, aims to remove tariffs on more than 300 environmentally beneficial products after efforts at the WTO collapsed.[11] The European Union has developed its *Generalised System of Preferences* (GSP) under which tariffs can be reduced to zero. The system has different tiers, such as the EU's *Everything but Arms* (EBA) for least developed countries which offers duty-free access for most products, or the "GSP+" arrangement which offers zero duties to countries that meet certain human rights, labour, and governance standards.[12] To benefit from these tariffs, exporters must meet specific rules of origin and consignment conditions, as outlined in the relevant GSP scheme. Although the UK has left the European Union, it has transposed similar arrangements into its tariff regime.

Non-tariff measures, such as technical regulations and eco-labelling schemes, are also being leveraged to promote sustainable production. These include setting emissions thresholds for industrial goods, mandating energy efficiency standards, and requiring lifecycle assessments. Subsidies have become a central feature of green industrial policy. Whilst the US *Inflation Reduction Act* is now in abeyance in many areas, it inspired others, such as Japan, Canada, and the EU, to follow suit with their own subsidy frameworks to remain competitive in the global green economy.[13] In addition, the 'common approaches' of export credit agencies across OECD member states[14] are framed in terms of the International Finance Corporation's *Performance Standards*[15] and therefore reflect a range of environmental and social norms. The purpose of export credit is to support a country's national economy by making it easier and less risky for its companies to export goods and services. This is achieved through financial support like loans, guarantees, and insurance provided by government-backed agencies, which can include protecting exporters from non-payment by foreign buyers and helping overseas buyers finance purchases. Ultimately, export credit aims to boost an exporting country's competitiveness in the international market and therefore uses sustainability to augment this.

However, the proliferation of sustainability-linked tariff waivers, subsidies, insurance and guarantees raises questions about trade fairness and compliance with the WTO rules.[16] Critics argue that such measures can distort competition and risk triggering *"green trade wars"* unless coordinated internationally.[17] Such measures, while environmentally sound, can create trade friction if they diverge significantly across jurisdictions. The challenge lies in harmonizing standards to avoid fragmentation.[18] During 2025, for example, China[19] tabled the need for greater integration of international carbon standards, such as ISO 14064[20] and ISO 14067,[21] within trade agreements.

But one of the most impactful of all trade measures will be the move to sustainability-based tariffs, such as those based on the carbon emissions of specific industrial processes linked to imported products. These are commonly called 'border carbon adjustment' approaches.

## 9.2    Border Carbon Adjustment Approaches

The European Union's *Carbon Border Adjustment Mechanism* (CBAM) could become one of the most consequential innovations at the intersection of trade and climate policy. Only time will tell. Introduced as part of the EU Green Deal, the CBAM seeks to prevent "carbon leakage"- the relocation of production to countries with weaker climate regulations - and to ensure that imported goods face the same carbon costs as those produced within the EU.[22]

Under the CBAM, importers of certain carbon-intensive goods such as cement, steel, aluminium, fertilizers, and electricity must purchase certificates reflecting the carbon price that would have been paid had the goods been produced under the EU's *Emissions Trading System*.[23] This approach should level the playing field between domestic and foreign producers and incentivises global emissions reduction. Despite its conceptual clarity, implementing the CBAM from 2027 onwards poses significant technical and political challenges. Accurately measuring embedded emissions across complex global supply chains is difficult, especially in regions with limited emissions data. Questions also arise over how to treat countries with subnational carbon policies, partial emissions pricing, or inadequate reporting mechanisms.[24]

At COP30 in Belem in November 2025, the CBAM became one of the most contentious of all climate issues.[25] The EU climate chief Wopke Hoekstra said he was happy to discuss the CBAM, but would *"not be lured into the suggestion"* that the measure is aimed at restricting trade.[26] It remains unclear whether the CBAM fully complies with the principle of non-discrimination[27] under the *General Agreement on Tariffs and Trade* (GATT).[28] Critics, including major economies such as China and India, have described CBAM as a "green protectionist" measure that penalizes developing countries unable to afford rapid decarbonization.[29] The CBAM's costs will likely be passed along to European consumers as free ETS allowances are phased out. However, proponents argue that these costs are justified by the broader economic and environmental benefits: protecting domestic industries, preventing carbon leakage, and reinforcing global decarbonization incentives.[30]

For developing economies, the CBAM presents both risks and opportunities. Africa, for example, has minimal heavy industry today but enormous renewable energy potential. If properly leveraged, African economies could become major exporters of low carbon electricity or hydrogen. Yet, according to the African Union, the CBAM currently offers limited recognition of such advantages, focusing primarily on current emissions rather than potential for clean energy transition.[31] The CBAM could entrench global inequalities unless it evolves to reward clean production potential in emerging economies. The development of a data-driven, fair emissions accounting system - including recognition of subnational or sectoral carbon policies - could benefit both Africa and Europe.[32] Asian economies - particularly China, India, and Indonesia - are among the most affected by the CBAM due to their reliance on carbon-intensive exports. Some argue that the mechanism undermines their "right to development"[33] and fails to account for historical emissions by industrialized nations. Indonesia, for instance, has criticized EU environmental trade laws as "regulatory imperialism".[34]

In the United States, policy debate around carbon pricing remains polarized. While federal adoption of carbon border adjustment measures is unlikely in the short term, individual states such as California have expressed interest in forming "carbon clubs" with like-minded regions to coordinate carbon pricing.[35] However, constitutional constraints limit their ability to negotiate international agreements independently.

In the face of the criticism, European policymakers continue to emphasize CBAM's logical consistency: if Europe imposes a carbon price domestically, it must extend similar treatment to imports to maintain fairness and prevent industrial flight. Yet European officials acknowledge the need for simplification. Recent reforms have aimed to exempt low-volume importers: focusing enforcement on the top 10% of emitters. Under the October 2025 revisions, companies importing less than 50 tonnes of goods annually will be exempt from the CBAM obligations. According to the EU Commission, *this measure is expected to exempt approximately 182,000 importers, mostly SMEs and individuals, while still covering over 99% of emissions in scope.*"[36]

Trade-related environmental measures such as the CBAM must navigate a narrow legal path under WTO rules. While Article XX of the GATT permits exceptions for environmental protection, these measures must not constitute "arbitrary or unjustifiable discrimination." Whether CBAM meets this test remains contested and could eventually be adjudicated by the WTO's Dispute Settlement Body.[37] Beyond legality, the politics of perception are equally important. If sustainable trade instruments are seen as unilateral or exclusionary, they risk undermining global cooperation. Europe's credibility as a climate leader depends on its ability to frame the CBAM and similar measures as collaborative rather than coercive.[38]

In summary, the logic behind border carbon adjustment measures can be summarised as follows:

## Levelling the Playing Field for Domestic Industry

One of the clearest arguments in favour of border carbon adjustment approaches is their capacity to "level the playing field" between domestic producers subject to high carbon costs and foreign producers operating under weaker climate regimes. Without equalisation, ambitious climate policies risk reducing the competitiveness of firms in jurisdictions with strong mitigation targets. The *Remaking Trade Project*, led by Yale Professor Dan Esty and others, works from the premise that trade rules offer the most critical point of policy leverage for moving the world towards a sustainable future.[39] Measures such as the CBAM ensure that imported goods bear a comparable carbon price to domestic production, preventing low-regulation economies from gaining unfair cost advantages simply by not pricing emissions.

## Preventing "Leakage" and Safeguarding Reductions

Border carbon adjustment approaches are also justified as a defence against *carbon leakage* - the shifting of carbon-intensive production to countries with weaker policies. Leakage can undermine domestic climate action and even increase global emissions if production moves to more carbon-intensive locations. While empirical evidence for leakage under the EU ETS has been limited, this is largely due to the existing system of free allowances.[40] As these are phased out under the EU's strengthened ETS, leakage risks rise. CBAM is an "enabling policy" that allows the EU to decarbonise energy-intensive sectors while retaining industrial activity. Modelling results suggest that introducing the CBAM produces a modest reduction in non-EU emissions and leads to an overall decline in global emissions. Importantly, without the CBAM, political pressure may force lower carbon prices, potentially adding *up to 1 gigatonne of $CO_2$ annually* to global emissions and jeopardising EU net-zero goals.[41]

## Incentivising Global Sustainability Ambition

A third major argument is that border carbon adjustment approaches, such as the CBAM, help stimulate more ambitious climate action beyond borders. By imposing a cost on carbon-intensive exports to the EU, the CBAM encourages other countries to adopt effective carbon pricing or cleaner production methods to maintain market access. Border carbon adjustments can serve as a response to the free-rider problem in global climate governance, giving high-ambition jurisdictions strategic leverage to push others toward stronger policies. For export-dependent economies, aligning with EU-level carbon standards becomes economically attractive: potentially accelerating global technology diffusion and reducing long-term emissions.

## Enabling and Protecting High Domestic Pricing

Border carbon adjustments not only prevent emissions displacement but might also help sustain the political viability of high carbon prices. Without the CBAM, fears about competitiveness could suppress domestic carbon prices and derail the EU's 2050 net-zero trajectory. In the case of the EU, the CBAM might allow the region to strengthen its carbon trading scheme while phasing out free allowances, a reform essential to improving carbon-pricing efficiency and encouraging decarbonisation investment in heavy industry.

These interlocking rationales position border carbon adjustments as a potentially necessary instrument for achieving deep decarbonisation in an uneven global climate policy landscape.

## 9.3   Wider Import and Export Measures

Of course, the question then arises: if such an approach works for 'carbon', why not for other environmental and social issues. There are clearly a few reasons why the model does not translate easily: the measurability of carbon, clear methodologies for mitigation, the direct link to industrial processes, the political consensus, and so on. But it is worth pausing to consider how trade-based systems might be considered for a number of other pressing sustainability issues in the future, even if in very different form and scale from the CBAM. While the CBAM itself is carbon-specific, its underlying regulatory logic of internalising external costs, preventing equity-related "leakage" and using border adjustments to reshape incentives can be applied to other sustainability issues. Currently, nothing as systemic as the CBAM is proposed by the EU on other sustainability issues through the nexus of trade. However, a few developments are relevant:

## Commodity-Specific Approaches

One of the European Union's other most consequential sustainability measures is the *Deforestation-Free Products Regulation* (EUDR).[42] Perhaps because of its potential impact and concerns of major exporting countries, its implementation has been delayed more than once (at time of writing: until the end of 2026 for larger companies, and mid-2027 for SMEs[43]). The EUDR technically came into force on 29 June 2023 and covers certain commodities (palm oil, beef, soy, cocoa, timber, rubber) and derived products. The regulation requires due diligence by companies to demonstrate that such products do *not* come from deforested land or have not contributed to forest degradation since 2020.

Although the EUDR is European legislation, its implications are global. Whilst most sustainability standards for commodities are still managed on a 'mass balance' basis, i.e. percentage in must match percentage out of the sourcing system. But individual components of material are not tagged. EUDR moves beyond this to full traceability. Companies will need to show the full provenance of every item, and to verify that these products are compliant with relevant legislation of the country of production, including respect for human rights, and the rights of affected indigenous peoples. The legislation will be enforced by the competent authorities of each member state, reviewing the disclosures from the companies and related initiatives, such as the geolocation coordinates of relevant commodities. With the help of satellite monitoring tools and DNA analysis, they will check where products come from. If EUDR is shown to be effective over the years ahead, it might become the model for managing other commodities known to have significant environmental or social impacts.

In contrast, the implementation of the European Union's *Critical Raw Materials Act* (CRMA)[44] has not been delayed (at time of writing) possibly because of its national security and defence implications in addition to sustainability considerations. While not strictly trade-only, it has trade implications because it governs the supply of critical raw materials (imports, trade diversification) for the EU's green/digital transitions. To meet its sustainability and digital objectives, sourcing, processing and recycling critical raw materials in Europe and securing supply chains are the challenges ahead. The Act came into effect on 23 May 2024 and covers all relevant metals and minerals, such as the lithium, cobalt and nickel used to produce batteries; gallium used in solar panels; raw boron as used in wind technologies; titanium and tungsten used in the space and defence sectors. With the Critical Raw Materials Act, the EU explicitly aims to ensure secure and sustainable supply of critical raw materials for Europe's industry and significantly lower the EU's dependency on imports from single country suppliers.

## Import Controls

All countries ban the import of specific products and materials for reasons of public health, protecting domestic plant or animal life (including endangered species), protecting the rights of workers or communities, as well as other national interests or religious requirements. Arguably then, the nexus between import controls and sustainability has always been strong, even if not considered explicitly in those terms. Sometimes human rights are invoked explicitly in relation to import bans of specific products known to originate from specific suppliers or countries that might either be sanctioned or require heightened due diligence.

Over recent years, successive US administrations have used import bans to enforce its forced labour trade laws and issue *Withhold Release Orders* on specific cargos entering US ports.[45] The European Union is now considering something similar with its own *Forced Labour regulation* which entered into force at the end of 2024. How this will be applied in practice to both imports and exports by the European Commission and member states is to be determined. So far, the European Commission has indicated it will take a "risk-based approach to investigations focused on high-risk sectors, products, and regions". When a significant risk of forced labour exists and the importing company cannot demonstrate adequate due diligence, cargoes will need to be withdrawn or destroyed. During 2025, the Commission has indicated that it hopes to make use of technology, including AI and federated data, to both identify risks and set due diligence expectations of companies. Again, this is an approach, which if effective and politically acceptable, might influence what other sustainability measures are considered in the future.

## Due Diligence and Reporting

The now very tired joke in Brussels is that you can wait for an omnibus for a long time, and then six 'buses' arrive at once. As of the end of 2025, the EU 'omnibus' packages related to the Common Agricultural Policy, defence, chemicals, digital rules, as well as sustainability reporting and due diligence. Many of these are the very policy areas known to have had the greatest impact on business. The explicit motivation has been to enhance the European Union's competitiveness within global markets. The talk of Brussels during 2025 was the report of Mario Draghi, the former European Central Bank President, and "one of Europe's great economic minds".[46]

So, the omnibuses are not explicitly a sustainability-reduction agenda (although some would argue they have become this) but are clearly about cutting red-tape and bureaucracy. The two sustainability instruments most under the spotlight have been the *Corporate Sustainability Reporting Directive* (CSRD) and the *Corporate Sustainability Due Diligence Directive* (CSDDD). The former places a broad-based sustainability reporting requirement on those businesses within scope, following the logic of 'double materiality' outlined in early chapters. The later requires business to take a human rights and environmental risk-based approach to business relationships, and to act on knowledge of actual or potential harms. CSDDD became 'politically hot' during 2025, with the leaders of Germany and France publicly distancing themselves from the legislation, even though their two countries already have national precursors of the law.

I hope, for sake of collective sanity, that by the time you are reading this book, the scope and reach of both CSDDD and CSRD have been decided. As of November 2025, for CSRD, the employee threshold for companies within scope of the legislation would increase from 1000 to 1750 for large companies. For CSDDD, the employee threshold for companies to be subject to the due diligence requirements would be raised to 5000, and €1.5 billion global turnover, in most cases. The due diligence would take a "risk-based approach", where companies would only need to request information from business partners if there are grounds to believe adverse impacts have occurred or may occur. The "duty to terminate" business relationships would be replaced with a "duty to temporarily suspend" them in certain situations. There would no longer be any requirement for climate action plans. For sustainability's sake, the best outcome would be for every EU member state to align with something like the existing *German Supply Chain Act*, or something very similar, but it seems that politics might trump practicality and fairness.

From a trade perspective what is interesting is that these 'domestic' European requirements are considered salient enough to be a feature of trade negotiations, even with a degree of political symbolism. On 21 August 2025, the EU and the US published a joint statement titled *Framework on an Agreement on Reciprocal, Fair and Balanced Trade*.[47] This document sets out both tariff and non-tariff commitments, and places sustainability laws and standards (previously seen mostly in regulatory or domestic policy contexts) into the trade and market-access arena. In the joint statement, the EU commits that the CSRD and CSDDD will not impose "undue restrictions" on trans-Atlantic trade.[48]

## 9.4   Remaking Sustainable Trade

As sustainability becomes a central pillar of trade policy, businesses are entering a period of rapid regulatory, operational, and competitive change. Trade frameworks that once focused primarily on tariffs and market access now increasingly incorporate environmental and social criteria. This evolution creates both opportunities and risks that firms must navigate carefully.

### Rising Compliance Obligations Across Borders

New sustainability-linked trade mechanisms - such as the EU's *Carbon Border Adjustment Mechanism* (CBAM), national green tariffs, supply-chain due-diligence rules, and evolving technical standards - mean that businesses face a growing web of reporting, emissions accounting, and verification requirements. Even companies outside the EU or other major markets may be drawn into these systems if they export intermediate or finalise goods. As trade and climate policies converge, the cost of non-compliance will rise through denial of market access, penalties, and reputational risk.

### Pressure to Provide Credible, Standardised Data

Sustainable trade policy increasingly relies on quantifiable metrics - embedded carbon, lifecycle analyses, traceability, or labour/human-rights due diligence. Companies will need systems capable of generating consistent, auditable, high-quality data across entire global value chains. The WTO's new *Trade Policy Toolkit* and the push for data harmonisation through climate clubs and initiatives such as ISO 14064/14067 signal the trend toward uniform global reporting norms. Businesses must anticipate this trajectory.

## Exposure to Shifts in Market Competitiveness

Sustainability itself is becoming a competitive factor in trade. Firms with lower-emission production processes, transparent supply chains, or access to renewable energy may gain preferred access to markets or reduced tariffs, while carbon-intensive producers risk erosion of competitiveness under mechanisms like the CBAM or green-tariff regimes. Governments are increasingly supporting greener firms through subsidies, export-credit incentives, and green industrial policies, thus creating asymmetric advantages within and across markets.

## Geopolitical and Legal Uncertainty

Businesses should expect legal and political volatility. The CBAM and similar policies face potential WTO challenges, and investor-state disputes over environmental policy are rising. Companies may face operating uncertainty where sustainability measures are viewed as protectionist, particularly by emerging economies. The risk of fragmented or conflicting standards across jurisdictions may make long-term investment planning more complex.

## Expanding Scope: From Environment to Social Sustainability

Trade policy is starting to move beyond carbon and environmental concerns towards labour standards, human-rights due diligence, and supply-chain governance. Although a formal "social CBAM" is unlikely soon, the direction of travel is clear: rules embedded in the CSRD, CSDDD and similar frameworks are being treated as non-tariff barriers within trade negotiations. Businesses should therefore expect heightened scrutiny of working conditions, human-rights impacts, and value-chain management - not only environmental performance.

## The Need for Strategic Supply-Chain Reconfiguration

As sustainable trade rules expand, firms may need to reassess sourcing, logistics, and production strategies. For example, carbon-intensive suppliers may become costlier, high-risk, or even non-compliant. Businesses may also find new opportunities in regions with abundant renewable energy or favourable sustainability frameworks - such as the potential for African economies to emerge as exporters of low-carbon energy or materials.[49] Supply-chain diversification and resilience planning will become essential.

## An Era of Collaboration: But Also Expectation

Climate clubs, public–private partnerships, and international sustainability initiatives will increasingly shape the trade environment. Businesses will be expected not only to comply with but to participate in sharing data, aligning with global standards, supporting sectoral decarbonization, and engaging in capacity-building where they operate. Forward-thinking companies will treat these as opportunities to influence future rules and secure early-mover advantages.

Sustainable trade does not advance because consensus has been reached, but because access is increasingly conditioned. As carbon intensity, deforestation risk, labour standards, and due-diligence requirements are embedded into border measures and market rules, sustainability becomes a practical requirement for participation rather than a shared aspiration. Compliance is uneven, contested, and politically charged - but it is no longer optional. The result is a more fragmented trading system. Unilateral and plurilateral measures proliferate where multilateral agreement stalls. Adjustment costs are redistributed across borders, often falling hardest on those with the least capacity to absorb them. These tensions will persist. But fragmentation does not weaken enforcement; it accelerates it by allowing leading markets to move ahead and set conditions that others must respond to.

For business and government alike, the implication is straightforward. Trade is no longer a neutral conduit through which sustainability debates flow. It is the mechanism through which those debates are settled in practice. Market access increasingly depends on the ability to measure, disclose, and reduce environmental and social impacts at scale. Where this capability is absent, exclusion replaces negotiation. Trade therefore functions as a ratchet. Once sustainability criteria are attached to access, reversal becomes difficult, even where political support fluctuates. Systems are built, data requirements harden, and compliance infrastructures take root. Sustainability becomes embedded not through alignment of values, but through the accumulation of conditions.

The next chapter turns to infrastructure, where these trade conditions are locked in physically. If trade determines who may participate, infrastructure determines what can be produced at all. Once assets are built, sustainability choices are no longer debated - they are inherited.

## Notes


1. United Nations, *Secretary-General Proposes Global Compact on human rights, labour, environment, in address to World Economic Forum in Davos*, 31 January 1999.
2. Helene Cooper, *Globalization foes plan to protest WTO Seattle round trade talks*, Wall Street Journal, 16 July 1999.
3. John Ruggie, *Just Business: Multinational corporations and human rights*, 2013.
4. Daniel Esty, *Greening the GATT*, 1994.
5. Pascal Lamy, *Greening the WTO*, speech at Yale University, October 2007.
6. World Trade Organisation, *Trade and Environment*, website, 2025.
7. Daniel Esty, *personal communication*, December 2025.
8. OECD, 2023.
9. Reuters, *TC Energy says its $15 bln claim for Keystone XL project thrown out by US tribunal*, 16 July 2024.
10. UK Government, Department for Business and Trade, 2023
11. New Zealand Government, Ministry of Foreign Affairs and Trade, 2023.

12. European Commission, *Generalised Scheme of Preferences*, Trade and Economic Security, website, 2025.

13. See for example: Japanese Government, *Japan's green industrial subsidies*, Ministry of Economics, Trade and Industry, *2023.*

14. OECD. *Recommendation of the Council on OECD Legal Instruments Common Approaches for Officially Supported Export Credits and Environmental and Social Due Diligence* (The "Common Approaches"), 2012.

15. International Finance Corporation, *Performance Standards on Environmental and Social Sustainability, website* (last revised in 2011), World Bank Group, 2025.

16. Elena Cima and Daniel Esty, *Making international trade work for sustainable development: towards a new WTO framework for subsidies*, Journal of International Economic Law, 27(1), March 2024.

17. Noah Kaufmann et al., *Green trade tensions*, F&D Magazine, International Monetary Fund, June 2023.

18. See for example the Villars Framework for a Sustainable Trade System.

19. World Trade Organisation, *Strengthening discussions and cooperation on carbon standards*, Communication from China, 24 October 2025.

20. International Organisation for Standards, *ISO 14064* is a series of international standards that provides a framework for organizations and governments to quantify, monitor, report, and verify greenhouse gas (GHG) emissions and removals.

21. International Organisation for Standards, *ISO 14067* is an international standard that specifies the principles, requirements, and guidelines for quantifying and reporting the carbon footprint of a product (CFP).

22. European Commission, *EU Green Deal and CBAM framework, 2023.*

23. European Commission, *EU Emissions Trading Scheme*, Climate Action (website), 2025.

24. European Parliament, *CBAM implementation review and reform proposals, 2024.*

25. Politico, *EU strains to defend carbon levy as trade tensions engulf COP30,* 18 November 2025.

26. Politico, *EU strains to defend carbon levy as trade tensions engulf COP30,* 18 November 2025.

27. Goran Dominioni and Daniel Esty, *Designing effective border carbon adjustment mechanisms: aligning the global trade and climate change regimes*, Arizona Law Review, 65(1), 2023.

28. World Trade Organisation, *Russia initiates WTO dispute regarding EU's carbon border adjustment and emissions trading*, 19 May 2025.

29. Sanna Markkanen et al., *On the borderline: The EU CBAM and its place in the world of trade*, Institute for Sustainability Leadership, University of Cambridge, 2022.

30. Sanna Markkanen et al., *On the borderline: The EU CBAM and its place in the world of trade*, Institute for Sustainability Leadership, University of Cambridge, 2022.

31. African Union, African Union, *Sustainable industrialization and trade in Africa, 2024.*

32. United Nations Economic Commission for Africa, *Implementation technicalities of international carbon trade largely unresolved at the 2024 Bonn Climate Change Conference*, 19 June 2024.

33. The 'right to development' is not a universally accepted right. Indeed, the US took a reservation on this point in the 1992 Rio Declaration.

34. Gayatri Suroyo et al., *Indonesia accuses EU of 'regulatory imperialism' with deforestation law*, 8 June 2023.

35. California Air Resources Board, *Carbon pricing and cross-border cooperation, 2023.*

36. European Commission, *Simplifications for the Carbon Border Adjustment Mechanism*, Director-General for Taxation and Customs Union, 20 October 2025.

37. World Trade Organisation, *Russia initiates WTO dispute regarding EU's carbon border adjustment and emissions trading*, 19 May 2025.

38. Sanna Markkanen et al., *On the borderline: The EU CBAM and its place in the world of trade*, Institute for Sustainability Leadership, University of Cambridge, 2022.

39. Remaking Trade for a Sustainable Future Project, (website), December 2025.

40. Sanna Markkanen et al., *On the borderline: The EU CBAM and its place in the world of trade*, Institute for Sustainability Leadership, University of Cambridge, 2022.

41. Sanna Markkanen et al., *On the borderline: The EU CBAM and its place in the world of trade*, Institute for Sustainability Leadership, University of Cambridge, 2022.

42. European Commission, *Regulation on Deforestation-free Products* (EUDR) 2023/1115.

43. Mark Segal, *EU Countries vote to delay supply chain deforestation law for another year*, ESG Today, 21 November 2025.
44. European Commission, *Critical Raw Materials Act (CRMA)*, 2024/1252.
45. United States Government, *19 US Congress 1307, Uyghur Forced Labor Prevention Act* (2021), and *Countering America's Adversaries Through Sanctions Act* (2017).
46. European Commission, *The Draghi report: A competitiveness strategy for Europe*, October 2024.
47. Responsible Investor, *EU pledges CSRD, CSDDD will not impose 'undue restrictions' on US trade*, 21 August 2025.
48. European Commission, *Joint statement on a United States – European Union framework on an agreement on reciprocal, fair, balanced trade*, 21 August 2025.
49. See for example the work on "green competitiveness" by former WTO chief economist Ralph Ossa.

# 10

# Circular Infrastructure

Infrastructure is where sustainability stops being adjustable and becomes irreversible. Once assets are built, their resilience profiles are largely fixed for decades. This is true for power systems, transport networks, buildings, ports, water, and waste systems. Decisions taken at the point of construction, therefore, determine not only future costs, but future options. Under sustainability constraints, infrastructure is no longer a neutral platform for growth; it is the mechanism through which risk is locked in or designed out.

This irreversibility changes the politics of sustainability. Markets can reprice, trade can condition access, and technologies can evolve, but infrastructure commits societies to particular paths. Where assets are built for efficiency alone, fragility accumulates. Where they are built for resilience, redundancy, and circularity, sustainability becomes embedded by default. The consequences of getting this wrong are not abstract: they surface as stranded assets and escalating public costs. This chapter examines infrastructure as sustainability's point of no return. It focuses on how materials, design choices, maintenance regimes, and system integration determine whether economies can operate reliably under conditions of scarcity and volatility. If earlier chapters showed how sustainability is


J. Morrison, *Remaking Sustainability*, https://doi.org/10.1007/978-3-032-23755-2_10

enforced through exposure, insurance, trade, and access, infrastructure is where that enforcement becomes permanent.

Coming out of COVID, even the US, the most productive of the G7 economies, has rates of growth that are tiny compared with the 1950s, the era of the Eisenhower Interstate Highway System.[1] Watching old movies from the period, with the sleek sleeper trains in *'Some Like it Hot'* or *'North by Northwest'*; they seem to me like propaganda from some far distant alien planet. Nowadays, train journeys within the US, outside of the eastern seaboard, are a lesson in patience. They have, in part, fallen victim to the same Interstate system which has motorised America. I once made the mistake of going to our local station to take the Amtrak from Oakland to Los Angeles in the 1990s only to be told that no one in their right minds just turned up at the station at the appointed time. Rather, we should follow the train's journey on the (still early days) internet and come back to the station a few hours later. Catching a train felt more like looking for the steam from a ship's funnel over the horizon from a desert island. Over the past seventy years, US infrastructure has slowly decayed, plagued by underinvestment, politics, NIMBY-ism, and what Moss Kanter, the Harvard Business School Professor, called the curse of just being "dull".[2]

The American Society of Civil Engineers has been patiently prodding successive administrations to invest in US infrastructure.[3] They started issuing a scorecard in 1998, and it was all 'D's and 'D pluses' until recent years. In 2021, the Biden administration scraped a 'C minus', and the second Trump term a solid 'C' in 2025. The bipartisan support for the 2021 *Infrastructure Investment and Jobs Act* has been the main reason for this, and the $1.2 trillion of spending on infrastructure between 2022 and 2026. The next report card will be in 2029, and the score will heavily depend on what the Trump administration does in 2026–28 to build upon this slow and steady progress. The 2022 *Inflation Reduction Act* was also an important part of the stimulus and back-pedalling on climate-related resilience measures will not help the government's chances of ever scoring a 'B minus'.[4]

Not all infrastructure is in cities, but cities are already where most of us live and work.[5] Proximity seems to be a key precursor of innovation. In their book 'Abundance', Ezra Klein and Derek Thompson point to a paradox of the modern age.[6] Whilst many supply chains have become global, innovation remains local: it thrives in cities. They point to the 'return to office' diktats of many US corporations following COVID, the realisation that remote working was never going to be enough to drive productivity. Trust, in particular, seems to require proximity and human interaction. Remote working some of the time might be fine with people you already know, but for new relationships, face-to-face human interaction seems to be essential. Most of us will have noticed that the global physical conference circuit is fully back in place, even though remote conferencing is technically very possible. Airplanes once again feel very full. People don't just live and work in cities, they meet and innovate there as well.

Infrastructure debates, however, have looked very different in East Asia. China, South Korea, Japan, and increasingly Southeast Asia have long viewed infrastructure as a strategic asset rather than a discretionary expense. High-speed rail, ports, urban transit, water systems, and digital infrastructure have been deployed deliberately to raise productivity, integrate regions, and anchor industrial ecosystems. While not without excesses or misallocation, this approach has delivered scale, speed, and learning effects that most OECD economies have struggled to match. Dense urban clusters such as the Yangtze River Delta, the Guangdong-Hong Kong-Macao Greater Bay Area, Seoul–Incheon, Tokyo–Yokohama, and Singapore function as integrated innovation systems. These regions combine transport, housing, energy, and digital infrastructure at scale, enabling rapid experimentation and diffusion of new technologies.[7]

Globally, most of this urban architecture has yet to be built and cities require resources. Material consumption in construction is set to rise dramatically, with demand for steel, cement, and aluminium projected to double, triple, or quadruple by 2050. Even with ambitious decarbonization strategies, emissions from material production could reach 649 billion tonnes of $CO_2$-equivalent by 2100.[8] Waste statistics highlight the urgency. High-income nations produce more than one-third of global waste despite representing only 16% of the world's population.[9] In low-income countries, 93% of waste is disposed of illegally, and by 2050, waste generation in Sub-Saharan Africa is expected to more than triple.

Global municipal solid waste totalled 2 billion tonnes in 2016 and is projected to reach 3.4 billion tonnes by 2050 - a 70% increase.[10]

Yet circular materials – reusable, repurpose-able, or recyclable - remain underutilized, representing a major untapped potential. With about 30% of construction sector emissions occurring at the product stage, rapid action across the value chain is crucial. Therefore, there is a strong business case for circularity: a circular building maximizes resource efficiency and minimizes waste throughout its lifecycle.[11] This includes designing for durability, using secondary or renewable materials, enabling flexible and adaptable spaces, ensuring easy maintenance and repair, and facilitating disassembly and reuse at end-of-life. Tools such as lifecycle assessment, lifecycle costing, and digital material passports support the process.

So, there is a compelling case for circular infrastructure but undoubtedly also many barriers. Where then is the sustainability bedrock?

## 10.1  New Age Infrastructure

McKinsey estimates that a cumulative \$106 trillion in investment will be necessary through 2040 to meet the worldwide need for new and updated infrastructure. The required investment spans seven critical infrastructure verticals, with transport and logistics requiring the largest share (\$36 trillion), followed by energy and power (\$23 trillion), digital (\$19 trillion), social (\$16 trillion), waste and water infrastructure (\$6 trillion), agriculture (\$5 trillion), and defence (\$2 trillion).[12] Conventional infrastructure systems have been centralized, resource-intensive, carbon-heavy, and often rigid. Green infrastructure is not inevitable in every case, but it is highly advantageous in many. It offers an alternative built on environmental sustainability, circular resource flows, digital intelligence, and climate resilience. The critical distinction is that green infrastructure is not incremental, it is transformational.

Green infrastructure changes approaches to:

- Energy production, shifting from fossil fuels to renewables supported by storage and smart grids.

- Transportation, favouring electrified mobility, efficient logistics, and low-carbon fuels.
- Urban design, integrating nature, reducing heat, and improving stormwater management.
- Water systems, using decentralized purification and reuse to ensure security.
- Construction, advancing low-carbon materials, recycled aggregates, and improved efficiency.
- Natural ecosystems, positioning them as infrastructure assets rather than externalities.

These shifts reflect a broader truth: the global system must evolve toward models that are adaptive, distributed, and resilient rather than linear, extractive, and brittle. Freight transport and logistics account for about 8% of global greenhouse gas emissions, with road freight and aviation as dominant contributors.[13] Maritime transport and the global ports infrastructure sit at the centre of much of this. The shipping industry moves roughly four-fifths of the world's trade by volume and remains the indispensable foundation of globalization. Developing economies rely heavily on maritime networks, accounting for most seaborne exports and imports. As I noted in Chap. 6, ports act as the connective tissue linking global production systems, consumer markets, and logistics chains. They also straddle energy, manufacturing and transportation systems, making them some of the most environmentally impactful and climate-vulnerable nodes of the global economy.

Ports need to adapt to sea-level rise and weather extremes. This means adjusting existing facilities, such as elevating terminals, redesigning drainage systems, and modifying operational practices. It means better defences: constructing sea walls, storm barriers, levees, or breakwaters to protect port assets. And sometimes it means surrendering to the inevitable: relocating critical infrastructure when protecting the original site becomes too expensive or technically unfeasible. Studies have estimated that elevating US ports by two metres could cost between $60–80 billion, while raising 53 major Asia-Pacific ports between 1.6 and 2.3 metres would require $30–50 billion.[14] These figures will grow as climate impacts accelerate.

Infrastructure is increasingly blending engineered systems with natural solutions. Restoring wetlands, mangroves, coral reefs, and seagrasses can mitigate erosion, buffer storm surges, cool urban temperatures, and provide economic co-benefits such as fisheries, tourism, and carbon sequestration. The Port of San Diego has mapped the economic value of natural coastal systems and compared the upfront and long-term benefits of green adaptation options.[15] Their findings illustrate a broader truth: in many cases, nature-based solutions outperform concrete in both cost-effectiveness and resilience.

A port planned today will likely become operational in the late-2030s and continue functioning into the 2070s.[16] Meaning it must withstand decades of climate change. Sea-level rise, increasing storm surges, and coastal erosion are not theoretical but inevitable. Indonesia offers a stark example: Jakarta, one of the world's largest coastal cities, faces inundation risks by mid-century due to rising seas and land subsidence.[17] This has prompted the relocation of key government and economic functions to safer ground, demonstrating the scale of adaptation required globally.

The rapid growth of e-commerce has increased freight volume and stressed existing logistics networks. New green trade corridors - such as the emerging *India-Middle East-Europe Economic Corridor* (IMEC)[18] - demonstrate how transportation systems are being redesigned for efficiency and sustainability. IMEC's planned low-carbon rail and logistics infrastructure is expected to cut transport times by 40% along key trade routes, reducing both emissions and geopolitical vulnerability.[19]

## 10.2  Building for Public Purpose

Governments everywhere are needing to meet public demand for more affordable housing and a better quality of life in the built environment. Three quarters of the world's city infrastructure required by 2050 has yet to be constructed.[20] If by 2040 global temperatures have risen by an average of 2C (a best case scenario given current trends) then over 70% of the world's coastal regions will witness a sea-level rise exceeding 0.2 m.[21] Among the areas most vulnerable to flooding will be densely populated urban centres, including at least 136 coastal cities (those with a population exceeding one million in 2005).[22] More new cities will be added as the global population is projected to rise to 9.7 billion by 2050 and then stabilise at around 10.4 billion at the end of the century.[23] Inhabitants of the built environment, ranging from small communities to megacities, will bear the brunt of climate change impacts, including extreme heat stress, severe weather events, and rising sea levels. A 2C rise will bring deadly heatwaves and life-threatening events, unless there are radical alterations to the built environment, such as implementing cooler roofs and embracing greener urban design.[24]

Communities increasingly view environmental conditions as integral to well-being. Social movements and civil society demand equitable access to clean environments, pushing policymakers toward green solutions. The right to a healthy environment became an internationally recognised right in 2022 and air pollution ranks very high amongst public concern in almost every country.[25] Fine particles in polluted air can penetrate deep into the lungs and cardiovascular system, causing diseases including stroke, heart disease, lung cancer, chronic obstructive pulmonary diseases and respiratory infections. Industry, transportation, coal power plants and household solid fuel usage are major contributors to air pollution. But concerted action can be taken. In the Chinese capital, notorious for its smog, air pollution has fallen by a massive 64% over the past decade. Harmful nitrogen dioxide has fallen by 54% while sulphur dioxide has dropped by 89%. Beijing increased the number of 'good air days' from just 13 in 2013 to more than 300 in 2023.[26] Nevertheless, air pollution is still responsible for about 2 million deaths annually across the whole of China. Ambient air pollution alone caused more than 1 million deaths, while household air pollution from cooking with polluting fuels and technologies caused another million.[27]

Green buildings reduce energy consumption, lower greenhouse emissions, reduce water consumption, increase air quality, and provide an overall healthier living environment. The World Green Building Council reports better design and construction can:[28]

- reduce energy consumption by 30–40% compared to traditional buildings,
- reduce water consumption by 20–30%,

– reduce CO2 emissions by up to 35%,
– enable workers in green buildings to score 25% higher on standardized tests of planning and critical thinking abilities, and to be 16% more productive than those working in non-green buildings,
– result in 30% fewer 'sick building syndrome' symptoms such as headaches and respiratory irritation, and 6% higher sleep scores on average.

The economic advantages of green building are notable, typically resulting in lower operating costs over the long term. Additionally, sustainable features and certifications can enhance the resale value of properties, attracting eco-conscious buyers and tenants. The US Green Building Council has found that the average operating cost savings in the first year for new green buildings is 10.5%.[29] Over a five-year period, green buildings see an average operating cost reduction of 16.9%, and owners report that green buildings and renovations have an increased asset value of over 9%.[30]

Green building certification schemes, such as the Leadership in Energy and Environmental Design (LEED),[31] have also started to include social issues such as supply chain labour standards of construction materials. The challenge is to make social standards as compelling a requirement as those relating to the environment, and to get them to permeate an industry that is systemically very complex in many countries, with high levels of informality and family-owned businesses.[32] Statistically speaking, building sites are dangerous places to work in most countries, with a global mortality rate in excess of 100,000 deaths per year according to the global trade union, Building and Woodworkers International.[33]

Cities can take steps to improve air quality and to prevent and mitigate the worst excesses of pollution. But faced with the reality of an above 2C global temperature rise and the associated impacts on weather and sea-levels, cities must also adapt and become more resilient.[34] This means redesigning building materials, roofing systems, ventilation, green spaces, and heat-management strategies. As biodiversity declines, engineered systems must compensate even if this increases costs. Given how interrelated and interdependent ecosystems are, there are many bottlenecks that will arise over the years ahead.[35] For example, sedimentation from deforestation reduces reservoir lifespans; wetland loss increases flood risk and requires larger engineered defences; and soil degradation reduces yields and raises irrigation needs. Green infrastructure needs to address these pressures by integrating natural processes into design, reducing operating costs, and increasing system longevity.[36]

## 10.3 Material Constraints

A range of commodities is essential for the rapid construction taking place today. In most cities, the primary materials are brick, concrete, steel, timber, diesel fuel, and plastics. Though others, such as straw, clay, and bamboo, are used in different regions. Steel and concrete dominate urban construction because of their durability, longevity, and strength. However, both materials carry significant climate impacts: their production generates substantial embodied carbon, which accounts for emissions across a building's entire lifecycle, from construction to demolition.[37] Beyond climate impacts, the world faces growing material constraints in fresh water, arable land, timber, minerals needed for industrial supply chains, and biodiversity. Traditional infrastructure systems often rely on linear extraction models - dig, use, dispose - that are no longer viable at scale.

In the UK, most carbon-reduction efforts have focused on operational emissions, such as heating and cooling, rather than on construction. Yet concrete and cement alone contribute roughly 1.5% of the nation's total carbon emissions, with around 1000 production facilities and limited opportunities to cut this footprint by more than 13% in the near term.[38] UK steel production also relies heavily on blast furnaces, which emit more carbon than electric arc furnaces or emerging green hydrogen methods. Many specialists argue that the UK should expand its use of wood in construction due to the comparatively low carbon footprint of sustainably sourced timber. The UK's *Climate Change Committee* recommends increasing the use of timber-frame housing from 26% today to 40% by 2050. The International Energy Agency likewise urges substituting timber for steel, masonry, and concrete to reduce embodied carbon.[39] However, since the 2014 *Grenfell Tower* fire - where cladding failures played a major role - insurance premiums for tall timber buildings remain prohibitively high, creating a systemic barrier to wider adoption.

Other materials are also critical. Although metals like copper are used in smaller volumes than core building materials, they are critical for urban electrification. A single house can contain more than 200 kg of copper, and residential buildings account for half of global copper consumption. While the industry highlights this importance, its supply-chain oversight rarely extends beyond the smelter, leaving little traceability once copper enters the built environment.[40]

Sand is also a case in point. Second only to water in global extraction, it is indispensable to construction (concrete, mortar, and plaster), glass-making, industrial processes, and renewable technologies. Whilst sand is a naturally occurring and a far from scarce material, not all sand is usable for construction. Desert sand, abundant in the Gulf of Arabia, is too smooth and fine for most of the construction currently underway in countries such as Saudi Arabia and the UAE.[41] Instead, builders rely on river and marine sand for many jobs, which is increasingly scarce. The Gulf states must import construction-grade sand from Australia, India, China, and East Africa to support mega-projects like NEOM. Unsustainable sand mining has fuelled coastal erosion, damaged ecosystems, and increased vulnerability to storms. Sand exploitation can also fuel social conflict and illegal "sand mafia" operations around the world are associated with labour exploitation, including forced and child labour. Ensuring ethical and sustainable sourcing is now a priority for governments and investors.[42]

Increasingly, downstream sustainability standards, such as LEED certification, will ask questions of the upstream and how sustainably commodities are procured. The European Union's efforts in relation to timber, under the Deforestation Regulation discussed in Chap. 9, might eventually become the benchmark for other natural materials. This will draw more attention to the ecosystems that underpin these resources.

# 10.4  Remaking Sustainable Infrastructure

Economics may ultimately be the strongest force making green infrastructure highly likely if not inevitable. As outlined in earlier chapters, over the past decade the cost of key elements of renewable energy have plummeted: solar PV costs are down nearly 90%, wind energy down over 60%, and battery storage costs are declining rapidly. In many regions, renewable energy is now the cheapest form of new electricity generation. By contrast, fossil fuel systems face volatile prices, geopolitical risk, and regulatory headwinds. The financial logic increasingly favours renewables. Even in the US, where the federal government has pulled many of the incentives, renewable energy is often the logical choice in Texas, California, and an increasing number of other states.

In addition to the reducing cost of renewables, high-carbon energy sources are facing increasing costs as old assets deteriorate.[43] Infrastructure failures expose critical vulnerabilities due to ageing, inadequate maintenance and extreme weather conditions. In 2005, Hurricane Katrina caused more than 1300 fatalities around New Orleans.[44] The death toll was exacerbated by neglected maintenance and care of the main levee. This resulted in massive destruction and made the disaster much worse. Short-term funding of maintenance can lead to a vicious cycle of reactive repairs which are often more costly than preventive measures. In the UK, the 2019 flood in Yorkshire could have been mitigated by timely levee maintenance. In the absence of it, damages exceeded £100 million. Environmental factors in Brazil fed into the collapse of the Mariana dam in 2015 as well as the company's decision to keep raising the height of the existing dam. A UK High Court ruling in November 2025 concluded that this was the "direct and immediate cause" of the dam's collapse, which killed 19 people, polluted the river and destroyed hundreds of homes, meaning BHP (the co-parent company that was headquartered in the UK at the time) is liable under Brazilian law.[45]

Repairing damage can cost exponentially more than preventing it. However, infrastructure maintenance often goes unnoticed and is politically unattractive until failures — and their socio-economic impact - bring the cost of inaction to the public's attention. Yet resilience isn't just about existing vulnerabilities. Infrastructure must be prepared to withstand risks, expected and unexpected. But it cannot be viewed in isolation. It is a system of systems. Failure in one area can trigger cascading effects across others. Timely strategic investments in infrastructure resilience can address future social, economic, and environmental risks and bring significant long-term benefits. Infrastructure resilience is not just about saving money; it is about improving efficiency, outcomes, and lives. To achieve this, a shift in perspective to prioritise resilience is required.

*Remaking Sustainability* in infrastructure through traditional methods is increasingly inefficient, especially as climate risks intensify and global economic needs evolve. Research shows that every dollar invested in resilience produces between four and ten dollars in avoided losses.[46] Green infrastructure incorporates resilience from the start, lowering long-term operational and maintenance costs. Countries that prioritize such investments also lay the groundwork for fast-growing economic sectors, including electric vehicle manufacturing, green hydrogen production, sustainable construction materials, energy-efficient housing, and digitally enabled logistics systems.

However, transitioning to a circular economy will require significant upfront capital. According to the World Green Building Council, approximately €230 billion will be needed to adapt physical assets and infrastructure.[47] Yet the long-term benefits far outweigh this investment. By 2040, the circular economy could generate €1.5 trillion in value through new markets, cost savings, and reduced emissions. Adopting circularity in the built environment offers a way to decouple economic expansion from carbon emissions. Globally, such a transition could yield up to $4.5 trillion in benefits by 2030. In Europe, it could generate €1.8 trillion annually, amounting to a 7% GDP increase.[48]

Technological progress is also reinforcing and accelerating the infrastructure transition. Electrification is becoming a unifying technological platform across infrastructure. Electric vehicles and heavy-duty transport, heat pumps replacing fossil-based heating, and electrified industrial processes are all key considerations for any infrastructure transition. On top of this, technology enables smart buildings and district energy systems, distributed renewable generation, and helps electric systems integrate seamlessly with renewables. Technological advances also bring green infrastructure closer. New advances include low-carbon concrete, recycled and green steel, engineered timber, advanced polymers and composites, and carbon-negative materials. Such innovations reduce embodied carbon, improve durability, and expand design possibilities. Microgrids, modular wastewater plants, distributed energy systems, and compact waste-to-energy units allow scalable infrastructure development, especially vital for remote or rapidly growing regions.

The world could replace all its high-carbon and polluting infrastructure like for like if it wanted to, but why would it? As the American Society of Civil Engineers know, investment in infrastructure is a long-game issue. They only produce their score card every four years, each time a new presidential administration is elected, and scoring has only edged upwards from a D to a C in the space of nearly thirty years. Shorting sustainability in infrastructure is of course possible but lacks many incentives. One moment of clarity in the US is September 2026 and the expiration of the 2021 *Infrastructure Investment and Jobs Act*. Readers of this book will know what I don't at time of writing: the extent to which sustainability is factored into the new round of investment? Of course, this means cutting through the political rhetoric and looking at what is really going on and where the bedrock has emerged. My prediction is that issues of climate resilience cannot afford not to be a key consideration. Beyond the US, almost everywhere beyond the US, sustainability in infrastructure is here to stay. Even within the US, at the subnational level, circular infrastructure remains a growth industry.

The three chapters in this section of the book have looked at different value chain perspectives. Security of supply is in nexus with sustainability (Chap. 8) is clearly a big business concern, but it is also increasingly an issue of national security too. Sustainable trade policy (Chap. 9) is led by governments but directly impacts on business through a variety of incentives and disincentives across borders. This chapter (Chap. 10), the final of the three, has shown that sustainable infrastructure is the collective interest of national and sub-national government, as well as business, and communities themselves. *Remaking Sustainability* requires a stronger synthesis between all aspects of the value chain. It is inevitable that sustainability will become an integral part of both the upstream and downstream of commodities, materials, products, services, and associated infrastructure. Security of supply will keep sustainability centre-stage as will the need to strengthen resilience in the face of environmental and geopolitical challenges. Better data will be required to achieve the coherence and traceability required for managing sustainability throughout complex value chains: the subject of the next chapter (Chap. 11), the start of the section on sustainability bedrock in technology.

## Notes

1. S&P Global, Infrastructure: *What once was lost can be found – the productivity boost*, 4 May 2020.
2. James Surowiecki, *System Overload*, The New Yorker, 11 April 2016.
3. American Society of Civil Engineers, *Infrastructure's upward momentum reflected in report card*, 25 March 2025.
4. S&P Global, Infrastructure: *What once was lost can be found – the productivity boost*, 4 May 2020.
5. John Morrison and Giulio Ferrini, *Human rights as a key to unlock a Just Transition for the Built Environment*, in Savitri Bisnath, Morten Kjaerum and Martha Davis, Human Rights Economies and Subnational Governance, 2026.
6. Ezra Klein and Derek Thompson, *Abundance: How we build a better future*, 2025.
7. Wu Changhua, *personal communication*, January 2026.
8. Ellen MacArthur, *Completing the picture: How the circular economy tackles climate change*, Ellen MacArthur Foundation, 2021.
9. World Bank Group, *What a Waste 2.0: Global snapshot of solid waste management to 2050*, September 2018.
10. World Bank Group, *What a Waste 2.0: Global snapshot of solid waste management to 2050*, September 2018.
11. World Green Building Council, *The Circular Built Environment Playbook*, May 2023.
12. McKinsey, *The infrastructure moment*, 9 September 2025.
13. World Economic Forum, *Global logistics emissions council*, 12 December 2024.
14. Jasper Verschuur and Austin Becker, *The overlooked sustainability trade-offs of port adaptation at scale*, PLOS Climate.19 August 2025.
15. Port of San Diego, *Blue Economy*, (website), November 2025.

16. World Economic Forum, *Global logistics emissions council*, 12 December 2024.
17. United Nations, *Sinking City*, UNFCCC, 29 July 2022.
18. IMEC International, *India-Middle East-Europe Economic Corridor (IMEC)*, (website), November 2025.
19. IMEC International, *India-Middle East-Europe Economic Corridor (IMEC)*, (website), November 2025.
20. https://worldgbc.org/article/how-can-the-built-environment-ensure-the-environmental-transition-leaves-no-one-behind/
21. Intergovernmental Panel on Climate Change (IPCC), *Sixth Assessment Report*, Working Group I: The Physical Science Basis, 2021.
22. https://www.wri.org/insights/ipcc-15deg-report-we-need-build-and-live-differently-cities
23. https://www.un.org/en/global-issues/population#:~:text=The%20world%20population%20is%20projected,and%2010.4%20billion%20by%202100
24. https://www.wri.org/insights/ipcc-15deg-report-we-need-build-and-live-differently-cities
25. John Morrison and Giulio Ferrini, *Human rights as a key to unlock a Just Transition for the Built Environment*, in Savitri Bisnath, Morten Kjaerum and Martha Davis, Human Rights Economies and Subnational Governance, 2026.
26. World Economic Forum, *In 10 years, Beijing has drastically cut air pollution*, (website), 2025.
27. World Health Organisation, *Air pollution in China* (website), 2025.
28. World Green Building Council, *The Circular Built Environment Playbook*, May 2023.
29. US Green Building Council, *Benefits of green building*, (website), November 2025.
30. US Green Building Council, *Benefits of green building*, (website), November 2025.
31. US Green Building Council, *Benefits of green building*, (website), November 2025.
32. Grace Farms Foundation's "Design for Freedom" initiative https://www.designforfreedom.org/
33. Building and Woodworkers International, *BWI Construction Hazards Fact Sheet*, (website), December 2025.

34. John Morrison and Giulio Ferrini, *Human rights as a key to unlock a Just Transition for the Built Environment*, in Savitri Bisnath, Morten Kjaerum and Martha Davis, Human Rights Economies and Subnational Governance, 2026.

35. John Morrison, *The Just Transition: a systems-thinking approach to managing climate action*, 2024.

36. Kathy Willis, *Good nature: improve your health and happiness with nature – one simple step at a time*, 2024.

37. Environmental Audit Committee, *Building to net zero: costing carbon in construction*, UK House of Commons, 11 May 2022.

38. Environmental Audit Committee, *Building to net zero: costing carbon in construction*, UK House of Commons, 11 May 2022.

39. International Energy Agency quoted in: Environmental Audit Committee, *Building to net zero: costing carbon in construction*, UK House of Commons, 11 May 2022.

40. John Morrison, *The Just Transition: a systems-thinking approach to managing climate action*, 2024.

41. Institute for Human Rights and Business, *Gulf Sustain*, 2026.

42. Institute for Human Rights and Business, *Gulf Sustain*, 2026.

43. Rowena Mason, *UK wasting 'tens of billions' on crumbling infrastructure and badly run projects*, The Guardian, 16 January 2024.

44. Institution of Civil Engineers, *Maintenance matters: what is the true cost of infrastructure failure?* October 2024.

45. Iona Wells, *UK court finds mining firm liable for Brazil's worst environmental disaster*, 14 November 2025.

46. World Green Building Council, *The Circular Built Environment Playbook*, May 2023.

47. World Green Building Council, *The Circular Built Environment Playbook*, May 2023.

48. World Green Building Council, *The Circular Built Environment Playbook*, May 2023.

# Part IV

## Bedrock in Technology

# 11

## Better Data

Sustainability becomes enforceable when it becomes legible. Without reliable data, physical limits cannot be priced, trade rules cannot be applied, insurance cannot be underwritten, and infrastructure risks cannot be managed. Under these conditions, sustainability remains rhetorical - invoked, audited, and reported, but rarely acted upon. As systems automate, this ambiguity collapses. Decisions increasingly depend on what can be measured and compared at scale. Better sustainability data leads to higher assurance and verification; that in turn allows banks, insurers, procurement platforms, and regulators to plug sustainability metrics directly into decisions. This allows for automatic penalties or exclusions when thresholds get crossed; and once the infrastructure runs that way, firms can't "opt out" of sustainability performance without opting out of markets, financing, or contracts. The operating system of the economy will increasingly require this data.

This shift is already under way. Sustainability data is being embedded into financial risk models, procurement systems, trade compliance, insurance underwriting, and regulatory enforcement. Firms, projects, and even countries that cannot demonstrate environmental and social performance increasingly find themselves unable to access a share of growing



J. Morrison, *Remaking Sustainability*, https://doi.org/10.1007/978-3-032-23755-2_11

markets, capital, or coverage. This chapter examines why existing sustainability data systems fail under this pressure, and why incremental improvements are insufficient. It shows how fragmented reporting, audit-based verification, and misaligned incentives systematically obscure risk rather than reveal it. It then turns to what replaces them: data architectures capable of supporting accountability at scale. If infrastructure locks sustainability into physical assets, data is what makes those commitments operational across institutions and machines. It is the first of three chapters that focus on what might be called the 'technology bedrock': the development in different aspects of digital technology that are helping to make the sustainability agenda inevitable.

## 11.1 Technology-Enabled Data

There is nothing new about data, but technology seems to offer an era of better data to come. We know that data is the lifeblood of good business. It shapes how strategy is set, how performance is judged, and how progress is measured. Yet when it comes to environmental and social sustainability, data has often arrived late to the table: fragmented, inconsistent, and difficult to trust. Many organizations still treat sustainability data as something peripheral to financial management, a parallel stream that runs nearby but rarely joins the main current. That is beginning to change. Across sectors, companies are learning that sustainability data is not an ethical accessory. Reliable environmental and social data makes it possible to understand how issues such as resource use, risk exposure, and stakeholder expectations affect profit and resilience. Even so, the journey toward better data is uneven. Surveys of global executives repeatedly show that most organizations doubt the completeness or accuracy of their sustainability data.[1] Many still rely on manual collection, spreadsheets, and assumptions rather than objective systems or verified sources. All too often, businesses are unwilling to disclose data due to its poor quality, for commercial reasons, or for fear of increased liability – or a mixture of all three.

The companies that have made the greatest strides toward sustainability over the past thirty years did not wait for perfect data. When I worked at The Body Shop International, now over a quarter of a century ago, our data gathering was far from optimal, but we pushed forward the sustainability agenda, nevertheless. But today we are now on the cusp of a new era when 'walking the talk' is a precondition for any leadership position, and that the disclosure of data will increasingly not sit solely within the control of companies in any case. Some have called this an era of *double materiality*: that companies must measure and disclose not just the external impacts on a business' performance ('financial materiality'), but also the business' own impacts on the environment and society ('impact materiality'). This is the basis of standards such as the European Union's *Corporate Sustainability Reporting Directive* (CSRD)[2] covered in Chap. 4. New forms of technology, in particular AI, also play a critical role in driving the data agenda, as we will come to later in this chapter and then more fully in the next.

## 11.2  A Short History of Green Data

Every revolution in accountability has begun with better data. Financial reporting emerged from merchants' ledgers; public health reforms followed the spread of epidemiological data; climate action gained urgency only when global carbon and temperature datasets became irrefutable.[3] The wider sustainability movement is the next chapter in that same story.

The origins of sustainability reporting can be traced back to the early 1960s,[4] when the latest concerns over humanity's impact on the planet began to take shape. It should always be remembered that this consciousness has existed for hundreds if not thousands of years amongst many indigenous peoples but has in many ways been rediscovered by the industrialised world. Rachel Carson's *Silent Spring* exposed the dangers of chemical pesticides, catalysing public resistance and leading to the U.S. ban on DDT, as I invoked in Chap. 1.[5] For the first time, a social–environmental movement challenged the unchecked pursuit of industrial profit and established a moral link between corporate behaviour and ecological well-being. Kenneth Boulding's essay, *The Economics of the Coming*

*Spaceship Earth*,[6] provided the first theoretical framing of this relationship. Boulding contrasted the exploitative *"cowboy economy,"* driven by limitless production, with the *"spaceship economy,"* in which finite resources and waste capacity must be managed responsibly. This metaphor positioned economic growth and environmental limits as inherently interdependent, a principle that underpins modern sustainability thinking.

In 1972, the Club of Rome's report *The Limits to Growth* deepened the debate.[7] Using early computer modelling, it predicted ecological and economic collapse if exponential population and industrial growth continued unchecked. The report's lead author, Donella Meadows, would then go on to develop the basis to how systems-thinking can be applied to sustainability challenges, a focus of my last book.[8] Institutional foundations also emerged. The United Nations Environment Programme (UNEP) was established in 1972 following the *Stockholm Conference on the Human Environment*, creating a global forum for environmental governance.[9] Subsequent conventions such as the *Convention on international trade in endangered species of wild fauna and flora* (CITES) in 1973,[10] and the *Bonn Convention* in 1979,[11] institutionalized early environmental cooperation. Together, these events built the intellectual and institutional groundwork for linking corporate behaviour, environmental impact, and social responsibility.

The 1989 Exxon Valdez oil spill in Alaska demonstrated the potential economic consequences of environmental negligence. Exxon settled in 1991 for over a billion dollars at the time, with funds disbursed in three discrete parts: the criminal plea agreement ($25 million), the criminal restitution ($100 million), and the civil settlement ($900 million).[12] This disaster marked a turning point: investors and the public began demanding transparent information on companies' environmental impacts. In response, environmentalists and investors formed the Coalition for Environmentally Responsible Economies (CERES) in 1989,[13] publishing the *Valdez Principles*—the first comprehensive code of corporate environmental conduct. These principles, emphasizing pollution prevention, biosphere conservation, and transparency, became the ethical foundation for later sustainability frameworks. Legal reforms followed, such as the

US *Oil Pollution Act* in 1990, which imposed stricter liabilities and operational standards for oil companies.[14]

Momentum continued globally. The 1992 *Rio Earth Summit*[15] promoted collaboration among governments, businesses, and civil society to integrate environmental and development goals, leading to the creation of the UN *Sustainable Development Commission*. Key critical thinkers of the time included Wangari Maathai, and Vandana Shiva. Throughout the 1990s, environmental accounting evolved into *sustainability accounting*, supported by growing recognition that financial reporting alone could not capture an organization's total impact. In 1998, John Elkington introduced the *Triple Bottom Line* framework - "people, planet, profit" - arguing that businesses must measure success across social, environmental, and economic dimensions.[16] This approach reframed corporate accountability, establishing the expectation that organizations should report not only their financial results but also their broader contributions to sustainable development.

Then came the proliferation of standards and frameworks, such as the *Global Reporting Initiative*,[17] the *Carbon Disclosure Project*,[18] the rise of ESG indices under which there is now a plethora of data of varying quality,[19] and national regulations. Each sought to make sustainability measurable and comparable. Yet this well-intentioned explosion created its own complexity. Companies faced overlapping requests for data, multiple reporting calendars, and diverging definitions. The result has been a new kind of noise: abundant data, but little coherence.

## 11.3  Too Many Trees to See the Wood

We are now at a turning point. The volume of sustainability data has grown exponentially, but its reliability has not always kept pace. Consolidation of standards is essential; the question is whose standards? To answer this, it is important to start with the story behind the data and why the status quo is very much a broken data system. The existing system has plenty of data, but it is heavily silo-ed, sometimes of poor quality, not shared, often not acted upon, and often not disclosed.

A quick look at social sustainability data perhaps illustrates the point well. Businesses seem truly surprised when incidents of forced labour or child labour emerge from their supply chains. They shouldn't be, or put another way, they should not be surprised that the risk of the human rights abuse exists, rather that it has been discovered. For example, the 28 million workers categorized as being the victims of forced labour are scattered across the globe[20] but there are several economic practices that draw them towards the global supply chains of international companies. These practices include the behaviour of recruitment companies, the charging of recruitment fees, withholding of passports, forced overtime and so on.[21] None of these risk factors are necessarily definitive proof of forced labour when taken individually, but together they can be indicative. Whilst forced labour can exist in any supply chain, anywhere, work exploitation is often highest when the workers are out of sight and out of mind, unable to organise themselves into trade unions or seek other forms of representation. It should be of no surprise that forced labour is very prevalent in some forms of agriculture, the deep-sea fishing industry, or amongst domestic workers for example. Yet when allegations of forced labour emerge, in the Tuna fishing industry for example aboard Taiwanese registered boats, and linked to British supermarkets, it is still greeted with shock.[22]

So why isn't the data preparing us for what is really going on? The truth is, there is plenty of data about the systemic risk of forced labour in the deep-sea fishing fleet and sometimes specifically linked to Taiwan.[23] The data is out there in NGO reports, media articles in several languages, trade union investigations and so on. But all too often the people managing corporate supply chains are either unaware of all this data or see it as contextual if it does not directly relate to the supply chain of their own company. And here lies the rub, the data collected by companies relating to their own supply chains is mainly through the social audits of workplaces and we know that at best, social audits, are a blunt tool. Social audits provide a momentary picture of working conditions - typically a single day, at a single site. Auditors visit pre-announced (or even unannounced) but undertake only short inspections. Exploitation and coercion are dynamic phenomena, and abusive employers can hide abuses temporarily. Conditions may change immediately after the audit team leaves. Therefore, audits capture compliance at a point in time, not always the *systemic risks* that cause abuse.

And companies have limited resources and might have tens of thousands of 'first tier' suppliers. But the most serious abuses often occur in subcontracted or informal layers, including home-based work, small workshops, or migrant labour brokers. These layers often fall outside the scope or jurisdiction of audit protocols. Therefore, even when discovered in a specific supply chain, exploitation can be pushed deeper into the shadows rather than eliminated, either moving workers to another company's supply chain or even more precarious forms of work.

Those of us working in social sustainability see this repeatedly. The knee-jerk response to child labour in the supply chains of sportswear in the 1990s led to many suppliers being dropped at short notice, but this did not necessarily help the workers at all. Evidence showed that girls and young women reemerged in more exploitative forms of work in agriculture or even prostitution. Until the most recent coup d'etat in Myanmar in 2021, I was able to visit the nascent apparel sector in and around Yangon, employing up to 700,000 workers, mainly women.[24] But where are these women now? The data that has been gathered suggests that many have migrated to Thailand, Malaysia, Laos, Cambodia, and China, for work, with less protections and higher risks of forced labour in some contexts.[25]

Another example that I know quite well is that of the Kericho tea plantation in Kenya, formerly one of Unilever's main tea suppliers. It was until recently the largest private sector employer in the country, and certainly the highest employer of women. Despite certification by a well-known sustainability auditor, labour practices had hardly evolved since colonial times, when the plantations were established. The supervisors of the women were almost exclusively men, and there were reports for many years of systemic abuse, including a culture of sexual favours, harassment, and violence.[26] When the first complaints arrived at the company, they were at first contested. Only upon investigation did it become clear that such abusive practices were rife. Kudos to the company for learning from this and disclosing this in their 2017 human rights report,[27] but this example illustrates another limitation of much social sustainability data. It is not systemic, and the burden of proof sits with the victims of abuse even in situations where the prevalence is so high that statistically the company should expect it to be there even if their social auditing is not identifying it.

This schism between what is known to be systemically true, and the pretence that specific supply chains are clean unless evidence arises that suggests otherwise, is only made worse by the lack of disclosure, analysis and understanding of the true nature of systemic risks. Companies fear they will be penalised if they are honest about the pervasive nature of these risks, and therefore they do not disclose them. If companies disclosed the true risk of forced labour in their supply chains, then all of the mandatory reporting under the UK, Australian and Canadian Modern Slavery Acts would be far more comprehensive than it is today, with some notable exceptions.

Now, there are not sufficient incentives or requirements in place for companies (or investors) to know what is really going on in their supply chains, or if they do know, to disclose that they know. This is one of the many arguments for further legislation, such as the original version of the European Union's *Corporate Sustainability Due Diligence Directive* (CSDDD)[28] and the *Corporate Sustainability Reporting Directive* (CSRD),[29] both much watered down by the end of 2025, but a start, nevertheless. The *German Supply Chain* Act[30] is one example of how the balance begins to shift when governments expect companies to proactively look for these risks in their supply chains, and to penalise them not for what they find, but for not looking in the first place. The earlier French due diligence law (*loi du vigilance*)[31] did not do this sufficiently.

Let's see if a better array of incentives start to emerge for the collection and use of sustainability data from the combination of measures the European Union has now developed (as outlined in Chap. 9), ranging from tackling deforestation, carbon trading, and forced labour, to the due diligence and reporting requirements already mentioned. All these laws will work if the right kind of data becomes available and is used effectively. Under its Forced Labour regulation, the EU Commission will include a forced labour risk database as part of the guidelines published in June 2026.[32]

# 11.4  Federating Data

## The Current Broken Data System

The current data system for managing sustainability issues in supply chains is at best suboptimal and sometimes even counterproductive.[33] Most social audits are paid for by the companies being audited or by the brands sourcing from them. This creates an inherent financial and reputational conflict of interest. Audit firms may feel pressured to issue favourable reports to retain clients. As already mentioned, factories sometimes prepare for audits by coaching workers, falsifying records, or temporarily improving conditions.[34] The result is that data credibility is compromised, and 'audit fatigue' sets in across supply chains.[35] Social audits often fail to capture the worker's voice. Interviews may be brief, conducted in management's presence, or limited to a few representatives. Migrant, temporary, or undocumented workers – often the most vulnerable - may be excluded altogether. Fear of retaliation can silence honest reporting meaning the workers most affected by abuse rarely shape the evidence used to address it. Sometimes, workers too can be complicit in hiding true levels of overtime for fear of losing income.

Environmental and social audit results too are siloed, typically shared only with the commissioning client. There is no universal data standard or central repository for audit findings although shared audit platforms do exist in some sectors (particularly apparel and electronics) and are obviously a step in the right direction.[36] Platforms include: *Sedex*, *Amfori*, the *Social and Labor Convergence* programme, Cascale's *Higg Index* tools, the *Fairwear Foundation*, the *Fair Labor Association*, the *Responsible Business Alliance*, and the *Open Supply Hub* (which as its name suggests is open source). But beyond these, different buyers commission different audits, sometimes duplicating effort or using incompatible checklists. All too often, lessons are not aggregated across industries or regions, so systemic patterns remain invisible.[37] The result is that knowledge about risks remains proprietary, and accountability is diluted. Across the sustainability landscape, fragmentation carries a cost measured in lost insight and missed opportunity. This in addition to the cost of auditing itself. The collective annual spend on social audits alone is estimated to be around $300 million from an industry currently worth about $20 billion and growing.[38]

There are also concerns about the cost of compliance. A survey of European companies showed that 51% said they spend or expect to spend over €100,000 a year on CSRD compliance, according to a survey by New York-based sustainability company Novata.[39] In particular, 29% said it will cost them between €100,000 and €250,000 per year, whilst 22% said it will cost over €250,000 annually. The findings of the report suggest that companies working with technology providers reported fewer issues with data collection and management. The use of technology, in particular AI, for such purposes is the focus of our next chapter (Chap. 12). Suffice it to say that the cost of implementation has been one of the main arguments used by those advocating to limit the scope of companies captured by CSRD to larger firms. Here the costs can be significant. The Financial Times[40] interviewed one undisclosed multinational in 2024 that claimed to have spent $18 million in the previous three years on automating its carbon emissions data and expected to spend another $50–$60 million over the next three to five years to comply fully with the CSRD. On top of this, it anticipated millions of dollars in annual costs for data compliance and auditing. The company also expected to have to comply with the Carbon Border Adjustment Mechanism (CBAM), at a cost of at least $500,000 a year.[41]

It is hard to verify these claims, as the company interviewed by the Financial Times was unwilling to go on the record. In November 2025, the CEO of Exxon, Darren Woods, did go on the record claiming that the potential liabilities under CSDDD would be "bone-crushing" and could cost the company billions of dollars and would give Exxon reason to leave the European market altogether.[42] The way the large accountancy and law firms have been marketing their own services in Brussels over recent years would indicate that the EU's sustainability compliance market will be worth a considerable amount. The question is whether this cost is worth paying, not just from the perspective of individual companies, but as a collective. Will it move the needle on sustainability? Will it generate the right kind of meaningful data that might yield insights into the kinds of impacts that might mitigate or prevent environmental or social damage, or restore and remediate that which has already occurred?

## A More Virtuous Data System

Whilst the current broken system might be expensive, it is not inevitably so. It is a design flaw: a legacy of systems built for isolation rather than integration. Overcoming it requires a new architecture for sustainability data, one that protects data sovereignty but enables connection. Other sources of data do exist. Governments conduct labour inspections even if these typically cover only a fraction of workplaces. Trade unions and NGOs document abuses but lack platforms for global sharing. United Nations agencies might also be active but will generally not want to embarrass the host government. Academics might publish rigorous analyses but are subject to the time lag of researching and peer review. Data aggregating companies are starting to provide services to help companies comply with forced labour and other related legislation, but this data is locked behind paywalls. Other forms of potential data, such as imagery from satellites, might or might not be available to some of these actors. Meanwhile, workers themselves – who have the direct experience of their own issues – are the providers of the largest potential source of real-time data.

The lack of incentives reinforces the problem. Businesses hesitate to disclose weaknesses for fear of reputational damage or legal risk. Governments guard information that might affect trade. NGOs and trade unions protect sensitive data to avoid endangering workers. Each has valid reasons, yet the result is the same: a broken ecosystem where risk multiplies in the dark. A world of bounded rationality as I discussed in Chaps. 2 and 3. Fragmentation does more than obscure exploitation - it sustains it. A company can claim ignorance of abuses in its supply chain because the information exists elsewhere. A regulator can delay enforcement because evidence is dispersed. A consumer can remain unaware because the signal never reaches the marketplace.

Data federation begins with a radical yet practical idea: data can remain where it is and still serve the whole. In a federated model, no single entity controls all information. Governments retain their inspection records. Corporations keep their supplier databases. NGOs and trade unions safeguard testimonies. Yet through common standards and secure protocols, enabled through new data technologies, these distributed datasets can speak to each other. Queries travel across the network, not raw data. The insights - patterns, correlations, risk indicators - are shared without compromising privacy or ownership. This approach has demonstrated significant potential in other policy domains, such as epidemiology. The triangulation of diverse data sets is also showing growing value on issues such as river pollution, illegal deforestation or fishing, or methane blooms arising from industrial processes – where satellite imagery can be cross-referenced with on the ground reports and inspections.

It is yet to be seen how well data federation might work on social sustainability issues but in theory it should help to disrupt some of the main negative feedback loops in the current system. The proposition is that federation dissolves the false trade-off between control and collaboration. Governments no longer fear exposing sensitive data; companies no longer fear competitors accessing proprietary audits; NGOs no longer fear breaches of confidentiality. Trust becomes the engine of participation. Federation mirrors how the internet itself evolved: decentralized, resilient, and scalable. It allows the sustainability ecosystem to mature beyond one-off pilots and data silos into a dynamic, continuously learning system. Each participant retains autonomy but contributes to a shared understanding of reality. It remains to be seen how far federated data might progress and how much the costs of reforming data collection drop once technology is applied.

## 11.5  Remaking Sustainability Data

What it the costs and the data insights were better distributed through the system and yielded higher value and actionable insights? The more sustainability data exists, the more everything must orbit around it. As datasets expand, analytical tools, benchmarks, and rating systems amplify their influence. Banks, insurers, and procurement platforms will increasingly automate decisions using sustainability data inputs. In such a data-driven environment, opting out will mean being excluded from automated systems of trust and trade. The goal of better data is not only knowledge but movement. When data becomes trustworthy and shared, it creates a self-reinforcing cycle - a virtuous loop where trust fuels participation, participation yields insight, insight drives action, and action delivers impact.

Federated data systems are already being used by businesses. In healthcare, organizations such as the National Health Service (NHS) in England are implementing federated data platforms to connect patient information across different hospital systems,[43] improving care coordination and research while maintaining strict privacy controls. In finance, banks and financial institutions use federated learning for collaborative efforts like fraud detection and credit risk modelling without sharing raw, sensitive customer data. In retail and E-commerce, companies like Walmart and Netflix use it to gain a unified, real-time view of customer behaviour across online and in-store systems,[44] which helps power personalized recommendations and marketing campaigns. In technology, Google has used federated learning for its *Gboard* predictive keyboard, training algorithms on user devices without uploading private data to the cloud.[45]

The failures described in this chapter are not transitional problems. They are structural. Sustainability data systems designed for disclosure and reassurance cannot support enforcement, automation, or exclusion. As long as data remains fragmented, unauditable, and shaped by incentives to conceal rather than reveal risk, sustainability commitments remain performative. Under sustainability constraints, this is no longer tenable. What replaces these systems is not a single database or reporting framework, but a shift in architecture. Federated data systems - where information remains distributed but interoperable, verifiable, and machine-readable - are becoming a prerequisite for participation. They are slower, more political, and more contested than voluntary reporting regimes, but they can support real consequences. As these systems spread, sustainability stops being something organisations say and becomes something systems check.

This marks a qualitative change. Once sustainability data is embedded in automated decision-making - credit allocation, procurement, insurance pricing, border controls - the scope for negotiation narrows sharply.

Actors without credible data are not argued with; they are filtered out. Sustainability becomes enforced not through persuasion, but through system design. The next chapter turns to artificial intelligence, where this logic accelerates. AI systems amplify whatever data architectures they are built upon. Where sustainability data is robust, AI can strengthen resilience and efficiency. Where it is weak, automation scales error, bias, and harm. The question is no longer whether better data is desirable, but whether sustainability systems are being built on foundations capable of bearing the weight now placed upon them.

## Notes


1. Cameron Saunders, *Report emphasizes lack of trust with ESG among businesses*, Sustainability magazine, 26 January 2023.
2. European Commission, *Corporate responsibility reporting*, DG Finance, (website), 25 November 2025.
3. James Lawrence Powell, *Scientists reach 100% consensus on anthropogenic global warming*, Bulletin of Science, Technology & Society: 34(4), 20 November 2019.
4. Soner Gokten et al., *The historical development of sustainability reporting: a periodic approach*, Ze współpracy z zagranicą (International Cooperation), 107 (163), 2020.
5. Rachel Carson, *Silent Spring*, 1962.
6. Kenneth Boulding, *The Economics of the Coming Spaceship Earth*, in H. Jarrett (ed.) 1966. Environmental Quality in a Growing Economy, pp. 3–14, 1966.
7. Donella Meadows et al., *The limits of growth*, MIT/The Club of Rome, 1972.
8. John Morrison, *The Just Transition: a systems-thinking approach to managing climate action*, 2024.
9. United Nations, *UN Conference on the Human Environment*, Stockholm, 5–16 June 1976.
10. United Nations, *Convention on international trade in endangered species of wild fauna and flora* (CITES), 1973.
11. United Nations, *Convention on the Conservation of Migratory Species of Wild Animals (CMS)*, 1979.

12. US Government, *Exxon Valdez Oil Spill*, National Oceanic and Atmospheric Administration (NOAA), (website), 2025.

13. CERES, *Coalition for Environmentally Responsible Economies (CERES)*, 1989.

14. US Government, *Summary of the Oil Pollution Act*, US Environment Protection Agency, (website), 2025.

15. United Nations, *UN Conference on Environment and Development (UNCED)*, 1992.

16. *John Elkington, Cannibals with Forks: the Triple Bottom Line of 21st Century*, 1997.

17. Global Reporting Initiative, *The global leader for sustainability reporting*, (website), 25 November 2025.

18. Carbon Disclosure Project, *CDP's 25th year*, (website), 25 November 2025.

19. Responsible Investor, *ESG data: too much or not enough?* 9 May 2023.

20. International Labour Organisation, *Forced labour, modern slavery, and trafficking in persons*, (website), 25 November 2025.

21. Institute for Human Rights and Business, *Global Forum for Responsible Recruitment*, 2025.

22. Financial Times, *The dark truth behind supermarket tuna*, 21 November 2025.

23. For example, Greenpeace International, *US tuna cans linked to reports of forced labour of Indonesian fishers*, 9 December 2024.

24. Eurocham Myanmar, *Myanmar Garment Factsheet*, version 2.0, November 2023.

25. Personal communication with in-country researchers during 2025.

26. SOMO, Special report: *PG Tips and Lipton tea hit by 'sexual harassment and poor conditions' claims*, 13 April 2011.

27. Unilever, *Human rights progress report*, 2017.

28. European Commission, *Corporate Sustainability Due Diligence*, 25 July 2024.

29. European Commission, *Corporate responsibility reporting*, DG Finance, (website), 25 November 2025.

30. German Government, *Gesetz über die unternehmerischen Sorgfaltspflichten in Lieferketten* (German Supply Chain Act), Federal Ministry of Labour and Social Affairs, 1 January 2023.

31. French Government, *Loi de vigilance*, governed under the Commercial Code (Articles L. 225-102-4 & L. 225-102-5), 2017.

32. European Commission, *The Forced Labour Regulation*, (website), December 2025.

33. Sarosh Kuruvilla, *Private Regulation of Labor in Global Supply Chains: Problems, Progress and Prospects*. Cornell University Press, 2021.

34. Ruoxin Gao, Ruina Yang, Li Li, *Individual or joint audit? Managing supplier social responsibility with extortion risk*, International Journal of Production Economics, 290, 2025.

35. Human Rights Watch, *Obsessed with audit tools, missing the goal*, 15 November 2022.

36. Mark Jaeger, *How many social audits are enough? Worldwide Responsible Accredited Programme (WRAP)*. 16 October 2023.

37. Shift Project, *From audit to innovation, advancing human rights in global supply chains*, August 2013.

38. Several market analysts value the global social audit industry around $20 billion in 2025, such as The Business Research Company, Research and Markets, and SEO Titan.

39. Novata, *CSRD Survey 2024: From strategy to spend: how companies are preparing for CSRD compliance*, 2024.

40. Andy Bounds, *Companies count the cost of compliance with green regulation*, Financial Times, 16 May 2024.

41. Andy Bounds, *Companies count the cost of compliance with green regulation*, Financial Times, 16 May 2024.

42. Sharon Kits Kimathi, *Sustainable Switch Climate Focus: Exxon CEO wants EU sustainability law scrapped*, Reuters, 20 September 2025.

43. UK Government, *NHS Federated Data Platforms*, NHS England, (website), December 2025.

44. Odyssey, *Streamlining how you shop: Walmart and GraphQL*, (website), December 2025.

45. Andrew Hard et al., *Federated learning for mobile keyboard prediction*, Google Research, 2018.

# 12

# The AI Nexus

*The [AI] revolution will not be televised*[1]

Artificial Intelligence (AI) changes business not by introducing new goals, but by automating processes and decisions. Its impact upon the workplace has already begun worldwide even if it has yet to become an issue of public debate. Machine learning systems are transforming a broad range of operations, from financial allocation, procurement and logistics, to risk assessment, and compliance. So too with sustainability.

This shift builds directly on the data architectures described in the previous chapter (Chap. 11). AI systems do not reason independently about sustainability; they operationalise the data they are given. Where sustainability data is robust, interoperable, and credible, AI amplifies accountability and efficiency. Where it is weak or biased, AI accelerates error, and potential harm. 'Rubbish in, rubbish out'. In either case, automation narrows the space for human discretion. AI also inherits the physical constraints of the systems it optimises. Data centres demand natural resources and energy, tying AI directly to the security-of-supply constraints explored in Chap. 8. Far from being immaterial, using AI at scale



J. Morrison, *Remaking Sustainability*, https://doi.org/10.1007/978-3-032-23755-2_12

intensifies competition for scarce resources and embeds those constraints into decision-making systems.

AI is becoming one of the primary mechanisms through which sustainability is applied across economies. The question is no longer whether AI will shape sustainability outcomes, but how quickly automation will harden today's assumptions into tomorrow's operating reality.

The exponential increase in capacity and speed leads experts to predict that within the next decade, AI agents will complete in instants a large fraction of software tasks that currently take humans days or weeks.[2] Hyperscale operators—companies such as Amazon Web Services (AWS), Google, Microsoft, and Meta—dominate this landscape, each racing to build larger and more energy-intensive data campuses. These investments bring local economic benefits—jobs, land development, tax revenues, but also significant environmental impacts with associated requirements for land, massive amounts of water for cooling, high electrical loads on local grids, heat pollution, and construction-related emissions. Some countries, such as the Netherlands, Ireland, Singapore and Chile, all put temporary pauses on new data-centre approvals to manage grid constraints and sustainability concerns.

This chapter explores the AI–sustainability nexus, a relationship marked by profound dualities. AI is simultaneously an engine of resource consumption and a tool for resource efficiency; a catalyst for climate solutions and a driver of climate risk; a powerful tool for advancing human rights but also a significant threat to employment, human autonomy, privacy and our agency as individuals. It is a consumer of minerals, water, and energy, but also potentially a means to govern those same systems intelligently. In many ways, this is all too much for one chapter of a book, but my aim here is not to deep dive into all the various opportunities and threats of AI. But rather within the specific inquiry of this book ask how AI raises the saliency of sustainability issues within any business or organisation. And as part of sustainability's new bedrock, how we might build upon it.

# 12.1 The Double-Edged Sword

Within two years of the release of ChatGPT in late 2022, governments had issued national AI strategies, while businesses restructured entire business models around large-scale machine learning. But there is a physical reality behind the digital, as there had been for big data and blockchain over the previous decade. Only each time tech advances so, it seems, does its environmental footprint. A ChatGPT prompt can consume ten times the electricity of a Google search.[3] Each prompt, image, or analysis rests on real machines, with servers, graphics processing units (GPUs), data halls, and cooling towers—all drawing electricity, water, minerals, and labour across global supply chains.

## The Heavy Footprint

In the data halls, GPUs have evolved to become general purpose parallel processors, handling a growing range of applications and supporting demanding use cases. While more traditional central processing units (CPUs) offer a small number of cores, GPUs offer thousands, allowing them to better support parallel operations.[4] High-performance GPUs run continuously for weeks or months. Training a frontier-scale model can consume over 1000 megawatt-hours, the annual electricity use of 120 US homes and emit more than 500 tonnes of carbon dioxide. Thus, the central paradox emerges: AI may be one of humanity's most potent sustainability tools, but also one of its fastest-growing sustainability burdens.

The capital allocations made by some of the main developers of data centres and associated AI during 2025 have been eyewatering, with aggregate business expenditure comparable to the gross domestic product of an entire small country. AWS spent over \$100 billion on datacentre and AI infrastructure in 2025 alone, the largest investment in the world.[5] Microsoft allocated \$80 billion, largely to AI-enabled data centres integrating renewable energy where available.[6] Google dedicated \$85 billion, including substantial expansion across India, North America, and Europe to meet AI demand.[7] Meta invested over \$70 billion in 2025, with nearly

1 GW of new compute capacity coming online.[8] The total CapEx across all companies exceeded $650 billion in 2025 alone. The Wall Street Journal attributes half of the entire growth of the US economy during 2025 to the growth in AI.[9] There has been talk of an "AI bubble", but if there is a bubble, it is far from bursting as I write this book.

Already, the total electricity consumption of data centres is around the same as the annual consumption of a whole nation the size of France. Projections foresee a doubling or tripling during 2026 if demand continues unchecked. AI-driven data centres rely heavily on evaporative cooling, which consumes very large quantities of water. All too often it is potable freshwater that is used, as saline water is corrosive and presents many more technological challenges.[10] UNEP warns that AI infrastructure could soon use six times more water annually than Denmark. In regions already facing drought, like Arizona, Nevada, northern China, and parts of India, the expansion of hyperscale data centres generates tension between local communities, agriculture, and global technology firms.

GPUs and servers require rare earth elements, as well as a number of transition minerals: high-grade copper, silicon, cobalt, lithium, nickel, gold and silver for interconnects. A single 2-kilogram computer may require 800 kilograms of raw materials mined, transported, and processed across global supply chains. E-waste becomes a second-order crisis, intensified by rapid hardware obsolescence. As AI models scale, servers are replaced on accelerated timelines. The number of new data-centre GPUs shipped grew exponentially from a base of over four million units in 2023. When discarded, many devices enter informal recycling sectors in the global south, where environmental protections are generally weaker. There are also social consequences that spikes in mining, energy extraction, and data-centre construction can impose on workers and local communities.


## The Sustainability Upside

But despite its social and environmental costs, AI also offers extraordinary potential to support sustainability outcomes at scale. On the issue of addressing climate change alone, there are several applications emerging.[11] Leveraging AI models, it is possible to enhance the design and implementation of climate policies by producing advanced insights, forecasts, and evaluations of complex policy scenarios and their real-world effectiveness. In addition, AI strengthens long-term resilience and adaptation by using large-scale simulations to model and anticipate how ecosystems may evolve over time. It can also enhance early warning systems for extreme weather events—such as floods and wildfires—so governments and communities can take timely, preventive action to reduce damage, save lives, and lower economic costs.

Machine learning is also transforming electrical grids. One early example is how DeepMind's reinforcement learning reduced Google's data-centre cooling energy by up to 40% in 2016.[12] Today, according to the International Energy Agency (IEA), AI-based forecasting could unlock 175GW of grid capacity through smarter management.[13] Wind and solar integration improves when AI predicts fluctuations in generation hours in advance. AI accelerates climate modelling, allowing scientists to simulate atmospheric processes at finer resolution. In vulnerable geographic regions, such as Sierra Leone or Indonesia, AI-powered weather prediction systems help communities prepare for storms, floods, and droughts. With agriculture consuming 70% of global freshwater, AI-driven tools improve precision irrigation, fertilizer use, and pest detection. Solutions like *Plantix* and *Climate Corporation* reduce environmental impact while improving yields.

Water utilities use AI leak detection to save billions of litres of water annually. AI-enabled acoustic monitoring systems, such as *Rainforest Connection*, detect illegal logging using repurposed devices and machine learning.[14] *Global Fishing Watch* employs satellite data to expose unregulated fishing operations.[15] Deep-learning models identify individual animals from images, supporting conservation research at unprecedented scale. AI's potential contribution to the United Nations Sustainable Development Goals (SDGs) is vast. Studies suggest around 80% of the SDGs could benefit from AI support, particularly cleaner energy and sustainable cities.[16]

AI holds the promise of helping to optimize supply chains, reduce waste, and design products for longevity. In manufacturing, predictive maintenance prevents equipment failures. Routing algorithms in logistics cut fuel consumption. These efficiencies contribute to carbon reduction strategies and ESG reporting, providing investors with real-time data on environmental and social performance. Financial institutions increasingly use AI to evaluate corporate sustainability claims and direct capital toward genuinely low-carbon activities.[17]

## 12.2  Sustainability Safeguards

The sustainability challenges of AI are in part understood. Some major tech companies now pledge 100% renewable energy procurement, with carbon neutrality or negativity by 2030–2050, new efficiency standards, and water stewardship programmes. Microsoft, for example, has paired some new data-centre projects with renewable energy procurement,[18] though the company's massive 2025-era spend still carries significant environmental implications. Google's multi-billion investments in AI/data-centre hubs highlight both the scale of expansion and the urgency of strengthening sustainability measures, especially in water-scarce areas of India and the southwestern US.[19] Some other firms outside the hyperscaler space have made notable progress. For example, Hitachi Vantara's virtual-storage platform cuts clients' data-centre power use by 30–40% and helped BMW reduce its data-centre carbon footprint by 70%.[20]

But despite global enthusiasm for AI, governance remains uneven and reactive. Over 190 countries have adopted UNESCO's ethical AI principles, which include environmental considerations, but implementation varies.[21] There are also several regulatory trends. In the European Union, mandatory disclosure of energy and water now exist for large data centres. China now has standards targeting 100% clean energy for data centres by 2032. Some US states have emissions disclosure and local siting controls even if these are challenged by the federal government. And some other countries have imposed temporary moratoria in grid-stressed regions as already mentioned above.

Yet national AI strategies often lack robust environmental safeguards, a gap UNEP warns is "*as dangerous as the lack of ethical ones.*"[22] Efficiency is a powerful lever. Techniques such as model pruning, quantization, low-precision arithmetic, and edge computing can radically reduce energy use with minimal performance sacrifice. On the hardware side, innovations in photonic computing, neuromorphic chips, advanced semiconductors, heat recycling systems, all show promise for lowering energy intensity. Researchers at Queen Mary University, for instance, have explored recycling waste heat from data-centre facilities for campus heating, demonstrating circular design thinking.[23] But AI relies on the same minerals that power the clean-energy transition. This interdependency creates both competitive pressure and opportunities for synergy. High-performance data centres require extensive copper wiring and cooling infrastructure. Analysts estimate that AI alone could add up to one million tonnes of copper demand by 2030, a significant increase (15% of total demand) but still overshadowed by demand for renewable energy and electrification technologies.[24]

In summary, whilst national protections do exist in some jurisdictions, global standards on AI's physical footprint have yet to be reached. Until this happens, there will always be short-term advantage for governments willing to operate at the lowest levels of sustainability due diligence. Sustainability can be shorted under the cloak of sustainability.

## Real and Immediate Risks in AI Use

Perhaps even more challenging than AI's sustainability footprint are the dilemmas that come with its use.[25] These potential harms are well-documented, even if not well understood, and might be summarised into four areas:

1. *Exclusion through automation*

As sustainability constraints tighten, AI systems increasingly mediate access to capital, insurance, markets, public and private services, and employment. When these systems encode biased data, proxy variables, or incomplete representations of reality, exclusion becomes automated and scaled. AI technologies rely on massive datasets, including personal and sensitive data often collected or inferred without explicit consent. The systems often learn from historical data that reflect existing patterns of inequality. As a result, they can reproduce and amplify different forms of discrimination: racial, gender-based, socioeconomic, and more.[26] What were once contested human decisions become opaque system outcomes, with limited scope for appeal or correction.

### 2. *Opacity that weakens accountability*

AI systems often outperform human decision-making while simultaneously reducing explainability. As sustainability decisions become automated—across procurement, risk pricing, compliance, and optimisation—the ability to trace cause, responsibility, and error degrades. From the perspective of enforcing accountability, opacity creates three sustainability failures: impacts cannot be clearly attributed, accountability is delayed or displaced, and disputes become harder to resolve. When sustainability outcomes are contested, systems that cannot explain themselves lose legitimacy. Irresponsibly designed or poorly tested AI systems can produce outputs that are inaccurate, unsafe, or misleading. In critical contexts, such as medical diagnosis, transportation systems, or public policy, unreliable AI can threaten lives and public welfare. Opacity therefore becomes a governance and trust risk, not just a technical limitation.

### 3. *Lock-in through scale and speed*

AI accelerates decision-making and embeds it into systems operating at scale. Once deployed, models shape behaviour continuously, often retraining on their own outputs. Errors, blind spots, or flawed assumptions therefore propagate and harden quickly. In sustainability terms, this creates the following risks: path dependency in infrastructure, logistics, and investment; reduced opportunity for mid-course correction; and amplification of early design choices long after conditions change. Hyper-personalized content delivery, while convenient, can contribute to echo chambers, polarization, and diminished social cohesion. Ultimately this is not about AI failure, but about premature optimisation under uncertainty and a potential challenge to human agency and autonomy.

4. *Misallocation of resources under distorted signals*

AI systems optimise what they can observe. When sustainability-relevant factors—such as biodiversity, social cohesion, resilience, and informal economies—are poorly captured, models substitute proxies. Over time, optimisation against these proxies distorts real-world outcomes. These risk lead to capital flowing to what is measurable rather than what is material, efficiency gains that undermine resilience, and sustainability goals being technically 'met' while real-world conditions degrade. AI-generated deepfakes, synthetic media, and automated persuasion tools can distort public opinion, manipulate voters, or enable harassment campaigns, eroding democratic processes and public trust. This is a systemic mispricing risk, not a data hygiene problem.

The question then becomes how well these risks can be mitigated or prevented, and the central role of AI governance.

## 12.3   Governing the Automated

As artificial intelligence systems move from experimentation into core economic functions, the risks they pose shift in character. The most significant risks for sustainability are not speculative future scenarios, but immediate, systemic effects that arise when automated systems scale faster than governance, oversight, and data quality.[27] The two-way relationship between AI and sustainability require different governance responses: 'AI for sustainability' and 'the sustainability of AI' are different things. 'AI-for' largely depends on deployment incentives and adoption pathways: who pays, who benefits, what makes utilities or farmers or cities actually implement the tools, and how we avoid greenwashing-by-analytics. 'AI-of' depends much more on infrastructure rules and procurement standards: disclosure, siting, water stewardship, hardware refresh cycles, and the supply chains of chips and servers. As outlined above, bias and exclusion are the first of these effects. AI systems trained on incomplete, biased, or strategically curated data do not merely reproduce existing inequities; they harden them into automated decisions.[28] In sustainability contexts—credit allocation, supplier screening, insurance pricing, labour monitoring—this can result in systematic exclusion of actors who lack the data, capacity, or institutional visibility required by the model. These tacit discriminatory outcomes are rarely visible at the point of decision, but they compound rapidly across markets.

Opacity amplifies this risk. Many AI systems operate as 'black boxes', producing outputs that are difficult to interrogate or contest. When such systems are embedded in procurement, compliance, or risk assessment, errors and biases become difficult to detect and even harder to correct. Accountability diffuses across data providers, model developers, deployers, and users, creating gaps precisely where sustainability enforcement depends on traceability and trust. Automation also compresses response time. Decisions that once involved human judgement and delay are executed at machine speed, reducing opportunities for contextual adjustment or appeal. In sustainability systems, this acceleration matters. It can entrench flawed assumptions before governance frameworks have time to adapt, and it magnifies the consequences of poor design choices made early in deployment.

These risks explain the growing focus on AI governance frameworks. Initiatives such as the EU's *AI Act* and UNESCO's *AI recommendations* seek to establish guardrails around transparency, accountability, and risk classification.[29] Their importance lies less in their specific provisions than in what they acknowledge: once AI systems are embedded at scale, governance becomes reactive rather than preventive. Early standards therefore matter disproportionately. Several overlapping global initiatives have emerged, such as the *AI Safety Summits* beginning with the 2023 Bletchley Park gathering hosted by the UK Government,[30] The G7 *Hiroshima Process*,[31] now supported by the OECD, and UN efforts, including advisory bodies shaping global standards.[32] The OECD has also published due diligence guidance for the responsible use of AI based on its *AI Principles* as well as the *Responsible Business Conduct Guidelines for*

*Multinational Enterprises*.[33] More speculative concerns about frontier or existential risk reinforce this point rather than displacing it. Even without extreme scenarios, AI systems already shape economic incentives, information flows, and institutional behaviour. The lesson for sustainability is not that AI poses distant dangers, but that automation narrows the space for correction.[34] As systems scale, errors propagate faster than governance can respond.

## Tools for Responsible AI Governance

Achieving safe and responsible AI in society, as well as business. Requires concrete methods. Techniques such as *likelihood-free importance weighting* help reduce bias in model outputs and improve accuracy. While powerful, these methods require deep expertise and must be complemented by broader frameworks. Approaches like *Behavioural Use Licensing* enable developers to restrict unethical uses of their technologies, adding legal and social safeguards. But the need for human-centred oversight will also remain. Frameworks such as *Contestable AI*[35] incorporate transparency, explainability, and opportunities for human challenge or correction throughout a system's lifecycle. Meanwhile, human-machine evaluation techniques such as *Verifiability Evaluation* help humans assess the reliability of AI outputs even in resource-constrained settings.[36] No single tool can address all risks, effective governance requires combining approaches adapted to specific contexts, industries, and resources. Crucially, these tools must be tested, improved, and iterated in real-world settings.

The central governance challenge is therefore structural. Sustainability outcomes increasingly depend on systems that execute decisions automatically, using data and models that embed assumptions about value, risk, and responsibility. Where these assumptions are poorly governed, AI amplifies unsustainable outcomes with unprecedented speed and reach. In this context, governance is not about choosing whether AI should be used, but about determining the conditions under which its use becomes irreversible. Once automated systems shape access to markets, finance, and services, sustainability is enforced through code rather than policy. The remaining question is whether that enforcement reflects deliberate design or accidental consequence.

## 12.4  Making the AI Nexus Sustainable

In their study published in 2025, the London School of Economics (LSE) undertook a comparative analysis to try to determine whether AI was a net good or bad in relation to climate change.[37] They predicted that advancements in AI in power, transport and food consumption could reduce global emissions of greenhouse gases by 3.2 to 5.4 billion tonnes of carbon-dioxide-equivalent annually by 2035. When compared with the increase in data centre-related emissions generated by all AI-related activities (not just those related to decarbonisation), the authors found that the estimated emissions reductions in only these three sectors would outweigh increases from global power consumption of data centres and AI. Therefore, the utilitarian assessment would seem to weigh in AI's favour, at least from an environmental perspective.

Whilst AI is unavoidable and has huge sustainability potential, it does not resolve sustainability tensions. Once embedded in automated systems, sustainability criteria cease to be negotiated and begin to operate as filters. This is what makes the need for AI governance decisive. Unlike policy instruments or voluntary standards, automated systems are difficult to pause, reverse, or reinterpret once deployed. Models are trained, incentives align around their outputs, and organisational processes adapt to their logic. Errors propagate quickly, while accountability diffuses. Under these conditions, sustainability failures are no longer isolated; they are systemic.

Governance therefore matters most before automation hardens. Choices about data quality, system design, oversight, and accountability determine whether AI embeds sustainability constraints or undermines them at scale. Delay is not neutral. As AI systems proliferate, they narrow the space for correction by turning assumptions into infrastructure. AI marks a threshold in the sustainability transition. Data made sustainability legible. AI makes it executable at speed. The next chapter turns to quantum computing which might scale the issues discussed in this chapter to an unimaginable level whilst also bringing some distinct issues of its own. As Chap. 13 shows, the potential of quantum casts its shadow forwards in time, and we have already entered it.

## Notes


1. With apologies to Gill Scott-Heron.
2. Model Evaluation and Threat Research (METR), *Measuring AI ability to complete long tasks*, 19 March 2025.
3. The Washington Post/University of California Riverside, The hidden environmental costs of using AI chatbots, 18 September 2024.
4. Intel, *Why data center GPUs are essential to innovation*, (website), November 2025.
5. Financial Times, *Amazon to spend $100 billion this year in AI drive*, 8 February 2025.
6. Brad Smith, *The gold opportunity for American AI*, (blog), Microsoft, 3 January 2025.
7. The Guardian, *The trillion-dollar AI arms race is here*, 29 July 2025.
8. New York Times, *Meta raises its spending forecast on AI to above $70 billion*, 28 October 2025.
9. Wall Street Journal, *How the US economy became hooked on AI spending*, 24 November 2025.
10. Fiona McCarthy et al., *Cooling the cloud: a focus on the water usage of datacentres*, Bird & Bird, 11 April 2025.
11. Nick Stern, Mattia Romani, Roberta Pierfederici, et al. Green and intelligent: the role of AI in the climate transition. *Npj Clim. Action* 4(56), 2025.
12. Wired, *Google's DeepMind trains AI to cut its energy bills by 40%*, 20 July 2016.
13. International Energy Agency, *AI for energy optimisation and innovation*, 2025.
14. Tech Monitor, *How AI is helping to fight illegal logging*, 5 February 2021.
15. Global Fishing Watch, *New research harnesses AI and satellite imagery to reveal the expanding footprint of human activity at sea*, 3 January 2024.

16. United Nations, *Global issues: Artificial Intelligence*, (website), December 2025.
17. Chiara Senni et al., *Using AI to assess corporate climate transition disclosures*, Environmental Research Communications, February 2025.
18. Brad Smith, *The gold opportunity for American AI*, (blog), Microsoft, 3 January 2025.
19. The Guardian, *The trillion-dollar AI arms race is here*, 29 July 2025.
20. Hitachi Vantara, *Hitachi Vantara unveils inaugural sustainability report*, 22 April 2024.
21. United Nations, *Ethics of Artificial Intelligence*, UNESCO, (website), December 2025.
22. UNEP, *AI has an environmental problem, here is what the world can do about that*, 13 November 2025.
23. Construction management magazine, *Queen Mary University to install heat recovery at data centre*, 1 July 2024.
24. Reuters, *AI could add 1 million tons to copper demand by 2030*, 8 April 2024.
25. See, for example, David Leslie, *Understanding artificial intelligence ethics and safety: A guide for the responsible design and implementation of AI systems in the public sector*. The Alan Turing Institute, 2019.
26. Valentin Hoffman, *AI generates covertly racist decisions about people based on their dialect*, Nature, 28 August 2024.
27. See, for example, David Leslie, *Understanding artificial intelligence ethics and safety: A guide for the responsible design and implementation of AI systems in the public sector*. The Alan Turing Institute, 2019.
28. Valentin Hoffman, *AI generates covertly racist decisions about people based on their dialect*, Nature, 28 August 2024.
29. European Commission, *AI Act*, Regulation (EU) 2024/1689.
30. UK Government, *The Bletchley Declaration*, 1–2 November 2023.
31. Japanese Government, *The Hiroshima AI Process: leading the global challenge to shape inclusive governance for Generative AI*, 9 February 2024.
32. OECD, *G7 Hiroshima Process on Generative Artificial Intelligence (AI): towards a G7 Common Understanding on Generative AI*, 7 September 2024.
33. OECD, *OECD Due Diligence Guidance for Responsible AI*, February 2026.
34. Kars Alfrink et al., *Contestable AI by design: towards a framework*, Minds and Machines, 33, 2023.

35. Kars Alfrink et al., *Contestable AI by design: towards a framework*, Minds and Machines, 33, 2023.

36. European Research Council, *Researchers create innovative verification techniques to increase security in artificial intelligence and image processing*, 29 April 2024.

37. Nick Stern, Mattia Romani, Roberta Pierfederici, et al. Green and intelligent: the role of AI in the climate transition. *Npj Clim. Action* 4(56), 2025.

# 13

## Quantum

*Man kann auch ganz burleske Fälle konstruieren. Eine Katze wird in eine Stahlkammer gesperrt, zusammen mit folgender Höllenmaschine.*[1]

This is how German physicist Erwin Schrödinger put it in 1935 when arguing with Albert Einstein. In his mind he had constructed a machine to deny the audience insight into whether the cat was alive or dead at the end of an hour. Perhaps it could be both. Schrödinger's cat was hypothetical and luckily the experiment was never replicated in a laboratory. Its purpose was to illustrate the central duality of quantum mechanics.

You might be very surprised to reach a chapter on quantum computing in this book on sustainability. It is true, very little has been written about this intersection to date. You would be right to question whether it is truly part of *Remaking Sustainability*, at least for the period of the next few years. But I hope this chapter at least presents a coherent thesis as to why it is already a salient issue, not least in relation to encryption. There is certainly a buzz surrounding the issue at international conferences, you often need to elbow your way through policymakers and corporate executives to get a seat, or even for standing room at the back. This is incredible given how little is still known about the underpinning physics.[2]


J. Morrison, *Remaking Sustainability*, https://doi.org/10.1007/978-3-032-23755-2_13

Quantum computing enters the sustainability debate earlier than its maturity would suggest, not because it is widely deployed, but because its implications arrive in advance of its availability. Unlike many emerging technologies, quantum systems create risk long before scale: in security, optimisation, and strategic advantage. As with climate risk, the timeline of impact is misaligned with the timeline of response. Waiting for full maturity is therefore not neutral, it is a decision with consequences.

The most immediate of these consequences is cryptographic. Data secured under current encryption standards is already vulnerable to future decryption, incentivising the harvesting of sensitive information today for exploitation later. This threat extends beyond state security into finance, trade, infrastructure, and sustainability systems increasingly dependent on long-lived data integrity. Once trust in these systems is compromised, it cannot be easily restored. In this sense, quantum risk is already embedded in present decisions. Beyond security, quantum computing has the potential to reshape optimisation problems central to sustainability: materials discovery, energy systems, logistics, and chemical processes. These capabilities are uncertain in timing and scope, but their direction is clear. If realised, they would accelerate both the efficiency of sustainable systems and the concentration of advantage among those able to deploy them first. As with artificial intelligence, quantum promises amplification rather than correction.

Still nascent, quantum technologies promise breakthroughs in materials science, biology, chemistry, logistics, and energy systems[3]—fields directly tied to both business and sustainability. Yet, their development also introduces some of the same environmental and ethical dilemmas as we covered in Chap. 12 on AI. Quantum processors will require extreme cooling, consume significant energy, and involve complex manufacturing processes. As with AI more generally, policymakers must therefore consider a dual imperative: how to unlock quantum computing's potential for sustainability while ensuring the technology itself develops sustainably. Although AI and quantum computing are deeply related, they are also distinct. Quantum is not just more AI. It potentially will transform our relationship with nature in ways that we can still not predict, but some of the possible implications require concrete action now.[4]

This chapter therefore treats quantum not as a speculative future, but as a forcing function. Its early risks demand governance before deployment, and its potential benefits raise questions of access, control, and lock-in. Quantum belongs in the sustainability bedrock not because it is ready, but because some of its consequences are with us now.

## 13.1 Encryption Concerns

Encryption converts readable plaintext into unreadable ciphertext to protect sensitive information from unauthorized access. It is a foundational element of data security, helping organizations safeguard data and reduce the risk of breaches. By applying encryption algorithms, data is transformed into a format that cannot be interpreted without the correct decryption key held by authorized users.

Businesses pay a lot for encryption. On average it accounts for at least a sixth of a firm's total IT budget, although this varies considerably between the nature of business and perceived exposure to risk. One benchmark suggests an average annual spend of about $525 per employee on data security measures.[5] Small businesses often spend very little, nearly half of small businesses spend less than $1500 a month on cybersecurity. But most large corporates pay considerably more. Large financial institutions can have massive budgets. For example, J.P. Morgan spends over $600 million every year just on cybersecurity.[6] During 2025, 13% of organizations reported breaches linked to their AI models or applications. Among those affected, 97% lacked adequate AI access controls. Most incidents occurred within the AI supply chain through compromised applications, APIs or plug-ins, often resulting in widespread data exposure (in 60% of cases) and operational disruption (in 31%). These trends suggest that AI systems are becoming increasingly attractive targets. The global average cost of a single breach is over $4 million according to an IBM study.[7]

For the reasons above, it is not surprising that data security appears on the corporate risk register of every company I know. Any threat to this security is therefore of material concern. Given how central data systems are to nearly all business operations (as I discussed in Chap. 11), data capture or corruption is highly material. The list of major data breaches affecting businesses and governments continues to grow, and now has touched the lives of nearly every citizen and consumer in one way or another.[8] So it is of profound importance that experts in quantum computing now predict that the vast power and speed that non-binary processing will bring will easily crack the mathematical models upon which current encryption is based (models that often make use of the irregular nature and complex factorisation of very large prime numbers). Although the impact of this risk might still be ten years away, it would be of such profound disruption and existential threat that companies need to start mitigating it now.

Some hackers are capturing encrypted data today with codes they can't break with current computers for the possibility that quantum computing will allow the data to be used within the next decade. 'Harvest now, decrypt later' means that no business or institution can feel they are not already at risk even if they have no further data breaches over the coming years.[9] *Post-quantum cryptography* (PQC) algorithms are currently under development, and future proofed technologies will be available over the coming years for a price. Each company will need to make its own cost-benefit analysis as to which procedures and systems it upgrades. But for this reason alone, I hope I have persuaded you to read the rest of this chapter and how this might affect the sustainability agenda. Let's start with the briefest dip into the basics.

## 13.2  Quantum Advantage

At its core, quantum computing differs fundamentally from classical computing. Traditional computers use bits, which represent information as 0 s or 1 s. Quantum computers, by contrast, use quantum bits—or qubits—that can exist in a superposition of states, meaning they can represent both 0 and 1, and everything in between, simultaneously.[10] When multiple qubits become entangled, their states are then correlated. Quantum computers exploit these properties—superposition, entanglement, and interference—to explore vast solution spaces in ways classical machines cannot.[11]

For policymakers, the distinction is not merely technical. It defines the scope of 'quantum advantage': the point at which quantum systems outperform classical supercomputers for meaningful problems. The global race to reach this milestone has produced a diverse ecosystem of architectures: superconducting qubits (used by IBM and Google), trapped ions, photonic qubits, and neutral atom arrays (developed by Pasqal, QuEra, and others).[12] Each approach carries distinct implications for energy use, scalability, and environmental impact.

Current quantum computers fall into the *Noisy Intermediate-Scale Quantum* (NISQ) era machines, with tens to hundreds of qubits but without full error correction.[13] These systems are experimental yet already being used for quantum simulations and algorithm testing in materials, finance, and logistics. As fault-tolerant quantum computers emerge later this decade, their ability to model complex molecular interactions, optimize industrial processes, and accelerate energy innovation could redefine the boundaries of sustainability science. Quantum computing's sustainability potential is often juxtaposed with its environmental cost. Certain quantum systems, especially those based on superconducting qubits, must operate near absolute zero temperatures—around 15 millikelvin—requiring cryogenic cooling and continuous power input. These extreme conditions raise legitimate concerns about carbon intensity and life-cycle emissions.

Projects like TechUK's *Quantum Campaign* have highlighted that while quantum machines consume substantial energy for cooling, their computational processes, once stabilized, should require minimal energy to execute operations.[14] Moreover, alternative architectures are emerging that drastically reduce or eliminate cooling demands. *Photonic quantum computing*, as developed by ORCA Computing,[15] and *neutral atom systems*, such as those built by Pasqal,[16] operate at or near room temperature, offering pathways toward 'sustainable-by-design' quantum systems.

Several policy developments are needed. Governments are likely to establish reporting standards for the power consumption and carbon footprint of quantum computing facilities, like those being developed for data centres today (as covered in Chap. 12). Planners will also incentivize the co-location of quantum facilities with renewable energy sources and circular cooling systems. Environmental and social impact assessments will be required along the full lifecycle: quantum hardware production, operation, and decommissioning. As the sector scales, aligning quantum infrastructure with national sustainability targets will be essential. A standardized carbon attribution framework for quantum workloads, allowing organizations to measure and offset emissions, might also be a near-term policy goal.

## 13.3  Quintessentially Qubit

The promise of quantum computing lies in solving problems that classical systems find intractable. Quantum isn't one technology: it's a family. Many of these applications are directly linked to sustainability, such as optimizing energy, biological impacts, materials, and resource systems for maximum efficiency and minimal waste. The following potential applications illustrate how quantum advantage could translate into transforming sustainability.

### Energy Efficiency and Smart Grid Optimization

Modern energy systems face an optimization challenge: balancing variable renewable generation with fluctuating demand while minimizing losses. Quantum algorithms, particularly *quantum approximate optimization algorithms*, should be able to evaluate millions of potential grid configurations simultaneously, identifying optimal load balancing and transmission strategies far faster than classical methods.[17] Pilot studies suggest that quantum-enhanced optimization could cut grid energy losses by up to 10–15%, improving renewable integration and stability. Policymakers might prioritize quantum-energy testbeds that integrate quantum computing with real-world grid data, enabling national utilities to test and deploy solutions as the technology matures.

## Green Chemistry and Materials Discovery

Chemical simulation is one of quantum computing's most transformative applications. Traditional computers approximate molecular interactions, but quantum systems should be able to model them directly, enabling the discovery of new catalysts, low carbon materials, and high-density batteries. For example, quantum simulations could accelerate the design of solid-state batteries, hydrogen storage materials, and carbon capture solvents. McKinsey's modelling suggests that quantum-enabled chemistry could reduce global $CO_2$ emissions by over 7 gigatons per year by 2035 through advances in these domains.[18] This represents a policy opportunity to link quantum innovation with industrial decarbonization strategies, particularly in sectors such as steel, cement, and energy storage.

## Climate Modelling and Prediction

Accurate climate modelling requires immense computational power to simulate complex atmospheric interactions. Quantum computing could drastically improve both speed and resolution, enhancing early-warning systems for extreme weather events and supporting climate adaptation planning. Quantum-enhanced simulations may allow real-time modelling of regional climate impacts, improving infrastructure resilience and disaster preparedness. National meteorological agencies will begin integrating quantum-assisted modelling frameworks into their research pipelines, supported by international collaborations such as the *Open Quantum Institute*[19] and the *European Quantum Flagship*.[20]

## The Water–Energy–Food Nexus

Sustainability challenges are interconnected. The Water–Energy–Food nexus illustrates how scarcity in one domain affects the others (as I discussed in Chap. 8). Quantum sensing and quantum simulation technologies can play a pivotal role in managing these interdependencies. For instance, quantum sensors show promise in detecting underground freshwater sources, monitoring soil moisture, and assessing aquifer health with unprecedented precision. Startups like PlanetAI Space are already exploring quantum machine learning techniques for satellite-based groundwater detection,[21] while Quantum Mads is applying quantum algorithms to optimize wastewater treatment and bioreactor efficiency.[22]

## Health, Biosciences, and Planetary Wellbeing

Quantum computing's impact on drug discovery and genomics extends beyond healthcare. It also might contribute to global sustainability by enabling equitable access to medical innovation and reducing the environmental costs of pharmaceutical production. The Finnish company, Algorithmiq, is amongst those pioneering quantum platforms that simulate molecular interactions to shorten drug development cycles, lowering R&D energy consumption and resource use.[23]

## Decarbonizing Industry

It is well known that some industrial processes—cement, steel, ammonia, and hydrogen—are amongst the highest carbon emitters but are also among the hardest sectors to decarbonize. Quantum computing could unlock new pathways for cleaner production in the following materials:

- Cement: by simulating alternative "clinker" materials at the molecular level, quantum systems could identify compounds that achieve the same binding strength with drastically lower $CO_2$ emissions.[24]
- Hydrogen: quantum models of electrolysis could optimize catalyst–membrane interactions, potentially improving energy efficiency and reducing hydrogen costs by up to 35%.[25]
- Ammonia: quantum simulation of nitrogenase enzymes, nature's own nitrogen fixers, could enable low-temperature, low-pressure ammonia synthesis, potentially cutting costs by up to 60% compared to traditional Haber–Bosch processes.[26]

- Batteries: quantum chemistry might help create cathode and anode materials with 50% higher energy density, accelerating electric vehicle adoption and grid-scale storage.[27]

These breakthroughs, if they come to pass, would have cumulative potential. McKinsey projects that quantum-enabled industrial innovation could abate over 7 gigatons of $CO_2$ annually by 2035: a figure comparable to the current emissions of the United States and the European Union combined.[28] For policymakers, this necessitates cross-sector collaboration frameworks where governments, corporates, and quantum research hubs co-develop pilot projects targeting emissions-intensive industries. Our decarbonisation strategies should not be contingent on quantum computing, but nor should they be blind to the potential.

## The Digital Carbon Footprint

While quantum computing may reduce emissions in industry, its broader integration into digital infrastructure raises new questions about the energy footprint of computation itself as it does for existing forms of AI (see Chap. 12). Data centres already account for roughly 1–1.5% of global electricity use, and AI workloads are accelerating that demand. But quantum computing could mitigate this through computational efficiency. Once operational, quantum systems can execute specific tasks, such as database searches or optimization, orders of magnitude faster, potentially offsetting the growing energy costs of classical data processing. And so, the energy demand of quantum might be no greater than existing AI data centres on a like for like basis, but if quantum technologies were to become omnipresent this would add demands of scale.

## 13.4  Future Sustainability Entanglements

Quantum algorithms aren't inherently less or more efficient, some require hybrid workflows (quantum together with classical processing), which can offset any theoretical energy savings. Error correction multiplies hardware requirements dramatically (potentially millions of physical qubits per logical qubit). Some quantum simulations may consume more total energy than equivalent classical approximations when full system costs are considered. If 'quantum advantage' is pursued without regard to energy advantage, the result could be computational power for its own sake not greater sustainability.

Some of the other salient issues have yet to be defined but are likely to include manufacturing process, material sourcing and disposal, and mechanisms to attribute carbon costs to quantum-enabled services. Those quantum technologies (particularly superconducting qubits) that require extreme cooling will consume very large amounts of electricity if cryogenic compressors are used continuously. When multiplied across commercial data centres, this could become as energy intensive as traditional supercomputing. Therefore, unless such systems are powered by renewable energy or replaced by room-temperature quantum architectures (like photonics or neutral atoms), their environmental footprint could be substantial.

Quantum computing might concentrate focus onto specific critical minerals even more than for the supply chains of traditional computing. Superconducting qubits currently use niobium, aluminium, and silicon. Ion-trap systems rely on high-purity vacuum chambers and lasers that require rare-earth elements. Cryogenics and electronics often involve hazardous coolants and complex metal alloys. If the sourcing and disposal of these materials are not managed responsibly, quantum devices could replicate the unsustainable patterns of classical electronics, including e-waste, toxic waste, and resource depletion. Access to these minerals is already shaping geopolitics. For example, niobium off-take agreements in Canada already command higher prices for US customers than Brazilian competition in part for reasons of energy-security and sustainability considerations. The US has yet to develop its own niobium resources, whilst China's are relatively low-grade. Greenland represents significant niobium potential, feeding into the US Government's political posturing witnessed at the start of 2026.

The deployment of quantum computing will also need to be intentional. Without coordinated action, the benefits of the technology could concentrate in a few economies or exacerbate global inequalities in technological access. A key governance challenge is the absence of standards for quantum sustainability. If quantum R&D is concentrated in wealthy nations; without access-sharing mechanisms, the 'quantum divide' could exclude developing countries from climate-solving, centralize intellectual property in a few corporations, and create quantum monopolies that widen global inequality.[29] As with other forms of AI, quantum innovation requires inclusive access, open data sharing, and global research collaboration to be sustainable in any social sense.

Quantum computing can either accelerate the green transition or become another high-energy, high-inequality technology, it depends entirely on governance and intent. It is possible—indeed likely—that without strong environmental and ethical frameworks, early quantum infrastructure will grow unsustainably, mirroring the mistakes of data centres, AI, and semiconductor industries. The challenge for policymakers is to guide quantum computing through a sustainability lens from the outset: define green standards, link funding to environmental performance, and make sustainability—not just speed—a core metric of quantum computing's success.[30]

With this, the technology bedrock section of this book is complete (Chaps. 11, 12, and 13). Data makes sustainability legible. Artificial intelligence makes it automated. Quantum alters the timelines of trust, optimisation, and control. What matters most is that quantum, like artificial intelligence and data infrastructure before it, is not seen as neutral. It embeds assumptions, priorities, and exclusions into systems that will be difficult to unwind. Once adopted at scale, quantum-enabled optimisation and security architectures will shape decision-making long after political intent has shifted.

Taken as a whole, Chaps. 4, 5, 6, 7, 8, 9, 10, 11, 12, and 13 have shown the complexity of ways that sustainability is firmly entangled into the bedrock of contemporary economic reality. There is no viable pathway forward for either business or society that does not have sustainability at its core. The is the basis for *Remaking Sustainability*. The next sections of the book now pivot to assess the different ways in which business itself should marry its internal systems to this external reality. Chapters 14, 15, and 16 look at the leadership, systems, and impacts of business as part of this bedrock and Chaps. 17, 18, and 19 at how this must be explained and communicated.

## Notes


1. Ewrin Schrödinger, *Die gegenwärtige Situation in der Quantenmechanik (The Present Situation in Quantum Mechanics), Naturwissenschaften, 23 (48), November 1935.*
2. Paul Davis, Quantum 2.0: *The past, present, and future of Quantum Physics,* 2025.
3. Paul Davis, Quantum 2.0: *The past, present, and future of Quantum Physics,* 2025.
4. Paul Davis, Quantum 2.0: *The past, present, and future of Quantum Physics,* 2025.
5. Business.com, *The cost of cybersecurity and how to budget for it,* 2 June 2025.
6. J.P. Morgan Asset Management, *Executing an integrated oversight framework,* (website), November 2025.
7. IBM, *Cost of a Data Breach* report, 2025.
8. Wikipedia, *List of data breaches,* (website), November 2025.
9. Freshfields Technology Quotient, *Quantum disentangled 1: 'harvest now, decrypt later',* 9 December 2025.
10. Paul Davis, Quantum 2.0: *The past, present, and future of Quantum Physics,* 2025.
11. Paul Davis, Quantum 2.0: *The past, present, and future of Quantum Physics,* 2025.
12. New Scientist, *IBM creates largest ever superconducting quantum computer,* 15 November 2021.
13. Quantum Insider, *What is NISQ Quantum Computing?* (website), 24 September 2025.
14. Tech UK, *Could quantum computing hold the key to sustainability?* 30 June 2021.

15. Orca Computing, *ORCA Computing Delivers First Photonic Quantum Computing System to UK's National Quantum Computing Centre*, 11 June 2025.

16. Pasqal, *The power of Neutral Atoms Quantum Technology*, (website), 20 May 2024.

17. Kostos Blekos et al., *A review on Quantum Approximate Optimisation Algorithm and its variants*, Physics Reports, 1068, 2 June 2024.

18. McKinsey & Company, *Quantum computing might just save the planet*, 18 May 2022.

19. Open Quantum Institute, (website), December 2025.

20. European Quantum Flagship, (website), December 2025.

21. PlanetAI Space, (website), December 2025.

22. Quantum Insider, *From theory to impact: winning quantum for society challenge startups take on the planet's greatest challenges*, 14 April 2025.

23. Algoritmiq, (website), December 2025.

24. McKinsey & Company, *Quantum computing might just save the planet*, 18 May 2022.

25. McKinsey & Company, *Quantum computing might just save the planet*, 18 May 2022.

26. McKinsey & Company, *Quantum computing might just save the planet*, 18 May 2022.

27. McKinsey & Company, *Quantum computing might just save the planet*, 18 May 2022.

28. McKinsey & Company, *Quantum computing might just save the planet*, 18 May 2022.

29. Amal Kasry and Rachel Won, *Democratizing quantum science through sustained action*, Nature Reviews: Electrical Engineering, 12 November 2025.

30. Quantum Insider, *Expert predictions on quantum technology 2026*, (website), 30 December 2025.

# Part V

**Delivering Remade Sustainability**

# 14

# Systems Leadership

Systems leadership is the bedrock competence required to operate under sustainability constraints. Organisations now function inside systems that enforce limits through finance, insurance, trade, data, and technology, alongside sustainability regulation. Leadership that fails to account for this reality does not merely fall short: it becomes operationally unviable. The preceding chapters have shown how sustainability has moved from ambition to implementation and accountability. Capital is reallocated, insurance is withdrawn, market access conditioned, reporting and due diligence are mandated, infrastructure is locked in, and intelligence increasingly automated. Under these conditions, the assumption that leaders can optimise individual objectives in isolation no longer holds. Decisions propagate through tightly coupled systems, creating second- and third-order effects that cannot be managed through linear planning or functional silos.

This chapter therefore reframes leadership not as control, but as stewardship within constraint. Systems leadership is the capacity to recognise interdependence, anticipate feedback, and make decisions that remain viable across multiple timescales and domains.[1] It is most visible not in vision statements, but in governance structures, incentives, and the

© The Author(s), under exclusive license to Springer Nature Switzerland AG 2026

J. Morrison, *Remaking Sustainability*, https://doi.org/10.1007/978-3-032-23755-2_14

questions leaders choose to ask. As sustainability becomes embedded in systems that filter access and allocate risk, leadership failure increasingly takes the form of misreading the system or operating through bounded rationality—assuming others will act according to your own set of interests.[2]

## 14.1 Embracing Complexity

If sustainability were merely an isolated technical problem, significant progress might have been made by now. But as Chap. 2 describes, there are several planetary boundaries being crossed simultaneously. The climate is changing, water systems are destabilising, biodiversity is collapsing, chemical pollution is accumulating, and biogeochemical cycles are going awry. Together these form a network of systemic risk that no single lever can fix. And so, the first task of systems leadership is to acknowledge the complexity, not wish it away.

A survey of nearly 900 companies in 2023 by the Boston Consulting Group[3] reported that the effort to address sustainability was having a direct impact on how boards operate. More than two-thirds of board-level respondents (69%) answered that sustainability-related demands on their time were increasing. The share was higher for directors in the energy and finance and insurance sectors, at 77% and 74% respectively. A strong majority (79%) said their board had a very or entirely clear understanding of the strategic opportunities and risks sustainability presents. But only 29% completely agreed they have sufficient knowledge to effectively challenge management on sustainability plans and ambitions and exercise oversight on their execution. The greatest share, 66%, said that sustainability considerations should be fully integrated into business strategy. But just 38% reported that is the case today. And although roughly half also say that sustainability should be entirely integrated into the board agenda, less than 30% report that is happening currently. Two years after this study, in late 2025 when writing this book, there was no evidence to suggest that this skills gap has yet closed. Surveys continue to show that sustainability skills, alongside digital literacy, crisis management, and fortifying organisational resilience, remain a key skill set many boards are looking for.[4] And, if the intersection between these and other concerns is in itself THE issue, as a number of business commentators are saying, then it systems-thinking that is the skill most missing from many boards today.[5]

## The Courage to Sit with Complexity

For decades, leadership education has trained executives to breakdown big problems into smaller ones, isolate variables, apply frameworks, optimise. Complexity was treated as disorder to be tamed. But in today's world, false simplicity is more dangerous than complexity itself. Executives might learn this quickly when a water shortage halts a factory producing semiconductors; or a climate-driven hurricane triggers insurance withdrawal, which triggers mortgage contagion, which triggers supply-chain reconfiguration; or a government's retreat from sustainability regulation reshapes market incentives overnight, creating uncertainty more destabilising than the regulation itself. These are not failures of planning. They are evidence of systems shifting beneath our feet.[6] A systems-literate leader does not pretend to control all variables. They learn instead to recognise patterns, to look for feedback loops, to distinguish symptoms from causes, and both of these from correlation, and to anticipate cascading impacts.[7]

## Systems Are Made of Relationships, Not Parts

A business is not a collection of departments. It is a set of relationships between people, processes, technologies, markets, natural systems, political institutions, and social expectations. The same is true for supply chains: they are not 'chains' at all, but webs. The earlier chapters on value chains illustrated this with force. Global supply security (Chap. 8) now depends not just on logistics but on water, energy, minerals, and geopolitical stability. Trade rules (Chap. 9) increasingly incorporate sustainability criteria because value chains cannot be insulated from climate or social impacts. Emerging economies (Chap. 7), once treated as peripheral, are now central to growth, raw materials, manufacturing, and climate diplomacy. Insurance (Chap. 5)—long thought a backstop—is itself exposed to systemic failure as climate losses grow and risk models struggle. Systemic leadership means learning to see these connections and refusing to reduce them into one-dimensional metrics simply because traditional dashboards prefer linearity. The energy–water–food nexus, described in Chap. 8, demonstrates how interdependencies compound: energy needs water, water needs energy, food needs both, and each competes with the other under climate stress.

## Learning to Work with Multiple Temporalities

One of the core frustrations of sustainability practitioners is that business and politics operate on short cycles while climate and social systems operate on long arcs. Systemic leadership requires accommodating these contrasting temporalities. Short-term operational decisions include supply shortages, extreme weather events, or annual insurance premiums. Medium-term strategic concerns might be green capacity investment, or technological transformation. Long-term planetary thresholds are those set out in Chap. 2 with their irreversible tipping points and need for intergenerational equity. Leaders need to operate within all three timescales at once even if they are in tension with each other. Chapter 1 made this point sharply: the sustainability pushback is happening at the very moment long-term planetary risks are becoming more material. Leaders must hold both realities in their heads at once. This is the paradox of systems leadership: to act within the context of now, but while factoring in all longer-term consequences.[8]

## A New Humility

Humility is not often listed as a leadership competency, but in systems leadership it is indispensable. The "humble CEO" might sound like an oxymoron,[9] but humility is a requirement for operating under uncertainty.[10] The world is now too complex for any leader to claim omniscience. Instead, the leader becomes a steward of collective intelligence. Humility allows the leader to ask better questions, invite dissent, recognise blind spots, acknowledge uncertainty, avoid the seduction of false certainty, and—critically—to learn. And learning is the most important currency in a shifting system. Systems management is sceptical about "heroic top-down leadership" (even from so-called "sustainability CEOs") and central control in favour of collaboration across boundaries. Rather it values attributes (e.g. humility), mindsets (e.g. big picture), and skills (e.g. facilitation) needed to act in complex systems.[11] I will return to this point in the chapters on retelling sustainability (Chaps 17, 18, and 19), not to repeat the mistakes many sustainability leaders have made in demonising those with different opinions and claiming moral superiority.

## 14.2  Developing Sustainability Strategy

As previous chapters demonstrated, sustainability strategy can no longer be a separate pillar of corporate planning. It is becoming the organising logic of the business environment itself. To set sustainability strategy today is not to produce a list of targets or policies. It is to recognise the strategic architecture of systems: the way environmental, economic, financial, political, and technological factors interact, reinforce, or destabilise one another. A sustainability strategy grounded in systems-thinking is built on four building blocks: understanding the systemic context, finding the organisational bedrock, aligning long-term purpose with near-term decisions, and managing the nodes and bottlenecks.

### Understanding the Systemic Context

A company's sustainability strategy is shaped by the world around it, with a multitude of relevant factors. The earlier chapters described how quickly the context is shifting. Trade agreements increasingly include environmental and labour clauses long considered outside their scope (Chap. 9). Data and AI are transforming risk analysis, making previously "unknown" risks increasingly knowable (Chaps. 11 and 12). Quantum computing may upend entire sustainability modelling methods (Chap. 13). Global financial markets are moving toward clearer sustainability disclosure norms even as political pushback creates noise (Chap. 4). Emerging economies are reshaping global demand, supply, and sustainability norms simultaneously (Chap. 7). Insurance markets are faltering in high-risk regions, altering the price of capital and the feasibility of development itself (Chap. 5). Energy, food, and water systems are becoming more stressed and more interdependent, demanding integrated strategies rather than siloed plans (Chap. 8). A meaningful sustainability strategy must begin by mapping how these forces interact—not just in the business environment, but in relation to one another. A company does not operate within markets; it operates within systems of systems. I will return to this in the next chapter.

## Finding the Organisational Bedrock

In Chap. 3, the notion of "bedrock" emerged as a foundational metaphor: the operational conditions that a business cannot ignore without threatening its own viability. Systemic leadership requires grounding strategy in organisational bedrock, and raises a number of foundational questions:

- What must remain stable in order for the business to thrive?
- What parts of the business model are non-negotiable?
- What societal expectations cannot be ignored?
- What planetary boundaries define the operating envelope?
- What supply chain vulnerabilities cannot be hedged away?
- What financial risks are so systemic they require structural mitigation?

When sustainability is approached through bedrock rather than branding, the conversation changes. It becomes about operational resilience, capital allocation, market positioning, licence to operate, and future competitiveness. This is why sustainability strategy must not be the domain of the sustainability team alone. It must be co-owned by operations, finance, risk management, procurement, human resources, innovation, and fundamentally the board itself.

## Aligning Long-Term Purpose with Near-Term Decisions

One of the quiet tragedies in corporate sustainability is the proliferation of beautiful long-term aspirations that collapse when confronted with quarterly decision-making or short-term political pushback. A systemic sustainability strategy must bridge the gap between:

- the 30-year horizon of climate and other planetary thresholds,
- the 10-year horizon of capital investment cycles,
- the 3-year horizon of corporate strategy,
- the annual horizon of budgeting,
- and the daily horizon of operations.

To do this, leaders must build mechanisms that connect long-term purpose to short-term action. These mechanisms will come in many different shapes and sizes. Capital allocation rules can be written to reward long-term resilience rather than short-term earnings. Risk assessment frameworks should incorporate systemic risks, compounding risks rather than isolated probabilities. Scenario planning must address non-linear futures, not just incremental variations. Internal carbon or resource pricing need to align incentives with long-term externalities. Sustainability-linked compensation should bind leadership behaviour to long-term value creation. And putting in place cross-functional governance structures that prevent sustainability from being siloed. Without such mechanisms, even the most eloquent strategy becomes performative.

## Managing the Nodes

In Chap. 3, bottlenecks were described as the critical nodes in global systems: points where disruptions cascade with disproportionate impact (such as the Suez Canal, Hormuz Strait, data chokepoints, mineral dependencies). I confessed to preferring the term 'bottleneck' to the more visceral 'chokepoints' or 'pinch points', but they are essentially the same thing. Systemic sustainability strategy is, in part, the art of managing your nodes. Identifying where your business is exposed to systemic bottlenecks and diversifying supply and routes. Monitoring for geopolitical and planetary early-warning signals, stress-testing dependencies, and understanding which nodes can break you—and which you can influence. This node-focused view shifts strategy away from broad generalisations and toward targeted resilience. It also helps businesses distinguish between those risks that can be absorbed, those that can be mitigated, those that can be transferred, and those that are systemic and must be transformed. The last category—systemic risks—cannot be managed alone. They require sector-wide, cross-sector, or public–private collaboration. This is another example of where systemic leadership becomes both necessary and transformative. I give a few examples of such partnerships in the next chapter.

## Place-Based Delivery

Strategy also needs to incorporate the reality that the social licence of business operations is always defined locally in terms of interactions between what a business does and the workers, communities, consumers, and others it interacts with.[12] Even e-commerce or web-based services must fulfil in the real world. Therefore, strategies need to incorporate bottom-up approaches to sustainability as well as the top-down. Place-based strategies are a central part of the way some industries approach sustainability but not for most. The mining sector is an example of a business sector that understands its social licence in local terms, and places most of its own resources there.[13] This does not mean the sector always gets it right, recent disasters in Brazil, Australia or the DRC all show that the industry can fail locally, but place-based approaches remain the norm. Contrast this with other sectors, such as supermarkets, data centres, or much manufacturing, and things can feel much more top down. Many corporate climate transition plans remain at the entity level even though the impact of energy and other transitions will be felt locally. In fact, place-based approaches are the most important element of any 'Just Transition' paradigm.[14]

A systems approach to sustainability strategy needs also to incorporate bottom-up elements. This also needs to be woven into how systems are enacted as we will go on to consider implementation (in Chap. 15) and the metrics we develop (in Chap. 16). But now to consider other aspects of leadership, at board-level and oversight.

# 14.3  Board-Level Engagement

Systems leadership cannot exist meaningfully inside an organisation unless the board itself becomes systems-literate. This is not because boards must master climate science, hydrological cycles, insurance modelling, trade politics, or AI ethics. It is because traditionally boards are the only body that sees—by design—the whole organisation at once. Boards sit at the point where complexity becomes accountability: board executives and non-executives operate within the proximate (annual targets and operational challenges) but also the panoramic (long-term viability, corporate purpose, existential risk). The earlier chapters laid out in unambiguous terms how quickly that panoramic landscape is shifting. Boards that treat sustainability as a reputational sidebar to the "real work" of governance are not conservative; they are negligent.

## Fiduciary Duty Is Starting to Shift in Some Markets

The legal definition of fiduciary responsibility once revolved around narrow financial interests. But in practice—and increasingly in governance guidance—directors are expected to consider long-term enterprise value, including systemic risks and climate exposure. One example of this is English company law. In 2024, the *Financial Markets Law Committee* (FMLC) established that pension fund trustees can account for sustainability considerations without breaching their fiduciary duty.[15] Risks associated with climate change and related sustainability factors are considered financially material and so can be factored into investment strategies and risk analysis. The committee was commissioned by the UK government to clarify the fiduciary duty question as part of its *Green Finance Strategy*, unveiled in 2025. English company law now also integrates sustainability through requirements in the Companies Act 2006, particularly Section 172 (directors' duties to consider environmental/community impact alongside shareholder success) and mandatory climate disclosures for large companies, moving towards the new *UK Sustainability Reporting Standards* (UK SRS) based on the work of the *International Sustainability Standards Board* (ISSB),[16] with phased implementation bringing stricter ESG reporting and potential changes to director duties for greater climate accountability. Key regulations include reporting under the *Task Force on Climate-related Financial Disclosures* (TCFD), *Streamlined Energy & Carbon Reporting* (SECR), and upcoming frameworks like the UK's *Sustainability Reporting Standards* (SRS), shifting focus from voluntary ESG to mandatory and detailed sustainability disclosure.[17]

The UK is one of the markets that leads the way when thinking about sustainability as a corporate governance issue. Other jurisdictions have followed the pathway of mandatory sustainability reporting and/or due diligence, both of which will emerge as board level considerations from time to time. Early drafts of the European Union's *Corporate Sustainability Due Diligence Directive* did include references to director duties, but these were dropped during the redrafting process.[18] However, the UK and Australian *Modern Slavery Acts* both require board-level sign off for annual disclosures by the companies of their supply chains that fall within the scopes of legislation.[19] And wider board oversight requirements of sustainability are emerging as we will come to below.

## The Board as the Interpreter of Systemic Risk

Boards must now spend more time interpreting, not just approving. A system-literate board bridges the gap between sustainability expertise and enterprise strategy. It asks questions executives may be too close to see:

- *What assumptions does our business model make about water, energy, minerals, land, climate, stability?*
- *How resilient are those assumptions under stress?*
- *Which shocks can we absorb, and which ones would break us?*
- *Which dependencies have become single points of failure?*
- *Are we investing in capability or merely in compliance?*
- *How does our strategy align with planetary limits, political trends, and social expectations?*

These questions are not ideological. They are commercial.

## Board Composition Must Evolve

Most boards today still consist of individuals with backgrounds in finance, law, accounting, or general business management. These skills remain essential, but insufficient. Systems leadership at the board level may require adding capabilities in sustainability issues.[20] The precise archetypes any board might need will depend on the company size, business sector, geographical location and other factors. What is essential is not that a board covers every competence, but rather that it knows what it knows, and what it doesn't.[21] Additional expertise can always be brought in through board committees and external experts.

## The Rise of Sustainability Committees (and Their Limits)

Many boards have responded by forming sustainability committees. These can offer valuable insight and scrutiny, particularly when they are committees of the full board and where the board chair and CEO both participate.[22] They are an important component but are not the true measure of a systems approach. Even more important than a bespoke committee is whether the wider panoply of corporate governance also aligns with sustainability. Does the audit committee understand climate-adjusted financial risk? Does the risk committee understand systemic and cascading risks? Does the remuneration committee align incentives with long-term outcomes? Does the nomination committee appoint directors who understand the complexity of modern business? Does the entire board treat sustainability as a fundamental lens on every decision?

The pushback against sustainability, described in Chap. 1, has tested the level of board commitment to sustainability. It will continue to do so.

## 14.4  Oversight and Accountability

Effective governance is essential for firms seeking to embed sustainability into their strategy, operations and reporting. As regulators, investors and stakeholders increase scrutiny, robust governance enables organisations to implement sustainability commitments, manage reporting obligations and build trust. International and domestic rules are evolving quickly. In Europe, governance features prominently in the *Sustainable Finance Disclosure Regulation* (SFDR), a regulation which came into force in 2021 but is currently being simplified.[23] In the UK, financial regulators are adapting existing governance practices to sustainability, while the government is consulting on its own disclosure framework.

Good sustainability governance mirrors other organisational change initiatives. Clear allocation of responsibilities, strong oversight, relevant expertise and aligned organisational culture are critical. Boards hold ultimate responsibility for strategy and must have, or the ability to access, the knowledge needed to oversee environmental and social risks. Equally important is the "tone from the middle," ensuring sustainability commitments influence day-to-day decisions.[24] Firms may need to update decision-making processes, management information systems, and internal controls to track sustainability performance. Key standards reinforce these themes as we shall discuss in depth in Chap. 16. when we consider delivery and metrics. The *Task Force on Climate-related Financial Disclosures* (TCFD)—for example—highlights board oversight and management accountability for climate risks, integration of risk processes into governance, and alignment of remuneration policies with climate objectives. The *International Sustainability Standards Board* (ISSB) builds upon TCFD principles through IFRS S1 and S2, requiring governance disclosures on how entities monitor sustainability-related risks and opportunities.[25]

The SFDR requires Article 8 funds to invest in companies with good governance, encouraging firms to create policies to assess governance in investments.[26] Examples include regular reporting to boards, dedicated sustainability committees and explicit allocation of climate-risk responsibilities. UK initiatives further emphasise governance. The *Transition Plan Taskforce* (TPT) set expectations around board oversight, accountability, culture, incentives and skills for credible net-zero plans.[27] The UK's *Prudential Regulation Authority* now expects boards to possess appropriate expertise, create risk-aware cultures and, in some cases, assign climate responsibility to senior managers.[28] As rules tighten, firms already advanced in sustainability governance can refine their frameworks, while lagging firms should act swiftly to avoid greenwashing and meet stakeholder expectations. Governance must remain adaptable as sustainability standards continue to evolve.

## 14.5 Sustainability Remade Through Systems Leadership

Compliance alone can never create systemic resilience. The earlier chapters on industrial strategies (Chap. 6) and trade (Chap. 9) made this clear. Oversight in a systems framework requires boards and executives to ask:

- Do our activities reinforce or undermine long-term resilience?
- Are we reducing the systemic pressures that create risk in the first place?
- Are we aligning with emerging global norms or resisting them to our long-term detriment?
- Are we part of multi-stakeholder solutions, or free riding on others' efforts?

In essence, compliance ensures legality, but coherence ensures legitimacy and longevity. Metrics are essential, but insufficient. Too often, sustainability oversight becomes a numbers game: tonnes of $CO_2$, litres of water, gigawatts of energy, percentages of recycled content. These matter, as we shall discuss in Chap. 16, but they can create the illusion of progress while obscuring underlying systemic vulnerability. Choosing what to measure is, in itself, a strategic consideration. Undertaking the same measurements quarter by quarter, year on year, is unlikely to respond effectively to the dynamic nature of systems. Earlier chapters highlighted this disconnect. A region may reduce carbon emissions while becoming dangerously dependent on water-intensive energy infrastructure (Chap. 8). A supply chain may report responsible sourcing while relying on minerals extracted under unstable political conditions (Chap. 7). A company may publish ESG scores that look favourable while ignoring systemic risks that ratings agencies themselves struggle to capture, as described in Chap. 4. Systems leadership reframes oversight around meaning, not just measurement. It asks:

- *What story do these metrics tell about our trajectory?*
- *Where are the deeper vulnerabilities the metrics do not reveal?*
- *What assumptions underpin our targets, and are those assumptions realistic?*
- *Is the system around us improving, or only our corner of it?*

## Sustainability Leadership Is a Collective Endeavour

Perhaps the most profound shift concerns responsibility itself. Traditional leadership cultures allocate responsibility vertically: each manager is accountable for their silo. But systems do not respect silos. A water risk created by procurement becomes a financial risk for the CFO, an operational risk for the COO, a reputational risk for the CEO, and a strategic risk for the board. No single function can own a systemic problem.

Systems leadership does not guarantee success, but its absence guarantees exposure. As sustainability constraints tighten, organisations are judged less by stated commitments than by how coherently they operate within interconnected systems of capital, supply, regulation, and technology. Leaders who continue to treat sustainability as a peripheral concern, or who rely on linear models of control, will increasingly find their organisations filtered out by systems they do not fully understand.

The implication is not that leaders must become experts in every domain, but that leadership itself must be redesigned. Boards and executives are now responsible for interpreting systemic risk, aligning incentives across functions, and ensuring that decisions remain viable under conditions of uncertainty and constraint. This is not a question of virtue or belief, but of institutional fitness. Systems do not reward intention, they respond to structure.

Leadership, in this context, becomes the ability to act through leverage rather than direct control. It requires identifying where small interventions can shift system behaviour and where effort is wasted against immovable constraints. The next chapter turns to this question directly. If systems leadership defines the minimum competence for operating under sustainability constraints, leverage is how that competence is exercised in practice.

## Notes

1. UK Government, *Systems Leadership Guide: how to be a systems leader*, Department for Energy, Security and Net Zero and the Department for Business, Energy and Industrial Strategy, 12 January 2023.
2. John Morrison, *The Just Transition: A systems-thinking approach to managing climate action*, October 2024.
3. Boston Consulting Group, INSEAD, and Heidrick & Struggles, Sustainability shakes up the boardroom, 2023.
4. Corporate Governance Institute, *Most important boardroom skills 2025*, (website), November 2025.
5. Mary Johnstone-Louis, *Today's most crucial leadership skill is systems thinking*, Forbes, 26 April 2025.
6. John Morrison, *The Just Transition: A systems-thinking approach to managing climate action*, October 2024.
7. See the work of Donella Meadows and others I refer to in my previous book: John Morrison, *The Just Transition: a systems-thinking approach to managing climate action*, October 2024.

8. Terhi Chakhovich and Tuija Virtanen, *Accountability for sustainability—An institutional entrepreneur as the representative of future stakeholders*, Critical Perspectives on Accounting, 91, 2023.

9. Mariano Heyden and Matthew Hayward, It's hard to find a humble CEO. Here's why, The Conversation, 21 August 2017.

10. Jeff Wright and Olga Petrenko, *The nature of the humble CEO*, Sam Walton College of Business, University of Arkansas, 28 February 2022.

11. Paul Cairney and Claire Toomey, *Systems leadership: a qualitative systemic review of advice for policymakers*, European Commission, Open Research Europe, 10 January 2025.

12. John Morrison, *The Social License: How to keep your organisation legitimate*, 2014.

13. John Morrison, *The Social License: How to keep your organisation legitimate*, 2014.

14. John Morrison, *The Just Transition: A systems-thinking approach to managing climate action*, October 2024.

15. Financial Markets Law Committee, *Paper: Pension Fund Trustees and Fiduciary Duties—Decision-making in the context of Sustainability and the subject of Climate Change*, 6 February 2024.

16. IFRS Foundation, *About the International Sustainability Standards Board*, 2025.

17. Linklaters, *Quick Guide: Key Sustainability Disclosure Regimes: UK climate disclosure rules under Companies Act 2006*, 9 September 2025.

18. Andrew Johnston, *Corporate governance for sustainability: a popular but still unfilled agenda for change*, Judge Business School, University of Cambridge, 3 October 2024.

19. For example, Section 54 of the UK Modern Slavery Act 2015 obliges qualifying organisations to prepare a slavery and human trafficking statement for each financial year and sets how it must be approved and signed.

20. Corporate Governance Institute, *Most important boardroom skills 2025*, (website), November 2025.

21. World Economic Forum, *Engaging Affected Stakeholders: The Emerging Duties of Board Members*, Global Future Council for human rights, May 2022.

22. Chartered Governance Institute, *Should my company have a sustainability or ESG committee at board level?* Chartered Governance Institute UK and Ireland, 15 February 2024.

23. European Commission, *Sustainability-related disclosure in the financial service sector*, 20 November 2025.
24. Norton Rose Fulbright, *Governance and Sustainability*, August 2024.
25. IFRS Foundation, *About the International Sustainability Standards Board,* 2025.
26. European Commission, *Sustainability-related disclosure in the financial service sector*, 20 November 2025.
27. IFRS Foundation, *Transition Plan Taskforce resources*, (website), December 2025.
28. Bank of England, *Policy Statement 25*, 3 December 2025.

# 15

## Leveraging for Green

No organisation can deliver sufficient sustainability outcomes directly at scale. The business systems that determine environmental and social outcomes—capital markets, supply chains, regulation, technology platforms, and consumer infrastructure—are often too large, too distributed, and too interdependent to be controlled by any single actor. Under sustainability constraints, action therefore may occur indirectly, through leverage over systems rather than command over outcomes.

The preceding chapter (Chap. 14) reframed leadership as the minimum competence required to operate within these constraints. This chapter (Chap. 15) takes the next step. It asks how organisations influence systems they do not fully control, once sustainability has moved from aspiration to enforcement. Leverage is not a leadership technique or a strategic option; it is the only remaining way action scales when direct control is unavailable or undesirable. Leverage works by shaping incentives, norms, rules, and expectations so that system behaviour shifts without requiring universal alignment or central authority. It is most effective when applied selectively, at points where small interventions produce outsized effects. Misapplied, it dissipates effort, creates backlash, or accelerates unintended consequences. The challenge for





J. Morrison, *Remaking Sustainability*, https://doi.org/10.1007/978-3-032-23755-2_15

organisations is therefore not whether to use leverage, but where, when, and how to apply it so that action remains viable under tightening constraints.[1]

Leverage is one of the oldest concepts in human problem-solving. The notion that a small, well-placed force can move something many times its weight goes back to Archimedes in the third century BC: "*Give me a place to stand, and I will move the Earth*". According to Plutarch, when Archimedes was challenged to put his words into action, he arranged a series of pulleys and cogs that allowed him to pull a massive Syracusan ship from the water onto the beach.[2] Today, in business, the term is most often used in relation to financial markets, when borrowed money is used to augment the available capital, thus increasing the funds available for a (perhaps risky) investment. The complexity of financial leverage these days raises its own new forms of risk.[3]

But in sustainability, leverage is not just a mechanical or transactional idea; it is a strategic one. It asks a deceptively simple question: where can we act so that the whole system shifts, not just our corner of it? This aligns both with the systems-thinking theory of writers such as Donella Meadows,[4] and political scientists such as John Ruggie who incorporated the concept of leverage into the United Nations Guiding Principles on Business and Human Rights.[5] Exercising leverage is the way to address systemic issues which your business might not have caused, but risks and impacts to which your company has contributed or is directly linked to. Even beyond issues of responsibility, businesses can seek to build leverage for wider strategic effect. As the former CEO and board chair, Sir Mark Moody Stuart, would say: "*it might not always be our responsibility, but it is still our problem*".[6]

Chap. 14 argued that sustainability requires leadership that can hold multiple time horizons, read feedback loops, and build trust across interdependencies. Leverage is how that leadership manifests in practice. If systems leadership is the ability to see patterns, leverage is the ability to use those patterns. What follows is not an abstract framework but a practical answer to the question: how do we intervene in systems in a way that accelerates progress rather than fragmenting effort? Leverage in sustainability is not simply a matter of technique, it is also a matter of judgement. A lever only works if it is placed on something solid. A push only shifts the system if it is applied at the correct point. Thus, this chapter explores leverage through four lenses: *leveraging systems*: understanding where small interventions shift whole structures; *setting priorities*: identifying which levers matter most; *building virtuous cycles*, and finally the *collective action* that builds leverage.

# 15.1  Leveraging Systems

The earlier chapters have already hinted at some of these leverage points. Financial incentives and capital flows can lock markets into one trajectory rather than another (Chaps. 4 and 6). Supply nodes might become bottlenecks where a single disruption cascades across multiple sectors (Chap. 8). Rules-based systems such as trade, tax, standards, and disclosure can help to reorganise markets (Chap. 9), whilst technological shifts can change the very geometry of possibility (Chaps. 11, 12, and 13). Emerging-market leadership might also find new forms of leverage, where green growth trajectories leapfrog legacy systems (Chap. 7). If Chap. 14 was about seeing systems, Chap. 15 is about using them. System leverage is the ability to shift a system's behaviour by intervening at a point where small changes create cascading effects.[7] The approach can be sub-divided into three parts: *structural* leverage, *behavioural* leverage, and *symbolic* leverage.

## Structural Leverage: The Rules That Move Markets

Structural leverage represents the infrastructure of influence and includes a few different forms such as pricing mechanisms, regulatory frameworks, and trade regimes. When structural leverage shifts, everything else must eventually follow. The EU's *Carbon Border Adjustment Mechanism* (CBAM),[8] a focus of Chap. 9, is a good example of a measure that might have considerable structural leverage over the behaviour of many companies and other governments. Similarly, Chap. 6 showed how *modern industrial strategies*—whether in the EU, China, India, or intermittently in the US—are now directing trillions into clean industries through subsidies, tax credits, procurement guarantees, and strategic planning. When the state changes its rules, markets respond accordingly. Chapter 4 reminded us that private finance—despite its internal contradictions—continues to be leveraged by systemic forces: risk, disclosure norms, stranded-asset logic, and the basic self-interest of capital in long-term stability. Even the ESG backlash does not reverse the underlying structural exposure of finance to planetary instability. Structural leverage matters because systems behave as they are designed. If a system is designed to reward short-term extraction, it will extract. If it is redesigned to value long-term resilience, it will adapt.

## Behavioural Leverage: The Patterns That Shape Decisions

Behavioural leverage concerns the habits, expectations, and incentives that drive day-to-day behaviour in organisations. These can be both explicit or implicit, ranging from procurement norms and managerial incentives to organisational cultures and unwritten rules of what 'counts' or 'matters'. Much of this was discussed in Chap. 3 when I looked at the operational bedrock of the business. An operational leader can redesign KPIs and procurement processes far faster than a government can pass a law, precisely because behavioural levers are close to the ground. Behavioural leverage also matters because it compounds. A single change in procurement criteria—say, requiring all suppliers to disclose emissions—creates upstream pressure across dozens of companies. One company becomes a node of influence.

Behavioural leverage is the quiet power of norms. When enough organisations adopt a practice, it becomes standard. When it becomes standard, it becomes expected. When expected, it becomes required. And when required, it becomes structural. This is how sustainability often advances in practice: not through breakthroughs, but through creeping professionalisation.

## Symbolic Leverage: The Narratives That Shift Paradigms

Symbolic leverage is the least tangible but often the most powerful. It concerns stories, metaphors, and worldviews. It shapes legitimacy: what counts as credible, modern, or inevitable. In Chap. 1 we saw how the narrative around sustainability shifted from urgency to backlash to quiet pragmatism. Narratives influence everything: investor behaviour, political choices, public sentiment, employee engagement, and even the confidence of executives who fear accusations of *greenwashing* or *greenhushing* (that I will explore in Chaps. 17 and 18). Symbolic leverage can make certain actions thinkable—or unthinkable. For example, once renewable energy became associated with national pride, or electric cars became aspirational, investment has soared in a few markets. When circularity can be reframed as efficiency, then it starts to appeal to finance directors. If sustainability becomes synonymous with supply chain resilience, then this too builds increased leverage. Narrative is leverage because narrative mobilises whole organisations around purpose. It also gives permission, it grants leaders the legitimacy to act boldly. I will return to this point in Chap. 19.

## Where Leverage Points Hide

Leverage points are rarely where one expects them. They often hide within the complexity of any system. But they can leave us clues along the way. Places to look include points in the system where incentives no longer align, or bottlenecks that reveal themselves during times of crisis. Regulation itself brings its own leverage but can also bring opportunities to out compete competitors above the 'level playing field'. Sometimes there are new forms of efficiency that can be found when making procurement more sustainable that provide a competitive edge (Chap. 8), or AI-driven technological fixes for business operations that include sustainability impacts (Chap. 12). Leverage points also hide within temporal dynamics. Many sustainability challenges arise because feedback loops are too slow. By accelerating information (e.g., through better data), organisations shorten delays and open new leverage possibilities. This was a key insight of Chap. 11, where I looked at how better data improves foresight and reduces systemic blind spots.

## 15.2  Setting Priorities

If understanding the different forms of systems leverage is the first task, choosing where to apply that leverage is the second. Priority-setting is perhaps the most difficult discipline in sustainability, not because organisations lack options, but because they have too many. The earlier chapters of this book revealed the sheer breadth of the sustainability landscape, but no manager can lead across all fronts simultaneously. The question becomes: *which interventions matter most for us, in this moment, given our role in the system?* This is the difference between importance and primacy. Everything in sustainability is important, but not everything is primary. Primacy depends upon where the organisation is structurally exposed, where it has real influence, where it is uniquely positioned, where risks are most concentrated (including risk to people and risk to planet), where opportunity is greatest, where timing matters, and where action by one actor can unlock action by many. Primacy is contextual. It differs across sectors, geographies, and business models.

### Materiality and Saliency

Many of the sustainability standards referred to in earlier chapters of this book include some usage of 'materiality' as a prioritisation requirement, or 'double materiality' as a more recent concept sitting behind many of the European Union's legislative innovations. Double materiality requires both an 'outside in' (how external factors influence the financial performance of a company) and 'inside out' (how the company's activities impact upon the environment and stakeholders) perspective. It is the basis of many evolving reporting standards, including the EU's *Corporate Sustainability Reporting Directive* (CSRD).[9] The concept of 'saliency' is not referred to in international standards but is an important prioritisation tool when considering which issues to prioritise when undertaking human rights due diligence, for example.[10] It requires companies to consider 'risk to stakeholders' and not just 'risk to business'. It is therefore a critical concept when considering how to implement standards such as the EU's *Corporate Sustainability Due Diligence Directive* (CSDDD),[11] for example, or the due diligence of the *EU Deforestation Regulation* (EUDR),[12] *Critical Raw Materials Act* (CRMA),[13] or the EU *Forced Labour Regulation.*[14]

## Mapping Exposure: The 'Bedrock' Perspective

Chapter 3 introduced the idea of bedrock: the operational foundations that a company cannot erode without jeopardising its viability. Bedrock is where exposure is most concentrated or where dependencies are most brittle. For a manufacturing firm, bedrock may be energy, minerals, or logistics. For a food company, it may be water, land, or supply-chain resilience. For a digital firm, it may be data, energy, or geopolitical stability. And for society itself it is all of these, as set out in Chap. 2. The priorities emerge by identifying the primary bedrock and asking: *Which vulnerabilities of people and planet cannot be 'outsourced' or 'hedged'? What are our responsibilities in relation to these? Where are we most constrained? Which systemic dependencies are non-negotiable?* It is double materiality in practice.

## Prioritising by Systemic Centrality

A priority issue is one that, if solved, unlocks progress elsewhere. A non-priority issue is one that, even if solved, leaves the major constraints intact. Not all sustainability issues are equal in terms of systemic influence. Some are 'node issues': they sit at the centre of multiple systems and shape everything around them. Chapter 8 described water–energy–food interdependencies in precisely these terms: a disruption in one cascades across all three. Likewise, minerals and materials are central nodes in the energy transition (Chap. 8); trade regimes are central nodes in global supply flows (Chap. 9); grid capacity is a central node in industrial strategy (Chap. 6); data governance is a central node in risk management (Chap. 11); and insurance pricing is a central node in investment decisions (Chap. 5).

## The Solvability Criterion

Some sustainability challenges are structurally essential but beyond the control of any single organisation. These still require attention, but they may not be prime targets for immediate leverage for a company alone, requiring 'collective action'—see below. The level of responsibility of any business is defined by risk to people or planet, and the nature of the business relationship, but the nature of the action taken is determined not solely by importance but also by solvability—the focus of Chap. 16. A solvable issue is one where: action can be taken in the near term. Progress can be measured, influence can be exerted, coalitions can be built, investment can be justified, and intervention does not exceed organisational capacity. These might be called 'quick wins', where the momentum of some initial success unlocks additional forms of leverage in the future. This is why many companies focus early sustainability efforts on energy efficiency, procurement standards, and supply-chain transparency, because these interventions are likely to have early impact (as I will return to in Chap. 16).

## The Inevitability Test

A priority issue is often one where the organisation must eventually act, sooner or later. To determine inevitability, leaders often ask questions such as: *is regulation moving toward this direction? Are markets re-pricing this risk? Are customers shifting preferences? Are investors integrating this factor? Are competitors already adapting? Is the physical world or society changing in a way that makes inaction impossible?* When the direction of travel is clear, waiting might become a liability.

## Strategic Prioritisation in Practice

Most organisations will find that their sustainability priorities cluster into different domains: *Risk stabilisation*—ensuring operational resilience (e.g., supply chains, insurance, energy security). *Market positioning*—aligning with industrial strategies, emerging-market demand, and trade incentives. *Efficiencies*—cost-efficiency, energy efficiency, waste reduction, and resource productivity. *Growth and innovation*—entering green markets and leveraging technology developing new business models. A mature sustainability strategy is not one that tries to do everything. It is one that is ruthless about what matters now, what matters later, and what matters most.

Each business, each organisation, will develop its own tools for prioritisation. The above criteria are amongst those to be considered for a systems approach to sustainability. Ultimately managers are accountable for the priorities they set from the board downwards. Increasing attention will be paid to what these criteria are, and who decides this, over the years ahead.

# 15.3  Building Virtuous Cycles

A virtuous cycle is a reinforcing loop where one improvement amplifies another. For example, better data can help enable better decisions; better decisions drive better performance; better performance builds trust; trust unlocks investment; investment fuels innovation; and innovation accelerates impact. Many institutions have talked about the need to build virtuous cycles in policy areas as diverse as international development,[15] developing generative AI,[16] to economic growth.[17] In sustainability, virtuous cycles can transform the slow grind of incremental progress into accelerating systemic change.

## Why Virtuous Cycles Matter

Most sustainability strategies fail not because leaders lack ambition or insight, but because the system inside the organisation is not aligned with the system outside it. Progress arrives in fits and starts, interrupted by budget cycles, leadership turnover, crisis-driven distraction, policy shifts, resource constraints, or cultural inertia. Virtuous cycles counteract this turbulence by creating self-reinforcing momentum that continues even when political attention, market sentiment, or leadership priorities fluctuate. Earlier chapters hinted at these cycles. The industrial strategy chapter (Chap. 6) showed how stable policy attracts investment, and which then strengthens political support for more stable policy. The finance chapter (Chap. 4) highlighted how disclosure improves foresight, which reduces risk, which might unlock cheaper capital, and which then encourages better disclosure. The supply-chain chapter (Chap. 8) showed how transparency drives supplier improvements, which reduce operational risk, which improves sourcing confidence, and which strengthens supplier relationships. Examples from emerging markets (Chap. 7) illustrated how green industries create jobs, which create legitimacy, which drives further investment, and which accelerates growth.

The interconnections between climate change, pollution and food security hold potential not just for negative feedback loops, but also for positive change in one area to spread to others.[18] Deployment of renewable energy solutions, both centralized and decentralized, can improve not only energy supply but also access to clean cooking, heating and lighting for improved air quality and human health. Kenya would be a good example of a country that has made renewable energy the basis for transformation across many aspects of its economy.[19] South Africa has a much greater carbon footprint given its historic use of coal for energy generation, but current investments in the Limpopo and Free State regions suggest this might be changing.[20] The large-scale plan is to build out renewable capacity, not just to end load shedding, a legacy of overwhelmed twentieth century infrastructure, but to initiate a cycle that creates employment opportunities, bolsters socioeconomic development, helps enterprise development, ups wealth creation, whilst helping to offset carbon dioxide emissions and to save water. Time will tell if the South African government is successful here.

## Key Factors for Virtuous Cycles

Whether they are always virtuous in practice seems to depend on several factors which we now turn to *capability, financial allocation, trust, coherence*, and *momentum*.

Capability is one of the most underestimated assets in sustainability. Without skills, everything else collapses: goals, measurement, investment, innovation.[21] Capability can be determined by factors such as specialist knowledge, data literacy, or management skills. Capability is the first virtue because it creates internal confidence. Without it, organisations can often timidly avoid decisions. With it, they move. When capability grows, decision speed improves. When decision speed improves, performance improves and leadership ambition can increase. This might be the first virtuous cycle in any business or organisation seeking to enhance its performance in sustainability.

Financial capital can unlock scale. Once investment begins flowing into sustainability priorities—grids, nature, data, efficiency, supply resilience, circular manufacturing—performance becomes self-reinforcing. Earlier chapters showed how capital can shift systems: Industrial policy pulls private investment into new technologies (Chap. 6). Insurance withdrawal forces companies to invest in resilience (Chap. 5). Supply-chain disruptions trigger capital reallocations toward stability (Chap. 8). Emerging-market growth attracts global investors and accelerates green innovation (Chap. 7). Capital builds the flywheel. Once it spins, it resists reversal.

Trust is a form of currency. When organisations build credibility—with stakeholders such as investors, regulators, communities, employees, or suppliers—they gain more room to operate and innovate. Credibility grows when institutional claims are matched by evidence, mistakes are acknowledged early, commitments are fulfilled consistently, and transparency is maintained even under pressure. Such credibility strengthens the social licence of the organisation, allowing for stronger partnerships and higher levels of trust.[22]

Coherence is the hardest virtue and the most important. It means that decisions across finance, operations, procurement, HR, strategy, and innovation align with the sustainability goals. Incoherence is what happens when the Chief Financial Officer (CFO) cuts sustainability budgets while the Chief Operating Officer (COO) is trying to build resilience, or when procurement chooses cheap suppliers while the board expects ethical sourcing. Other examples would be when design teams innovate circular products while marketing promotes disposability, or when risk committees ignore climate exposure while the Chief Executive Officer (CEO) promises net zero. Incoherence kills progress. Coherence accelerates it. When internal systems reinforce rather than contradict each other, sustainability becomes a natural output of how the organisation operates.

Momentum is also a determiner of success. As I discussed above, virtuous cycles often succeed when momentum can be established. Often collective action can be an important way of achieving this.

## Plan A: A Case-Study in Building a Virtuous Cycle

There are many case-studies of how businesses have tried to make sustainability part of core business. One of the best, and long-standing, are the experiences of Marks & Spencer, the UK retailer, and its 'Plan A' programme. Initiated in 2007 by the then CEO, Sir Stuart Rose, as strategy for reducing the company's impact on the planet. According to the company website nearly twenty years later: *"Plan A continues to play a pivotal role for the business, and our ambition to become a net zero business across our value chain by 2040 is an important part of our strategy to reshape M&S for sustainable, profitable growth."*[23] The approach now includes Foresty, Land, and Agriculture (FLAG) emissions, as well as non-FLAG emissions from energy and industry. In 2025, the company updated its Scope 3 emissions targets, accordingly, validated by the *Science Based Target initiative* (SBTi).[24]

Few companies have internal integration programmes that have lasted as long as Plan A has through successive leadership teams. It can be contrasted with the ebb and flow of some higher profile 'sustainability-hero' CEOs, whose former companies have been more fully in retreat since their departure. The progress under Plan A has been more incremental, and still focuses mainly on climate above all else, but it has become part of the operational DNA of the company. Part of the 'code' for success is definitely that whilst the company is not privately held, like some of the other sustainability leaders in the consumer goods sector such as Ikea, The John Lewis Partnership, Tetra Pak or Mars (all of which has compelling case studies of their own, some of which I know very well), it does own much of its supply chain—it is 'private label' (in much the way Ikea is). This is a big advantage when it comes to integrating sustainability, as it is the case for some other supermarkets such as Lidl.

When discussing Plan A with Mike Barry, a key leader in the process over much of the period, I am struck by how he describes it as a transformational process, and not one that regards sustainability purely in technical terms.[25] Managing transformational processes require a high level of emotional intelligence, with high levels of trust throughout the organisation, and a key eye on business efficiencies. Mike points to the 'horizontal' nature of Plan A—one of the few corporate initiatives that spanned both M&S's food and apparel businesses: seeing quality in a fully systemic way. The premium for product quality, particularly in terms of what we eat as food systems and are more closely aligned with failing health systems, is only likely to become more salient. This is also true of Waitrose supermarkets, part of the John Lewis Partnership, which places an increasing value on regenerative agriculture, in part driven by its private-label products from the Leckford Estate under company ownership but now also to 2500 farms in the company's supply chain.[26]

Plan A has become a useful shorthand for what many of the true sustainability leading companies do. Focusing on sustainability in systemic terms and building a set of internal and external incentives to help ensure continuity through adaptation and solid performance.

## 15.4  Sustainability Remade Through Collective Action

If leverage is the art of influencing systems, and prioritisation is the discipline of knowing where to intervene, then collective action is the reality that makes any of it possible. No single actor—government, business, civil society organisation, trade union, scientist, financier—controls the sustainability system. This is what makes sustainability so vexing. It is also what makes it transformative. Systems change is rarely a solo performance; it is an ensemble piece. The earlier chapters have shown, repeatedly, that sustainability challenges are intrinsically systemic. None of these systems can be steered by a single organisation, however powerful. So collective action is an essential part of using many forms of leverage. There are different forms: *internal coalitions*, collaboration across functions inside a company; *vertical coalitions*, collaboration up and down value chains; and *horizontal coalitions*, collaboration across competitors. Each type has its own leverage.

## Internal Coalitions: Breaking the Tyranny of Silos

The first form of collective action is often the hardest: getting your own organisation to behave like a system rather than a set of disconnected functions. Sustainability priorities—be they energy, water, resilience, procurement, data, labour practices or other—touch nearly every department. But internally, those departments often operate in silos, each with its own incentives and its own worldview. Breaking these silos is not a cultural nicety; it is a leverage requirement. For example: a Chief Operating Officer (COO) cannot redesign supply chains without the Chief Financial Officer (CFO)'s capital support; a Chief Information Officer (CIO) cannot improve data transparency without input from risk, operations, and procurement. Procurement cannot influence suppliers without clarity from the sustainability team; and the board cannot exercise oversight if information flows are fragmented. Internal coalitions are the least glamorous form of collective action, yet they produce some of the highest returns. They align incentives. They reduce duplication. They prevent well-intended efforts from working at cross-purposes. If you cannot coordinate internally, your capacity to influence externally is limited. There are many good examples of when a company has been able to galvanise sustainability in such a way, the 'Plan A' programme at the UK retailer Marks and Spencer being one of the better known.[27]

## Vertical Coalitions: Re-shaping Value Chains

The second form of collective action is up and down the value chain including suppliers, distributors, logistics partners, and customers. Vertical coalitions are where much of the real sustainability impact occurs, because value chains are where environmental and social footprints concentrate. Earlier chapters emphasised how value chains act as systems, not lines. The bottlenecks that destabilise supply—whether rare-earth minerals, water shortages, or port disruptions—always originate somewhere upstream or downstream, rarely inside the company itself (as I discussed in Chap. 8). Vertical coalitions allow companies to take systemic steps such as co-investing in resilience, harmonising standards, or sharing data on non-price related issues (see Chap. 11). When a major purchaser changes its procurement rules, entire industries move. This is leverage by volume.

There has been a succession of cross-industry and multi-stakeholder initiatives focused on environmental issues, upholding workplace and other human rights through supply chains over the past 30 years. Such approaches started in the *apparel sector* (such as the Fair Labor Association or the Clean Clothes Campaign), and in *electronics* (now the Responsible Business Alliance), but now cover a number of other sectors:

- *Critical minerals* (for example: the International Council on Mining and Metals, the Extractive Industries Transparency Initiative, the Aluminium Stewardship Initiative, the Global Batteries Alliance, the Copper Mark, the World Gold Council, the Initiative for Responsible Mining Assurance).
- *Agricultural products* (such as: the Roundtable on Sustainable Palm Oil, the Sustainable Cocoa Initiative, the Marine Stewardship Council, the Forest Stewardship Council, the Sustainable Rice Platform).
- *Energy* production (such as the International Petroleum Industry Environmental Conservation Association, the Global Wind Energy Council, the Solar Stewardship Initiative).
- Digital rights (the Global Network Initiative, or the Freedom Online Coalition); as well as specific high-risk contractors such as *security pro-*

*viders* (the Voluntary Principles on Security and Human Rights, or the International Code of Conduct for Private security Providers).
- The *Sports industry* (the Centre for Sport and Human Rights).
- *Recruitment agencies* (such as the Global Forum for Responsible Recruitment).

The effectiveness of such approaches has been evaluated at different points of time, but critical factors include the ability of members to hold each other accountable and for the collective action to influence standard-setting with both home and host governments.

## Horizontal Coalitions: The Unusual Power of Competitors

Horizontal coalitions, cooperation among competitors and other actors within specific markets, are often the most controversial, but they are also among the most impactful. Competitors face the same structural constraints, the same regulatory risks, the same physical pressures, and often the same investor expectations. They also share a deep need for level playing fields. When competitors work together on pre-competitive issues they reduce systemic friction. Think of examples such as renewable-energy buyers' alliances, sector net-zero pathways, joint circular-economy initiatives, shared charging infrastructure for EVs, industry-wide methane standards, and agricultural coalitions to support regenerative farming, These efforts can create what Chap. 6 called catalytic industrial strategy: shaping markets through coordinated signals and shared investment. Critically, horizontal coalitions also de-risk government action. When industries coordinate, policymakers might feel empowered to set more ambitious rules. This is leverage through alignment.

There are many examples of such horizontal coalitions. I personally have been involved in several:

- that relate to the UK (such as the Ethical Trading Initiative), and other European countries (other Ethical Trading Initiatives, **'entreprises pour les droits de l'homme'**),

- Bangladesh (the Accord on Fire and Building Safety), Myanmar (the Myanmar Centre for Responsible Business), Colombia (‘**Centro Regional de Empresas y Emprendimientos Responsables**’),
- the Gulf States (Gulf Sustain),[28]
- but we could add to the list the ‘Better Work programme’ of the International Labour Organisation,[29] or the national chapters of the United Nations Global Compact,[30] or the National Contact Point system of the OECD.

Often meetings will need to start with a reminder of what can and cannot be discussed according to national anti-trust (or monopolies) legislation, possibly with a neutral party observing to guarantee fair play.

Collective action is a natural consequence of prioritising leverage as the main means of addressing sustainability and other business issues from a systemic perspective. Arguably, its benefits have yet to be fully appreciated. Even legislative approaches acknowledge the norm-setting advantages of industry-wide or multi-stakeholder processes that governments are often unable to perform on their own. In my previous book on a systems-thinking approach to the Just Transition, I attempt to set out the key advantages of collective action in systems terms.[31] One key element is the reduction of what the economist Herbert Simon coined as ‘bounded rationality’—the limitations on each organisation’s world view from their corner of the system. Collective action can allow different stakeholders to challenge each other’s preconceptions and to better understand each other’s constraints and incentives. In this way, the limits of bounded rationality can be pushed back, allowing for trust and stronger partnerships to develop, even between unlikely bedfellows.

Leverage does not guarantee success, but the absence of leverage guarantees irrelevance. In systems that increasingly enforce sustainability through access, pricing, and automation, organisations that rely on direct control, voluntary alignment, or fragmented initiatives will struggle to influence outcomes that now operate at system scale. Leverage is how leadership translates intent into impact when authority is limited and constraints are real. The preceding sections have shown that leverage is not a single tool, but a set of mechanisms that operate structurally, behaviourally, and symbolically. Its effectiveness depends on prioritisation, sequencing, and an honest assessment of where influence is possible and where it is not. Poorly chosen leverage wastes political capital and erodes credibility; well-chosen leverage reshapes system behaviour with an effective use of effort.

The next chapter (Chap. 16) turns to the most important consequence of applying leverage: real-world impact. Irrefutable data about outcomes, using the most legitimate metrics, is what separates bedrock sustainability from 'greenwashing' and 'greenhushing' (the focus of Chaps. 17 and 18 respectively).

## Notes

1. Donella Meadows, *Thinking in Systems*: A Primer, 2008.
2. Plutarch, *Life of Marcellus, 7–8*, Parallel Lives, written sometime between 90–120AD.
3. Satyajit Das, *The increased complexity of modern leverage raises risks*, The Financial Times, 23 January 2024.
4. Donella Meadows, *Thinking in Systems*: A Primer, 2008.
5. United Nations, *UN Guiding Principles on Business and Human Rights*, Human Rights Council, 2011.
6. Mark Moody-Stuart. *Personal communications* around 2011.
7. Donella Meadows, *Leverage points: places to intervene within a system*, Donella Meadows archives, (online), November 2025.
8. European Commission, *Simplifications for the Carbon Border Adjustment Mechanism*, Director-General for Taxation and Customs Union, 20 October 2025.
9. European Commission, *Corporate responsibility reporting*, DG Finance, (website), 25 November 2025.
10. United Nations, *Guiding Principles on Business and Human Rights*, Human Rights Council, 2011.
11. European Commission, *Corporate sustainability due diligence*, Directive 2024/1760, 25 July 2024.
12. European Commission, *Regulation on Deforestation-free Products* (EUDR) 2023/1115.
13. European Commission, *Critical Raw Materials Act (CRMA)*, 2024/1252.

14. European Commission, *The Forced Labour Regulation*, Internal Market, 2024/3015, 27 November2024.

15. Christine Lagarde, *Building a Virtuous Cycle*, International Monetary Fund, 7 June 2017.

16. Ishit Vachhrajani, *Building a Virtuous Cycle: Your path to maximising value from generative AI*, The Guardian, 7 August 2024.

17. McKinsey & Company, *A virtuous cycle for topline growth*, 1 February 2015.

18. Tafadzwanashe Mabhaudhi, *Harnessing the energy nexus for good needs systems leadership*, World Economic Forum, 13 October 2025.

19. Stefan Dercon, *Gambling on development: why some countries win and others lose*, 2023.

20. Tafadzwanashe Mabhaudhi, *Harnessing the energy nexus for good needs systems leadership*, World Economic Forum, 13 October 2025.

21. Stefan Dercon, *Gambling on development: why some countries win and others lose*, 2023.

22. John Morrison, *The Social License: How to keep your organisation legitimate*, 2014.

23. Marks and Spencer (M&S), *Plan A*, (website), January 2026.

24. Marks and Spencer (M&S), *Plan A*, (website), January 2026.

25. Interview with Mike Barry, February 2026.

26. John Lewis Partnership, *Farming for Nature*, (website), February 2026.

27. Marks and Spencer (M&S), *Using systems thinking to make sense of complex real-world sustainability challenges*, (website), November 2025.

28. During my time as CEO of the *Institute for Human Rights and Business*, 2009–2025.

29. International Labour Organisation, *Better Work programme*, (website), November 2025.

30. United Nations, *UN Global Compact*, (website), November 2025.

31. John Morrison, *The Just Transition: A systems-thinking approach to managing climate action*, October 2024.

# 16

# Real World Impact

As sustainability moves from aspiration to enforcement, impact becomes the basis on which decisions are made. Capital is allocated, insurance withdrawn, market access conditioned, and reputations contested not on the strength of commitments, but on evidence of real-world outcomes. What cannot be demonstrated at scale is discounted, challenged, or ignored. In this context, impact is everything. And with impact come metrics.

The problem is not a lack of data (as I discussed in Chap. 11). Organisations now generate unprecedented volumes of sustainability information, covering emissions, resources, labour, and governance. The problem is that much of this information was designed for (often limited) disclosure, not judgement. It describes activities rather than outcomes, performance within silos rather than effects across systems, and progress against targets rather than consequences in the world. As a result, it often fails to answer the questions that increasingly matter: who is affected, where, over what timeframe, and at what cost?

This chapter (Chap. 16) examines why measuring real-world impact has proven so difficult, and why that difficulty is now consequential. I argue that traditional approaches to sustainability measurement obscure





J. Morrison, *Remaking Sustainability*, https://doi.org/10.1007/978-3-032-23755-2_16

interaction effects, misrepresent risk, and weaken accountability as systems tighten. I then set out some of the alternative ways of seeing impact, at the levels of 'system' and then 'place', that better reflect how sustainability outcomes are produced and judged in practice. The objective is not to propose new reporting standards here, but to clarify how impact must be understood if sustainability is to remain credible under constraint.

Chapters 14 and 15 established the two halves of systems execution: the mindset that recognises interdependence, and the ability to intervene at points of leverage. This chapter builds the bridge to delivery. Real-world impact is where those ideas meet evidence. Setting the right goals is the first question to ask, and here business needs to learn from governments, academia and civil society as goals need to be coherent across all issues as well as stakeholder groups. Measuring impact is then the second concern and the larger part of this chapter. One tension that comes is the need to be concrete and specific within the silos of each sustainability issue, whilst also being able to aggregate these into common platforms. In the last section I go on to propose a few areas for potential additional metrics that cut across the system, and the specificities of particular locations. In other words, five that relate to the macro, the health of the system itself, and an additional five that might be applied at the much more micro level: place-based interventions.

So many metrics! This is often the retort from practitioners who have to do the hard work of gathering and analysis, and from board members who long for dashboards with only the most strategic of metrics. But sustainability has many variables and false simplification is a risk in itself. As I have said already earlier in this book, embracing complexity is the starting point. Rather than complaining about the number of metrics, we should instead ask whether the metrics we have are meaningful and find better tools, through AI and otherwise, to integrate and manage the complexity of impact. As I discussed in Chap. 11 on better data, we need as much federated data as we can get from as many sources as possible.

# 16.1  Setting the Right Goals

In sustainability, setting the right goals can be uniquely challenging because the world they relate to is profoundly non-linear and increasingly unpredictable. Not everything is scientifically defined and measuring real world outcomes, especially for social issues, can be challenging. There is a danger that we prioritise the things we can quantify and neglect the things we cannot.

## Lessons from the UN Sustainable Development Goals (2015–2030)

The United Nations (UN) Sustainable Development Goals (SDGs) were agreed in 2015 with a fifteen-year delivery horizon. In its 2025 report, the UN Department of Economic and Social Affairs (DESA) reported two thirds of the way through this journey, ten years into implementation and five years from the 2030 deadline.[1] DESA described progress as "*real and substantial*," yet also "*fragile and unequal*". Amongst the areas of progress[2] are the more than 100 million children and young people gaining access to education; significant reductions in maternal and child mortality; and a 40% decline in HIV infections since 2010. An additional 45 countries had reached universal electricity access over the decade meaning 92% of the global population were connected.[3] 54 countries had eradicated at least one neglected tropical disease by the end of 2024 with hundreds of millions gaining access to safe drinking water.[4]

But the more general picture is not so positive. In Chap.1, I shared DESA's assessment that, according to the data available, only 35% of the 169 specific targets underneath the 17 goals were 'on track' to being met or moving moderately forward. Nearly half 'lacked sufficient progress', and 18% had actually 'regressed'.[5] But the global averages mask stark disparities across regions and countries. European countries are leading in SDG implementation, whilst many East and South Asian countries have been making the most progress, including Nepal, Cambodia, the Philippines, Bangladesh and Mongolia. Barbados topped an index tracking commitment to UN multilateralism, followed by Jamaica and

Trinidad and Tobago. The USA ranked last.[6] Despite their mixed record, it is hard to write off the SDGs. Only three countries did not submit national plans for advancing sustainable development in 2025: Haiti, Myanmar, and the USA.[7]

But the development economist Stefan Dercon argues that the goals themselves were always too ambitious, expecting every country in the world to follow a development trajectory akin to the modern history of Sweden rather than locally rooted and context specific 'development bargains'.[8] For this book, it is important to unpick the SDGs a little more from the perspective of the most powerful non-state implementer of all: business. Whether or not the SDGs are the right way for governments to proceed after 2030 is one question. But have the SDGs ever been the right way to measure the real-world sustainability impact of business?

## The Anatomy of a Business Sustainability Goal

When it comes to business, many companies in many parts of the world have endorsed the SDGs in one way or another. The accountants KPMG report that 74% of the world's largest 250 companies now include the SDGs in their sustainability reporting, with about one-third considering both positive and negative impacts. But a 'cherry picking' mentality applies in most cases, with only 10% of companies reporting against all 17 SDGs. Three SDGs remain the most popular for companies: SDG8 on *Decent Work and Economic Growth*; SDG12 on *Responsible Consumption and Production*; and SDG13 on *Climate Action*. Few companies prioritize SDG2 on *Zero Hunger*; SDG14 on *Life below Water*; or SDG15 on *Life on Land*.[9] It certainly feels strange that 90% of businesses do not feel that issues such as hunger or biodiversity are salient issues for them.

The question is does such cherry-picking by business matter? The SDGs were designed for governments and not businesses and there is no theory of transposition as might exist under other frameworks which have businesses more clearly in mind, such as the UN *Guiding Principles on Business and Human Rights*.[10] Some have developed specific measurable targets for businesses to come behind, such as the venture capitalist John Doerr's focus on climate change and related SDGs.[11]

To set the right goals, leaders must balance ambition, realism, systems thinking, and organisational capability. In earlier chapters, I discussed how narrow goals often misfire. For example, a net-zero target that ignores water scarcity collapses when factories lose access to water (Chap. 8). A decarbonisation plan that ignores industrial strategy becomes uncompetitive (Chap. 6). A human-rights policy that ignores climate mitigation risks overlooks some of the greatest potential social impacts, even more so if it also downplays resilience and adaptation measures.[12] Goals often fail not because they are unworthy, but because they are incomplete.

Sustainability goals in business require synchronising long-term planetary thresholds (Chap. 2), with medium-term investment cycles (Chap. 4), and short-term operational realities (Chap. 3). As I discussed in the previous two chapters (Chaps. 14 and 15), they should be structured for systems, not silos. Goals must be nested within real operations. If companies set goals using siloed frameworks alone, they replicate the very fragmentation that created systemic risk in the first place. Goals must also be tested against different sources of instability, in particular: *physical instability* (climate impacts, water scarcity, invasive pests), *geopolitical instability* (trade tensions, sanctions, conflict), *economic instability* (commodity volatility, capital re-pricing), *technological change* (AI energy intensity, grid constraints, mineral shortages), and potential *social instability* (inequality, migration, political polarisation). A robust goal is not one that is easy to achieve. It is one that remains valid when the world changes.

## 16.2  The Limits of Siloed Metrics

Most sustainability measurement frameworks were designed to make complex problems legible by breaking them into discrete components. Emissions, water use, waste, health and safety, and human rights are measured separately, often by different teams, using different data sources and reporting cycles. This approach has improved visibility, but it also embeds a structural weakness that becomes increasingly problematic as sustainability moves from aspiration to enforcement.

Siloed metrics assume that impacts can be understood and managed independently. In practice, sustainability outcomes are produced through interactions between systems. Decarbonisation affects water demand; water scarcity reshapes industrial location; labour practices influence resilience and productivity; land use decisions alter both emissions and livelihoods. When these interactions are measured separately, optimisation in one domain can generate unintended consequences in another. What appears as progress within a silo may undermine outcomes at system level.

This limitation is not theoretical. Net-zero strategies that ignore water stress have stalled projects and destabilised communities. Circularity initiatives that reduce waste but increase energy use have shifted, rather than reduced, environmental burden. Supply-chain audits that focus narrowly on compliance have displaced risk rather than reducing it. In each case, the problem is not the absence of data, but the fragmentation of insight.

Siloed metrics also struggle with scale and aggregation. They perform reasonably well within organisational boundaries, but poorly across value chains, geographies, and time horizons. As sustainability enforcement increasingly operates through finance, trade, and regulation, these boundaries matter less. Decisions are made based on system-level exposure, yet the evidence available remains organisation-centric and issue-specific. This mismatch weakens accountability and fuels dispute.

Attempts to address this through additional indicators or ever more granular reporting often exacerbate the problem. Proliferation increases complexity without resolving interaction effects, while raising costs and diluting focus. More data does not automatically produce better decisions if it reinforces silos rather than revealing connections.

The consequence is that siloed metrics are increasingly misaligned with how sustainability outcomes are judged in practice. They remain useful for operational management within defined domains, but they are insufficient for assessing real-world impact across systems. As enforcement tightens, the question is no longer whether impacts are being measured, but whether they are being understood in relation to each other. This is the gap that system-level and place-based approaches attempt to address. Without them, sustainability measurement risks optimising parts while degrading the whole - a failure mode that becomes more visible, and more costly, as constraints tighten.

## 16.3 Impact at the Nexus

The limits of siloed metrics become most visible where sustainability challenges intersect. Climate, nature, labour, and development outcomes do not evolve independently; they interact through shared systems of energy, land, water, capital, and governance. It is at these junctions that risk accumulates and where conventional measurement most consistently fails. Climate transition is a clear example. Decarbonisation strategies reshape water demand, land use, mineral extraction, labour conditions, and regional development patterns. Energy systems that reduce emissions may increase local water stress; renewable infrastructure may displace communities or strain biodiversity; mineral supply chains may shift environmental pressure rather than reduce it. When these effects are assessed separately, decisions that appear successful within one domain can generate instability elsewhere.

These interactions are increasingly material. Physical climate risk now coincides with social vulnerability, infrastructure exposure, and institutional capacity (as discussed in Chap. 5). Transition pathways that ignore this convergence face resistance, delay, or failure - not because goals are contested, but because consequences are unevenly distributed. The result is not simply trade-off, but compounding risk. The same pattern appears in digital and industrial systems. Data centres, electrification, and advanced manufacturing concentrate demand for power, water, land, and skilled labour in specific places (Chap. 12). Metrics that treat emissions, water use, employment, or community impact independently obscure these cumulative pressures. What matters in practice is not whether each indicator improves marginally, but whether the system remains viable under combined stress.

Attempts to address these dynamics through additional disclosure or more granular reporting often fall short. Granularity does not resolve interaction effects, and proliferation can distract from the core question: how risks and benefits combine across systems and places. Without an integrated view, decision-makers optimise components while destabilising the whole.

## Some Examples of Nexus Approaches

A systems-based approach requires disclosing differently, not more. It prioritises metrics that illuminate interdependencies rather than treating issues in isolation.[13] In mining and resources, nexus-aware reporting might combine water intensity per tonne of output with basin-level water balance, biodiversity overlaps and indicators of community grievance. Together, these metrics show whether operations are compatible with local ecosystem limits and community stability, often the most important determinants of long-term viability. In agriculture, integrated metrics such as water withdrawals per tonne, soil-health scores, regenerative practices and farmer-livelihood resilience link ecological stability with long-term supply-chain reliability. In textiles manufacturing, reporting on water use per garment, wastewater treatment performance, labour conditions and heat-stress exposure provide insight into how climate trends shape resource use, worker well-being and production continuity.

1. *The example of Climate Transition Plans*

Developing a nexus between climate and social issues is not optional; it is essential for ensuring that climate action succeeds rather than stalls (Chaps. 8 and 9).[14] The transition to a low-carbon world will reshape employment, infrastructure, consumption and lifestyles, and these shifts will have profound social consequences. As noted, the move toward *Net Zero* by 2050 will disrupt livelihoods - from the loss of jobs in carbon-intensive industries to pressures on agriculture, finance, and housing. If these impacts are ignored, transitions risk provoking resistance from workers, communities, and consumers, undermining the very climate action they seek to advance. Climate is thus inseparable from social realities. People are both perpetrators of, and victims of, climate change. Any transition that fails to grapple with inequality and perceptions of fairness will lack legitimacy. Indeed, climate action will only proceed at the necessary speed if affected stakeholders feel the outcomes are just. The paradigm of Just Transition captures this: unless stakeholders believe the process treats them equitably, they will oppose it through protest, voting, or refusal to cooperate.[15]

This is why climate action must be deeply social. Jobs lost in high-carbon sectors and job opportunities in growing green industries will not be geographically or socially aligned. Many communities most dependent on carbon-heavy sectors will be those most vulnerable to disruption. A Just Transition requires anticipating these imbalances and supporting reskilling, social protection, participation, and dialogue - placing people, not only emissions targets, at the centre. Ultimately, climate policies that do not account for social systems will fail, because climate action is a systemic challenge: everything connects to everything else. The Transition Plan Taskforce (TPT) framework, developed in the UK, goes well beyond emissions and includes equity and social requirements, which are crucial to achieving a just transition. Many companies producing transition plans aligned with the TPT disclosure framework are doing so for the first time, including HSBC, H&M, and Bayer.[16] Others, such as Unilever, are on their first major update. A growing number of firms are also submitting their plans to shareholder votes. While this increases scrutiny, it also demands expertise to evaluate the quality of these plans - expertise the finance sector does not yet consistently have.

In short, transition plans are rapidly becoming standard practice, but their maturity and level of sophistication remain limited. This picture is reinforced by the *Carbon Disclosure Project's* (CDP) assessment of 2023 disclosures.[17] Out of 23,000 participants, only 140 companies reported against all 21 of CDP's climate transition plan indicators. Given CDP's status as a credibility benchmark, this suggests that organizations continue to struggle with several core elements of transition planning. Neither TPT nor CDP have explicit 'nexus indicators' as such (yet) but they do understand the intersection of environmental issues. CDP's 'climate-water-forests' nexus would be one example of this, by integrating related questions into its comprehensive questionnaires and providing specific guidance on how companies can disclose these interdependencies. The *Taskforce on Nature-related Financial Disclosures* (TNFD) is another good example, explicitly working at the climate-nature nexus.[18]

TNFD does not prescribe a separate set of 'nexus metrics' but rather incorporates the climate-nature nexus within its existing metrics architecture.

## 2. *The example of Data Centres*

Artificial intelligence is expanding rapidly, with global spending expected to exceed \$2 trillion by 2026 (Chap. 12). But AI's growth depends on managing the 'AI-energy nexus': the interconnected pressures among energy, water, critical materials and the ecosystems that support them.[19] As data centres proliferate, electricity demand is soaring and still largely met by fossil fuels, raising risks around cost, stability and emissions. Cooling these centres also requires vast quantities of water, competing with agriculture and communities, especially in already water-stressed regions. Companies increasingly track *power usage effectiveness* (PUE), *water usage effectiveness* (WUE) - litres of water per compute unit or model trained, *renewable energy share*, and *exposure to peak-load conditions*.[20] These nexus indicators reveal how data centre growth interacts with local energy and water systems and whether expansion will compound regional pressures.

AI hardware also depends on critical minerals such as lithium, cobalt and rare earths, often sourced from areas with environmental damage, geopolitical tension and social conflict. The resulting displacement and biodiversity loss undermine public trust and threaten the industry's social licence.[21] Treating energy, water, minerals and nature as isolated issues only worsens trade-offs. Sustainable growth requires integrated strategies and potentially other forms of nexus metrics. Data centres need efficiency targets, renewable energy and water stewardship but they also need to measure community benefits and worker rights through their full value chain. Hence the need for integrated metrics.

Across industries there are many ongoing efforts to align and consolidate standards at present. This will prompt questions and open possibilities for smarter metrics. Silo-ed indicators still play a valuable role for reasons of measurement and accountability, but the need to be augmented by more dynamic systems-oriented approaches to measurement.

This leads us also to the third and final tier of metrics, those that relate to the system as a whole as well as specific nodes within it.

# 16.4  Systems Metrics

If sustainability outcomes are produced through interconnected systems, then impact must be understood at more than one level. Siloed metrics fail not only because they are narrow, but because they privilege organisational boundaries over the systems and places where consequences occur. To address this, nexus-metrics will increasingly be developed as discussed above. But beyond this lies the system itself and the possibility of measuring both macro and micro systemic impact.

It is useful to distinguish between two complementary ways of seeing impact: *system-level* effects and *place-based* effects. This distinction is not a framework or a reporting model. It is a diagnostic lens. Its purpose is to surface interactions, trade-offs, and distributional effects that are otherwise obscured when impacts are assessed only within functional or organisational silos. This thinking is very nascent but here are my thoughts,

## System-Level Impact

System-level impact describes how activities influence the behaviour, resilience, and trajectory of the systems on which outcomes depend. These effects often sit beyond the control of any single organisation, but they shape long-term viability and risk exposure. Five dimensions are particularly revealing when assessing system-level impact:

- Scale and trajectory - whether actions contribute to absolute reduction or improvement at the level of the system, rather than relative efficiency within a single actor.
- Resilience - whether interventions strengthen or weaken the system's ability to absorb shocks, adapt to stress, and recover from disruption.

- Lock-in and path dependency - whether decisions reinforce existing patterns or enable alternative pathways, particularly in infrastructure, technology, and capital allocation.
- Distribution of risk and benefit - how costs, benefits, and exposures are allocated across actors, regions, and time horizons.
- Governance and coordination effects - whether actions improve or undermine the capacity of institutions and markets to coordinate responses at scale.

These dimensions help explain why interventions that appear successful in isolation can generate negative outcomes at system level, and why some failures only become visible over time.

## Place-Based Impact

Place-based impact focuses on how sustainability outcomes are experienced in specific locations and communities. While system-level effects shape global trajectories, place-based effects determine legitimacy, social licence, and political durability.[22] Five considerations are particularly salient:

- Material outcomes for people - impacts on livelihoods, health, safety, affordability, and access to essential services.
- Environmental condition in context - changes in local ecosystems, resource availability, and exposure to environmental risk.
- Economic structure and capability - effects on employment, skills, and the long-term economic role of a place.
- Equity and inclusion - who bears the costs of transition, who benefits, and whose voices are marginalised.
- Institutional capacity - whether actions strengthen or erode local governance, enforcement, and delivery capability.

These dimensions explain why sustainability initiatives that perform well against global metrics can fail locally, and why place-blind optimisation often triggers resistance, delay, or reversal.

## Why This Lens Matters

Taken together, system-level and place-based perspectives reveal impact as relational rather than additive. Outcomes emerge from interactions across scales, not from the accumulation of isolated improvements. The purpose of this lens is therefore not to measure everything, but to ask better questions: where impacts accumulate, where they collide, and where they are displaced. As sustainability becomes enforced through capital, regulation, trade, and data-driven systems, these questions become unavoidable. Decisions are increasingly judged not by activity or intent, but by their consequences across systems and places. Impact that cannot be understood in these terms is difficult to defend, and increasingly difficult to ignore.

These system-wide and place-based considerations I have suggested here are just indicative. They are meant to complement and not replace the silo metrics and emerging nexus metrics already in existence. For there to be three tiers of metrics might feel like overkill; but also, already suggested in this book, complexity is not our enemy, rather it is false simplification, bounded rationality, and poor metrics that hold us back. Measuring impact does not guarantee good outcomes. But the absence of credible impact guarantees dispute. As sustainability becomes embedded in systems that allocate capital, access, and legitimacy, claims that cannot be substantiated at system and place level are increasingly challenged, discounted, or penalised. In this environment, measurement is not about precision for its own sake; it is about whether outcomes can withstand stakeholder scrutiny during times of pushback.

What follows in the next section are questions of accountability. When impact becomes decisive, false claims become liabilities, silence becomes risky, and narratives are tested against evidence rather than intent. Chapters 17, 18, and 19 examine these consequences directly. They show how greenwashing, greenhushing, and storytelling fail - or survive -once sustainability is judged not by what is said, but by what can be shown.

# Notes


1. United Nations, *Annual Sustainable Development Goals Report: 2025 edition*, UN Department of Economic and Social Affairs, 16 July 2025.
2. United Nations, *Annual Sustainable Development Goals Report: 2025 edition*, UN Department of Economic and Social Affairs, 16 July 2025.
3. United Nations, *Annual Sustainable Development Goals Report: 2025 edition*, UN Department of Economic and Social Affairs, 16 July 2025.
4. United Nations, *Annual Sustainable Development Goals Report: 2025 edition*, UN Department of Economic and Social Affairs, 16 July 2025.
5. United Nations, *Annual Sustainable Development Goals Report: 2025 edition*, UN Department of Economic and Social Affairs, 16 July 2025.
6. Martina Igini, *None of 17 UN SDGs on Track to Be Achieved By 2030*, Earth.org, 24 June 2025.
7. Martina Igini, *None of 17 UN SDGs on Track to Be Achieved By 2030*, Earth.org, 24 June 2025.
8. Stefan Dercon, *Gambling on development: why some countries win and others lose*, 2023.
9. KPMG, *Reporting on the UN Sustainable Development Goals*, 2022.
10. United Nations, *Guiding Principles on Business and Human Rights*, Human Rights Council, 2011.
11. John Doerr, *Speed & Scale*, 2021.
12. John Morrison, *The Just Transition: A systems-thinking approach to managing climate action*, 2024.
13. Lauren Smart and John Morrison, *How shared standards can help businesses and governments master the energy nexus*, World Economic Forum, February 2026.
14. John Morrison, *The Just Transition: A systems-thinking approach to managing climate action*, 2024.
15. John Morrison, *The Just Transition: A systems-thinking approach to managing climate action*, 2024.
16. ERM, *Ahead of the climate curve: leveraging climate transition planning for a low carbon future*, 20 September 2024.
17. Carbon Disclosure Project. *CDP, 2023*.
18. Taskforce on Nature-related Financial Disclosures, *About TNFD, (website)*, November 2025.

19. Lauren Smart and Sam Hsu, *The AI-Energy nexus will determine AI's impact. We must account for it better*, World Economic Forum, 1 December 2025.
20. Lauren Smart and Sam Hsu, *The AI-Energy nexus will determine AI's impact. We must account for it better*, World Economic Forum, 1 December 2025.
21. John Morrison, *The Social License: How to keep your organisation legitimate*, 2014.
22. This thinking draws on both of my previous books: John Morrison, *The Social License: How to keep your organisation legitimate*, 2014; and John Morrison, *The Just Transition: A systems-thinking approach to managing climate action*, 2024.

# Part VI

Retelling Sustainability

# 17

# Hanging Out the Greenwashing

Greenwashing has flourished in an era when sustainability has been voluntary, loosely defined, and weakly enforced. Claims could outpace delivery because there were few mechanisms to test them against real-world outcomes. When *Remaking Sustainability*, that condition no longer holds. As sustainability moves from aspiration to accountability, claims increasingly collide with data, regulation, trade rules, and legal scrutiny. What was once tolerated as marketing exaggeration now functions as a strategic liability. The shift is structural, not moral. Sustainability claims are no longer assessed primarily through reputation or intent, but increasingly through their materiality to system outcomes. Where claims cannot be substantiated at the level of impact—across value chains or geographies—they are challenged, discounted, or penalised. In this environment, greenwashing fails not because it is unethical (although it might be), but because it misrepresents risk and distorts allocation decisions in systems that are increasingly intolerant of false signals.


J. Morrison, *Remaking Sustainability*, https://doi.org/10.1007/978-3-032-23755-2_17

## 17.1  Greenwashing Is a Real Problem

The underlying problems with greenwashing are not just that it is misleading; it also creates systemic harm. These are some of the thoughts from business leaders I interviewed for this book:

- Greenwashing *"slows progress by promoting the illusion that change is already happening"*.
- It *"misallocates consumer spending"* away from genuinely responsible companies.
- It *"deepens public scepticism"*, making sustainability messaging less effective for all organisations.
- It discourages internal change, allowing harmful practices to persist under the guise of *"doing enough."*

This chapter examines why greenwashing will become unstable within bedrock sustainability. It is less concerned with the past behaviour of individual firms, but with understanding how systems now surface and correct misrepresentation, as sustainability outcomes become more consequential. An end to greenwashing is a key performance indicator for *Remaking Sustainability*.

## 17.2  Seduction through Non-material Means

*Le secret du succès, c'est la sincérité. Si vous arrivez à la simuler, vous avez réussi"*.[1]

*"The secret of success is sincerity, once you can fake that you've got it made"*.[2] But perhaps not for much longer. Greenwashing is best understood as the gap that has grown between what is claimed and what is materially consequential.

## Competitive Forces

I have claimed elsewhere in this book that companies report there is often not a 'sustainability price dividend' when it comes to what customers and consumers are willing to pay for products. This differs from what consumers actually say themselves in surveys. According to a PwC survey[3] of 20,000 consumers across 31 countries and territories in 2024, over 80% of consumers express willingness to pay up to 10% more for sustainable products. This intent does not always carry over into real behaviour but there is undoubtedly a growing sustainability market for value over pure price considerations (for example in growth of circular fashion or home furnishings), as well as competitive forces between companies and brands. Over 80% of consumers surveyed by Accenture[4] said that reusability or recyclability are important in product design, with nearly three quarters saying they were buying more environmentally friendly products than they did five years before, and 81% said they planned to buy more such products in the five years to come. So even if there is not always price advantage, there is growing competitive advantage in making sustainability claims for some products in specific segments of the market.

Companies recognise this growing market expectation and consumer trends, but not all are willing or able to meet it authentically. If competitors appear greener (even superficially), companies fear falling behind. Marketing departments may push for sustainability claims that operations cannot yet support. Achieving meaningful reductions in carbon emissions, resource use, or waste typically requires significant investment and organisational change. A 2022 global CEO survey[5] found that over half of executives admitted their organisations had engaged in some form of greenwashing, partly because meaningful sustainability transformation is difficult and required capital investment. The growth of greenwashing has tracked the growth of sustainability itself and perhaps is another indication of its salience.[6]

One of the best-known examples of deliberate and cynical greenwashing was that perpetrated by Volkswagen between 2009 and 2016. Volkswagen promoted its diesel vehicles as *"clean"* alternatives while installing defeat devices designed to cheat emissions tests.[7] During real-world driving, these vehicles emitted up to 40 times the legal limit of nitrogen oxides. Volkswagen's accumulated losses from the emissions scandal are more than 30 billion euros, estimated by the company itself in 2020.[8] The scandal resulted not only in fines but also in plummeting stock value and years of efforts to rebuild trust.

## Subtle Deflection

Greenwashing is often more subtle than the Volkswagen case. Many organisations report real activity but elevate aspects that are easy to communicate rather than those that are systemically significant. Packaging improvements are highlighted while core production emissions rise. Voluntary offsets are foregrounded while physical exposure increases. Recycling rates are promoted while absolute material throughput grows. In each case, the issue is not falsity, but misalignment between claim and consequence. For example, Coca-Cola repeatedly positioned itself as committed to solving plastic waste, promoting bottle recycling initiatives.[9] But lawsuits in Europe accused the company of misleading consumers about the environmental friendliness of its packaging causing the company to reconsider some of its claims.[10] When McDonald's replaced plastic straws with paper *"sustainable"* straws in 2019, investigations revealed the paper versions were not recyclable either.[11] Critics accused these companies of 'performative sustainability'.

Another example is airlines and carbon offsetting. Many airlines promote 'carbon-neutral flights' calculated through carbon offsets. Regulators have repeatedly challenged these claims, pointing out that offsets do not address the material impact of aviation emissions. In 2020, the airline Ryanair faced accusations by the UK *Advertising Standards Authority* of misleading consumers about sustainability claims for this very reason.[12] In the fashion industry, Dutch regulators criticised H&M's *"Conscious Collection"* for misleading consumers about environmental benefits,[13] resulting in the company retracting some of the claims. There are many other examples, including those within the construction sector that ignore the embodied carbon, or labour rights abuses, in the material supply chain, when extolling the low carbon use attributes of buildings.[14]

As data availability improves and definitions of materiality tighten, these misalignments highlighted above are harder to sustain. System-level indicators increasingly reveal when progress in one domain is off-set by deterioration in another, or when local improvements mask displaced impacts elsewhere. Claims that once appeared credible are reinterpreted as partial, misleading, or strategically selective. Through better data and legal requirements to disclose, sustainability claims can be adjudicated by stakeholders throughout the system. Such exposure will accelerate accountability through multiple channels simultaneously.

## 17.3  A Systemic Response

Across jurisdictions, regulators are converging on a simple principle: sustainability communication must be consistent with material impact and verifiable data.

Within the UK, for example, no one single piece of primary legislation has addressed the greenwashing issue, but the screws have been tightened through several regulatory levers. The UK's Competition and Markets Authority (CMA)'s *Green Claims Code* (2021) was written for consumer-facing "environmental claims."[15] Updates to consumer protection law via the *Digital Markets, Competition and Consumers Act* 2024 (DMCCA), gave UK regulators greater enforcement powers.[16] Sector-specific enforcement and guidance has also been developed; for example, the CMA issuing tailored guidance to the fashion industry in 2024.[17] The DMCCA (2024) allows the CMA to directly fine firms for misleading environmental claims, up to 10% of global turnover.[18] In addition, the *Financial Conduct Authority* (FCA)'s "anti-greenwashing rule" under its sustainability disclosure regime, is now applicable to financial services and investment products.[19]

Beyond the UK, France has gone further than most. The French *Climate and Resilience Law,*[20] passed in 2021, bans 'carbon-neutral' claims unless proven through actual emissions reductions or offset-based neutrality claims. The law introduces mandatory carbon footprint disclosure for many industries, with very aggressive bans on advertisements and large fines. The Netherlands *Authority for Consumers and Markets* (ACM)[21] is another leading regulator in Europe forcing companies to change misleading marketing or pay fines to environmental causes, including on airline carbon-offset claims. Norway's *Consumer Authority*[22] is another prominent example. Europe as a whole has been planning its own regulation with the EU *Green Claims Directive,*[23] though at the end of 2025 the directive was facing delays.[24] Beyond Europe, Canada and the US already have related legislation, and Australia, Japan and Singapore are known to be considering their own.[25]

The strongest regulatory models share four features. They all require mandatory evidence before companies make sustainability claims: not just 'don't lie', but 'prove it before saying it'. They all have high penalties, with fines of 4–10% of global turnover, which give board rooms reason to pause. They all have active enforcement, with regular sweeps of marketing claims, surprise investigations, and public 'naming and shaming'. Finally, they all place restrictions on offset-based 'carbon neutral' claims, previously offsets had been one of the biggest loopholes.

Within these markets, the direction of travel is clear. Claims are increasingly scrutinised for consistency with disclosed data and alignment with recognised definitions. They must be relevant to material risks and outcomes, and proportional to actual performance. This applies across advertising, financial disclosure, labelling, and corporate reporting. Enforcement is uneven and evolving, but the signal is consistent: sustainability claims that cannot be substantiated are treated as sources of market distortion. The effect is to shift communication from persuasion toward precision. Crucially, regulation operates alongside other market mechanisms. Investors, insurers, and supply-chain partners increasingly impose their own requirements, often moving faster than public authorities. The combined effect is not always uniform compliance, but reduced tolerance for misrepresentation across systems that depend on accurate information to function.[26]

## 17.4 Why Greenwashing Persists Even When It Fails

If greenwashing is becoming more costly, more visible, and more tightly regulated, it is reasonable to ask why it persists at all. The answer is not that organisations are unaware of the risks, nor that enforcement is insufficient. Greenwashing endures because, within many organisations, it continues to make internal sense, at least for a time. The system can still deliver some incentives.

As already stated, greenwashing does not always begin as a deliberate attempt to deceive. More often it emerges from a set of rationalisations that frame overstatement as temporary, defensive, or necessary. Claims are justified as a way of buying time for delivery to catch up; of managing external expectations while internal capabilities mature; of maintaining competitiveness in markets where peers appear to be making similar claims. In politically charged environments, exaggeration is sometimes defended as a way of signalling alignment without provoking immediate resistance. In these contexts, greenwashing is not experienced internally as dishonesty, but as risk management under pressure. Sometimes greenwashing is not always condemned by stakeholders at source as it shows social pressure is working.[27]

This logic is reinforced by the structure of many organisations. Sustainability commitments are often articulated by teams that do not control capital allocation, operational priorities, or delivery timelines. As a result, ambition can become decoupled from capability.[28] The language used externally reflects intention and aspiration, while the systems required for implementation remain fragmented, underpowered, or deferred. What appears as greenwashing from the outside is frequently the visible symptom of an internal governance gap: statements moving faster than systems, and narratives running ahead of decision-making.

Once this gap opens, organisations can become trapped in a cycle of escalation. Initial overstatement creates expectations that are difficult to reverse without reputational damage. Correction feels like retreat; qualification feels like failure. Each subsequent communication must therefore sustain or extend the original claim, even as internal confidence weakens. Greenwashing, in this sense, is rarely a single act.[29] It is a cumulative process, sustained through repetition, in which retreat becomes progressively harder and exposure progressively more likely. What began as optimism hardens into misrepresentation through inertia.

Regulation and enforcement, while essential, do not automatically break this cycle. They operate retrospectively, punishing false or misleading claims after they have been made. But greenwashing originates upstream, in incentive structures that reward signalling over delivery and speed over integration. Where executive accountability for sustainability outcomes remains diffuse, and where timelines for performance stretch beyond leadership tenures, the temptation to over-promise persists. Ending greenwashing therefore requires more than tighter rules; it requires changing how organisations decide what they are prepared to say before they are ready to deliver.

As scrutiny intensifies, however, this internal logic begins to fail. The costs of exaggeration rise, while the space for ambiguity narrows. Claims that once passed unchallenged are now tested against data, regulation, and lived experience. At this point, organisations face a choice. Some respond by aligning ambition more closely with capability, rebuilding credibility through restraint and delivery. Others draw a different conclusion: that if saying too much has become dangerous, it may be safer to say very little at all.

## 17.5  An End to Performative Sustainability

Greenwashing will increasingly fail because the systems that once tolerated it no longer do. As sustainability is adjudicated through data, materiality thresholds, and real-world outcomes, claims that do not correspond to consequence are discounted or penalised. This shift reframes sustainability communication as a risk-management problem rather than just a reputational one. Claims that exaggerate peripheral activity, rely on selective disclosure, or substitute symbolism for consequence distort decision-making in systems that depend on accurate signals. As capital, insurance, and market access become more tightly conditioned on demonstrable impact, these distortions are corrected—often abruptly and at cost.

Sustainability narratives that are not anchored in credible evidence increasingly trigger enforcement responses rather than trust.

The next chapter examines one predictable reaction to this environment: silence. As greenwashing becomes costly, some organisations retreat from public claims altogether. This comes at a time when others are also trying to short sustainability (Chap. 1), creating political and legal obstacles to disclosing social and environmental information. A perfect storm for silence it would seem. But 'greenhushing' is not a stable alternative to greenwashing. In systems that rely on disclosure, data, and accountability to function, absence of signal creates its own risks. What follows in Chap. 18 is the price of saying nothing.

## Notes


1. Attributed to the French novelist Jean Giraudoux, 1882–1944.
2. Translation of quote from French novelist Jean Giraudoux, 1882–1944.
3. PwC, *Voice of Consumer Survey*, 15 May 2024.
4. Accenture, More than Half of Consumers Would Pay More for Sustainable Products Designed to Be Reused or Recycled, Accenture Survey Finds, 4 June 2019.
5. Google Cloud, *CEOs are Ready to Fund a Sustainability Transformation*, April 2022.
6. Simon Schillebeeckx, *Why do we need more not less greenwashing?* Medium, 4 August 2020.
7. US Government, *Learn about Volkswagen Violations*, Environmental Protection Agency, last updated: 19 March 2025.
8. Reuters, *Volkswagen says diesel scandal has cost it 31.3 billion euros*, 17 March 2020.
9. Packaging Europe, *Coca-Cola to rework 'misleading' recycling claims on plastic bottles*, 15 May 2025.
10. Packaging Europe, *Coca-Cola to rework 'misleading' recycling claims on plastic bottles*, 15 May 2025.
11. BBC News, *McDonald's paper straws cannot be recycled*, 5 August 2019.
12. Mark Sweney, *Ryanair accused of greenwash over carbon emissions claim*, The Guardian, 5 February 2020.

13. ESG Today, *H&M to remove sustainability labels from products following investigation from regulator*, 14 September 2022.

14. John Morrison, *The Just Transition: A systems-thinking approach to managing climate action*, 2024.

15. UK Government, Greenwashing: *CMA puts businesses on notice*, Competition and Markets Authority, 20 September 2021.

16. Jessica Gardner, *Greenwashing under scrutiny: the CMA's new powers to tackle misleading environmental claims*, Fieldfisher, 1 May 2025.

17. UK Government, *Greenwashing: CMA issues tailored guide for fashion brands*, Competition and Markets Authority, 18 September 2024.

18. Jessica Gardner, *Greenwashing under scrutiny: the CMA's new powers to tackle misleading environmental claims*, Fieldfisher, 1 May 2025.

19. UK Government, *Handbook guidance on the Anti-Greenwashing Rule*, Financial Conduct Authority, April 2024.

20. Loi n° 2021–1104 portant lutte contre le dérèglement climatique et renforcement de la résilience face à ses effets, 22 August 2021.

21. Autoriteit Consument & Markt, (website), December 2025.

22. Forbrukertilsynet, (website), December 2025.

23. European Commission, *Green claims: new criteria to stop companies from making misleading claims about environmental merits of their products and services*, Environment, (website), November 2025.

24. Politico, *EU countries abandon anti-greenwashing talks after Italy pulls out*, 23 June 2025.

25. Curtis File, *Global greenwashing regulations: How the world is cracking down on misleading sustainability claims*, Sustainalytics, 14 November 2023.

26. Mao Xu et al. *Greenwashing and market value firms: An empirical study*, International Journal of Production Economics, 284, June 2025.

27. Simon Schillebeeckx, *Why do we need more not less greenwashing?* Medium, 4 August 2020.

28. Evan Farbstein and Alexander Schmidt, *Pairing good intentions with bad math can lead to unintentional greenwashing—and all its consequences*, 3 March 2025.

29. Khalil Feghali, *Greenwashing in the era of sustainability: A systemic literature review*, Corporate Governance and Sustainability Review, 9(1), 2025.

# 18

# Putting a Price on Greenhushing

As sustainability moves from aspiration to operational accountability, silence is no longer neutral. In systems that increasingly allocate capital, insurance, market access, and legitimacy based on disclosed impact, the absence of information is itself a signal.[1] Greenhushing—the deliberate retreat from public sustainability claims—emerges not as caution, but as a form of greenwashing itself. To decide not to talk about sustainability is a choice, and the wrong one to make if you are committed to reinforcing systems and not weakening them. According to regulators such as the *Australian Securities and Investments Commission* (ASIC), the trend toward greenhushing has become a structural problem in global markets.[2]

The term was first coined in 2008 to describe the act of companies intentionally withholding information surrounding their environmental initiatives, for fear of being called out. But the conditions that allowed organisations to say less without consequence have changed. Whilst it is tempting to keep quiet when anti-sustainability rhetoric is high, the longer-term consequences will be costly for the organisation as well as the system as a whole. As other chapters in this book have shown data systems are starting to aggregate signals across supply chains (Chap. 11); regulators test consistency between claims and performance (Chap. 17);



J. Morrison, *Remaking Sustainability*, https://doi.org/10.1007/978-3-032-23755-2_18

investors and insurers price uncertainty aggressively (Chaps. 4 and 5 respectively). In this environment, withholding information does not reduce risk—it reallocates it. Unexplained gaps are interpreted as unquantified exposure, weak governance, or misalignment with material outcomes.

This chapter examines why greenhushing becomes unstable once sustainability is enforced through data, regulation, and market mechanisms. It shows how absence of signal will be treated as a risk factor, how silence might erode access and credibility, and why retreating from disclosure ultimately narrows—not preserves—the space for action. In a more accountable systemic environment, saying nothing is no longer a safe alternative to saying the wrong thing.

## 18.1  Why Organisations Go Quiet

Organisations retreat into silence for what seem like understandable reasons. Legal uncertainty, inconsistent regulation, activist scrutiny, ESG backlash, and fear of misstatement all play a role. There has indeed been a trend for civil society organisations to target companies where there is at least some public performance data in order to send a message to businesses more widely. This has led to a disincentive to disclose amongst some companies—the 'first head above the parapet' syndrome. In such a context, senior managers (and particularly legal counsel) within companies can regard disclosure as a liability rather than a safeguard. Under voluntary regimes, where companies are given the choice whether to disclose or not, caution often paid off. The plateauing of performance under the *Corporate Human Rights Benchmark* between 2017–20 amongst Fortune 500 companies is evidence of this and was used as part of the European Union's rationale for mandatory due diligence.[3]

The anti-ESG sentiment in parts of the finance sector has also contributed to the muting, a key part of the current pushback I reflected upon in Chap. 1. Soon after the change of administration in the US in early 2025, the *Net Zero Banking Alliance* abandoned its pledge to limit global warming to 1.5C.[4] Then in October 2025, the Alliance, which had nearly 150 corporate members at its peak, voted to disband itself entirely.[5]

Research published by the South Pole consultancy suggested that many banks had adapted to placing sustainability within general risk statements rather than more detailed climate risk plans.[6] Companies, South Pole said, *"navigate a complex landscape where they can be sued for saying too little, and sued for saying too much".*[7]

## Audience Segmentation

Selective hushing has been quite common. Some NGOs won't speak to companies and vice versa due to ideological differences and prior experience. Many companies refuse to recognise trade unions until local laws force them to do so, whilst others proactively develop global framework agreements with international union bodies. I often hear from companies that 'investors don't ask the right sustainability questions', whilst the same investors bemoan the slow levels of improvement within the same company. Clearly sustainability has long been a walled conversation, with information often shared tactically and in silos. I used to advise one government department that had a hostile view of civil society organisations, whilst another department of the same government was trying to develop stronger sustainability relations with the same NGOs. So, selective hushing can happen in stages, for temporary periods, and for a myriad of reasons, with a huge quotient of bounded rationality.

Hushing with consumers is also quite common against a rising tide of consumer scepticism of business sustainability claims.[8] One 2025 study suggests that 52% of consumers believed that organizations are continually greenwashing their sustainability initiatives, up from 33% in 2023.[9] Therefore there is sometimes a reluctance to communicate with consumers even when decisions have been made on sustainability grounds to either end sourcing from a problematic country or company, or suspend sales of a particular product (such as a fish species) for reasons of biodiversity.[10]

But selective greenhushing can create internal confusion. When employees cannot see how sustainability fits into the company's identity, purpose, and strategic direction, they are less motivated to participate in environmental or social initiatives. This is clearly the view of the business leaders I interviewed for this book.[11] Employee buy-in requires not only action but communication of that action. Moreover, silence can create contradictions between what leadership says internally and what is communicated externally. This inconsistency erodes trust within the organisation and complicates cross-departmental coordination.

## Humility Becomes Hushing

There are a surprising number of acts of sustainability that never get communicated as such. I interviewed the former Managing Director of a UK fashion retailer who could not understand why they continued to use shoe boxes when reusing shoe pouches would save the company many millions and reduce environmental waste. So, he instigated a system of pouches that were returned to suppliers once the shoes were on display and reused up to 12 times. Instead of cardboard boxes filled with tissue paper, consumers were offered nice tote bags for their purchased items. There was a cost-saving benefit alongside a sustainability benefit. This, he felt, makes communicating about the example tricky. Very often the response can be *"well you would do that if it saves you money"*—devaluing the sustainability motivation. Such preconceptions advance the perverse premise that the only sustainability actions of any value are those that cost the business more money.

This hopefully will start to change in an environment where consumers too are linking sustainability to saving money, such as reused fashion items through platforms such as *Vinted*. There are some indications that younger consumers are also more likely to respond to business offerings premised on trusted information related to reuse and recycling. In the UK, for example, 36% of Gen Z and Millennials are spending more of their fashion budget on second hand clothes than five years ago.[12] In response, 74% of retail executives who don't currently offer resale are considering doing so.[13] It is hard to imagine any business model based on circularity succeeding in the absence of trusted information.

## 18.2  An End to Selective Disclosure

Greenhushing is often accompanied by selective disclosure: reporting what is safe, measurable, or favourable while omitting what is complex or contested. Under voluntary regimes, this approach was common and largely tolerated. Annual sustainability reports often included feel-good stories about recycling initiatives, biodiversity projects, or employee volunteering, while omitting or minimising the organisation's larger environmental risks or carbon impacts. This practice was not always malicious. Sometimes companies lacked the data or feared stakeholder judgment. Sometimes they genuinely believed small actions were worth celebrating. In Chap. 16, I reflected on the fact that most companies engage in 'cherry-picking' when communicating impact across the UN Sustainable Development Goals. There has been a 'cuckoo in the nest mentality' (one fat chick pushing the others aside) about what gets measured and communicated, and what does not. Climate mitigation has shaded out climate resilience and adaptation; climate itself has nudged aside other environmental issues such as biodiversity, water and land; and environmental sustainability has pushed many social sustainability issues out of the nest altogether.

Even if they remain in the cuckoo's nest, many companies prefer to see social sustainability issues in softer developmental terms rather than human rights, particularly in markets where human rights are perceived to be sensitive. Self-censorship is also a real risk, 'human rights' become 'harmonious relationships', 'worker rights' become 'worker welfare', and 'forced labour' statistics are underreported so as not to offend. I remember when the *Institute for Human Rights and Business* issued a report to try and persuade the *United Nations Global Compact* not to 'hush' its own first two principles (relating to human rights) back in 2010.[14] There are also many good environmentalists that prefer for social complexity to be downplayed, if not ignored, in the pursuit of pure green targets. Undoubtedly this is one of the reasons that *Just Transition* has struggled for so many years to get agenda space at UN climate meetings even after the concept was included in the preamble to the 2015 *Paris Climate Agreement.*[15]

Now there are a new set of sensitivities, with 'ESG', 'Climate' and even 'Sustainability' disappearing from conferences, annual reports and corporate communications for some US-based companies. It seems that the US, China and India have all become sensitive to different parts of the sustainability agenda, and so selective hushing is most definitely a temptation.

The partial nature of many reporting frameworks has also enabled partial disclosure, particularly the championing of climate mitigation above all other sustainability issues. The advance of climate frameworks such as the *Science-Based Targets initiative* (SBTi)[16] and the *Task Force on Climate-related Financial Disclosures* (TCFD),[17] have been a mixed blessing. They have indeed incentivised disclosure on carbon emissions but have allowed companies to focus mainly on issues of climate mitigation. This has created tiered hushing. I discuss this at length in Chap. 11 and efforts in the European Union and elsewhere to break down silos.[18] As *double materiality* definitions tighten and embrace a wider spectrum of environment and social issues from an agreed taxonomy, selective disclosure become more noticeable. Progress in one domain is assessed against deterioration in another; relative improvements are tested against absolute outcomes; local gains are weighed against displaced impacts elsewhere. What once appeared prudent is reclassified as partial or misleading. Selective silence interferes with coordination and misrepresents risk. As a result, as sustainability becomes more systemic, it will attract greater scrutiny rather than avoiding it.

## 18.3  Silence as Systemic Risk

### Silence Has a Cost

As accountability increases, so does the calculus on greenhushing. The problem is not that political and cultural pressures exist, but that silence does not resolve them. Withholding sustainability information will not remove scrutiny; it will shift its focus. In the absence of disclosure, external actors substitute inference for evidence. Investors, insurers, regulators, and civil society will increasingly fill gaps using proxy data, peer comparison, and worst-case assumptions. The absence of sustainability data is increasingly considered a red flag for investors, suggesting poor governance and inadequate preparedness for the rapidly changing regulatory environment. Recent research indicates this is as true in China[19] as it is in the European Union.[20] Investors do not expect perfection, but they do expect visibility. When greenhushing, risk is not reduced—it is amplified.

Up until now, legal advice has often accelerated retreat by prioritising minimisation of short-term exposure. But this framing treats disclosure as discretionary rather than structural. In systems that increasingly rely on sustainability data to allocate capital and access, silence itself becomes a material factor. What cannot be assessed is treated as uncertain and what is uncertain is penalised. Communications caution similarly misfires. Pulling back from claims may reduce the chance of misstatement, but it increases the likelihood of misinterpretation. Silence invites speculation about intent, particularly where prior commitments or public positions exist. The result is not neutrality, but heightened attention.

Greenhushing therefore reflects a mismatch between organisational risk perception and system response. It might be a rational short-term reaction to greater scrutiny, but an ineffective one over the medium and longer terms. Good sustainability legislation foresees this and places its weight on penalising an absence of disclosure and not just the consequences of poor performance the disclosure might reveal. This is a very sensitive balance between how much regulators reward 'knowing' and 'showing'. Reward the 'showing' too much and you might provide too much legal 'safe harbour' for companies who committed serious abuses, but over penalising companies for breaches can encourage legal counsels to hide things. This is a balance that has had to be struck in specific disciplines such as health and safety and anti-corruption measures, and so other facets of sustainability need to learn from these. You don't wait for workers to fall off high ladders before you penalise companies for allowing workers to operate unsafely. Or at least you shouldn't.

As sustainability outcomes are judged through federated data, as I discussed in Chap. 11, and processed with the increasing power of AI, discussed in Chap. 12, the business case for greenhushing should diminish.

Knowledge of real-life real-time performance will increasingly be 'out there' and outside of the control of any one company or even government.

The final chapter turns to what comes next. If neither exaggeration nor silence works, narrative becomes an operational responsibility. Organisations must rebuild sustainability narratives that are grounded in evidence, transparent about trade-offs, and resilient to scrutiny. Yet, creativity and freedom of expression are key to good storytelling. Chapter 19 examines how credible narratives emerge once sustainability is no longer a matter of belief, but of demonstrable consequence.

## Notes

1. The Economist, *The remarkable rise of "greenhushing"*, 29 July 2025.
2. Fiona McNally, *Australian watchdog warns firms against 'greenhushing' in response to regulatory crackdown*, Responsible Investor, 5 June 2023.
3. World Benchmarking Alliance, *The Corporate Human Rights Benchmark*, (website), December 2025.
4. Damien Gayle, *Banking industry's net zero alliance shuts down admit faltering climate commitments*, The Guardian, 3 October 2025.
5. Damien Gayle, *Banking industry's net zero alliance shuts down admit faltering climate commitments*, The Guardian, 3 October 2025.
6. South Pole, *Global financial institutions zero in on net zero, The South Pole 2025 Net Zero Report*, 2025.
7. South Pole, *Global financial institutions zero in on net zero, The South Pole 2025 Net Zero Report*, 2025.
8. UK Government, *Global sweep finds 40% of firm's green claims could be misleading*, UK Competition and Markets Authority, and the Netherlands Authority for Consumers and Markets, 28 January 2021.
9. Capgemini, *A world in balance 2024: Accelerating sustainability amidst geopolitical challenges*, Capgemini Research Institute, 2024.
10. I have direct experience of this from the UK supermarket sector.
11. Interviews conducted between October 2025 and January 2026.
12. ThredUp, *Resale Report*, 2024.
13. ThredUp, *Resale Report*, 2024.
14. Institute for Human Rights and Business, *The UN Global Compact and Human Rights—Developing a vision for 2020*, 18 October 2010.

15. John Morrison, *The Just Transition: A systems-thinking approach to managing climate action*, October 2024.
16. Science Based Targets, *Science Based Targets Network (SBTN) Framework*, (website), November 2025.
17. IFRS, *Taskforce for Climate-related Financial Disclosures (TCFD)*, 2023.
18. IFRS Foundation, *SASB Standards and other ESG frameworks*, (website), December 2025.
19. Fahd Alduais, *Unravelling the intertwined nexus of firm performance, ESG practices, and capital cost in the Chinese business landscape*, Cogent Economics and Finance, 11(2), 2023.
20. Economist Impact, *The Dispatch: climate risk doesn't mean risky business. Five insider insights from Climate Risk Europe*, 2021

# 19

# Stronger Sustainability Stories

Complex systems do not operate on data alone. They require shared interpretation. Narratives help organisations and societies decide what to prioritise, what to tolerate, and what to change. They translate complexity into action. Storytelling can be one of the most profound forms of *symbolic leverage*, as I discussed in Chap. 15. Stories create the *moral imagination* that allows humanity to be self-aware, self-critical, to learn from the lives of others, and to make the right choices.[1]

The question about which stories we tell, who tells them and about whom, is a question about power. Who controls the narrative controls much else.[2] If sustainability is now a form of orthodoxy, and I hope—like me—you have reached Chap. 19 with this conclusion, then there is a tension which immediately emerges. Orthodoxies are often built on a shared mythology—in particular a 'creation myth' of some kind. I briefly described the sustainability movement's own story in earlier chapters (Rachel Carson and so on). Clearly Rachel Carson, Wangari Maathai, and Vandana Shiva are all real people, and their works continues to inspire, but narratives are always selective. Who tells the story matters.

One of the limitations of orthodoxies, and another reason why I think that is what we have become, is the fact that there is a lack of humour and

© The Author(s), under exclusive license to Springer Nature Switzerland AG 2026
J. Morrison, *Remaking Sustainability*, https://doi.org/10.1007/978-3-032-23755-2_19

creative dissent within the movement itself. In her 2018 book, *Bad Environmentalism*,[3] Nicole Seymour pointed to the irony that environmentalists had become the pro-science lobby, very different from the time of Rachel Carson and the challenge to the integrity of environmental science during the 1960s. She argues that the political left in the US sowed the seeds of scepticism in science, which have now been embraced by the anti-sustainability lobby. It is the sceptics who are not just anti-science but are also the most ironic these days, perhaps with a slug of dark sarcasm. And it is the sustainability orthodoxy that is often framed as the po-faced humourless 'woke police', denying freedom of expression, and 'deplatforming' and 'cancelling' those with opposing views. The sustainability movement has lost its sense of humour.

This level of self-awareness matters hugely when it comes to telling better sustainability stories. If operational sustainability suggests that new narratives should all essentially be about corporate communication, then we have lost the creative narrative space completely. This has long been the case amongst consumer brands. They might have rottweiler-like corporate lawyers and corporate communication heads, but when it comes to selling products, they will go to advertising companies and other creatives and be much more 'loosey goosey'. It has long been this way in media and the creative industries, maintaining a firewall between the corporate and the creative. Of course, this separation is never absolute, media barons are known to ring their newspaper editors from time to time. But freedom of expression matters a lot in any society that wishes to be entrepreneurial and creative. It is all too easy to characterise sustainability as being increasingly authoritarian, with its laws and diktats, and that the freedom-fighters are now sceptics: the farmers driving their tractors into the centre Brussels or expressing themselves freely on social media.

And so, this chapter separates the sustainability story-telling requirements of society itself from those that relate to the responsibilities of the organisations charged with delivering it. The lessons for *Remaking Sustainability* lie in how to navigate the tensions that will continue to deepen between these two objectives given they are linked systemically. Freedom of expression never happens by accident. Those with power and authority must for go some of their actual or potential power to allow others to mock them and challenge the orthodoxy itself.

Authoritarian leaders are famous for their lack of a sense of humour and self-depreciation,[4] and sustainability can never afford to be like that.

## 19.1  Better Narratives for Action

Society needs better sustainability stories. Individuals such as David Attenborough or Greta Thunberg have taken us a long way but there is most definitely a plateauing, particularly in the dominant dystopian and 'doom and gloom' narratives surrounding climate change, plastics pollution, loss of biodiversity, and so on. 'It is indeed hard not to be dystopian when the science tells us we are heading to dystopia', is often the retort (who said environmentalists have no sense of humour). Those such as Nicole Seymour have always said we should be more diverse, subversive, and counterculture. The sustainability communications agency *Futerra* have developed a range of story-telling archetypes to encourage us to move beyond relying on just the 'end of the world' blockbusters, respectable scientists with power points, or 'national treasure' journalists with gorillas.[5]

Futerra call the dominant overstory the "*Frankenstein*" paradigm[6]—a dystopia that is a result of our own, governmental or business failings. They then chart three stories that are emerging to nuance or counter the dominant narrative, they name the first the "*Hunger Games*" which shows the youth rising and taking action. Then "*Iron Man*", which has technology coming to save us, and "*Eat Pray Love*": the idea of a global awakening. They also propose several new narratives for specific audiences, including "*Futurama*"—a merry utopia, "*Sand Talk*" with indigenous peoples and traditional storytelling; "*Modern Family*"— normalising sustainable activity, "*Lord of the Rings*"—the sustainability adventure and community; and finally "*Erin Brockovich*", character-led climate action.[7] This thinking illustrates the point that we don't need to be, or should we be, constrained by a singular narrative-type.

## Who Are We Speaking To?

Chapter 19 is not about telling a single sustainability story to a generic public. It is about narrative as an operational tool: how legitimacy, consent, and trust are built and sustained among the people whose acceptance, or resistance ultimately determine whether sustainability is delivered or blocked. The basis of any *social licence*.[8] The audiences that matter are therefore plural and differentiated. At the centre are affected communities and workers, who bear the costs and disruptions of transition first and who can withdraw social licence when trade-offs are obscured or unfairly distributed. Closely connected are employees and internal decision-makers, whose everyday choices translate strategy into practice, and senior business leaders, who allocate capital and take responsibility for consistency under pressure. For these groups, storytelling is not about optimism or persuasion, but about honesty, fairness, and clarity around constraints, risks, and trade-offs.

Beyond the organisation sit investors, regulators, and policymakers, who set financial and regulatory constraints and require narratives that demonstrate discipline, materiality, and defensible decision-making rather than aspiration. Equally important are the sceptical and fatigued middle ground—those not opposed to sustainability in principle but unconvinced by moralised or abstract claims—and civil society actors, who amplify, challenge, or legitimise narratives in the public sphere. In all cases, the stories that matter are those that reduce uncertainty, acknowledge real-world costs, and demonstrate competence under constraint. I suggest that sustainability will regain its social licence not through better slogans, but through narratives that support delivery, withstand scrutiny, and sustain consent among those who must live with the consequences.[9]

## Moving Beyond Awareness to Action

Several familiar sustainability narratives collapse once outcomes are judged rather than intentions. It is at this point that many of the classic narratives can fail. *Certainty narratives* promise clarity and linear progress in systems defined by non-linearity and feedback. They can fail when projections collide with physical limits, political resistance, or unintended consequences. *Heroic narratives* centre transformation on exceptional leaders, firms, or technologies. They can falter when outcomes depend on coordination across institutions, value chains, and jurisdictions rather than individual agency.[10] *Painless transition narratives* suggest that sustainability can be achieved without trade-offs, disruption, or loss. They unravel as distributional effects, cost burdens, and local impacts become visible.[11] *Inevitability narratives* frame transition as unstoppable and self-correcting. They collapse when progress proves uneven, contested, and reversible.

These narratives fail not because they are implausible in isolation, but because they cannot withstand scrutiny once systems test claims against evidence and experience. This is why lived-experience of sustainability impacts really matters and sharing these stories is likely to be more influential than just narratives of sustainability intent by experts.[12] One overriding take-away is that any perception that sustainability leaders are 'preaching' is extremely toxic and will quickly turn off most audiences. Above all things, sustainability is not a religion and should not be seen as such.

But some ideas are emerging about what works. One emerging narrative shifts the focus from minimizing harm to actively restoring systems. *Regeneration* emphasizes renewal: healthier soils, revived ecosystems, and revitalized communities. Rather than asking people to do less, it invites them to imagine doing better. *Regenerative agriculture*, for example, tells a story not just of reduced erosion or lower emissions, but of farms that become more resilient, productive, and biodiverse over time. *Urban rewilding projects* highlight the return of wildlife, improved mental health, and new economic opportunities through tourism and recreation.[13] These stories replace scarcity with possibility.

Another new narrative centres on *justice*—not as a story of perpetual victimhood, but as one of leadership and innovation. Communities that have historically been excluded from investment are increasingly at the forefront of clean energy, climate adaptation, and social enterprise.[14] Examples include *community-owned solar projects* that reduce energy costs while building local wealth, or *Indigenous-led land management practices* that lower wildfire risk and restore ecosystems. These stories reframe justice as collective flourishing, showing that addressing inequality strengthens society as a whole.

Urban sustainability narratives are also evolving. Instead of framing change as restriction—fewer cars, smaller homes, reduced consumption—new stories emphasize quality of life. Walkable neighbourhoods, shaded streets, accessible public transport, and vibrant public spaces are presented not as sacrifices, but as improvements. The link between nature and health is a powerful point of connection, for example the role of plants and vegetation in the bult environment. There are now numerous studies showing the physical and mental health benefits of the natural environment when integrated into living and workspaces.[15]

Cities that prioritize people over traffic often experience cleaner air, stronger local economies, and greater social connection. When sustainability is associated with beauty, health, and joy, it becomes aspirational rather than burdensome.

## 19.2  Better Narratives for Responsibility

The delivery of sustainability requires governments, businesses and civil society organisations working in partnership, and also holding each other to account. But institutions are not well trusted in the modern world. Edelman's *Trust Barometer* for 2025, showed that 61% of the 33,000 respondents interviewed globally (in 28 countries) had a moderate or high sense of grievance, which is defined by a belief that government and business make their lives harder and serve narrow interests, and wealthy people benefit unfairly from the system.[16] The Edelman research investigated trust levels within four quadrants of society: business, media, government and non-governmental organisations (NGOs) but did not focus on attitudes to sustainability specifically. While this sense of grievance is not good news for any form of organisation, it is least bad for business. Those interviewed saw businesses as the most competent and ethical constituency relative to governments, the media and NGOs, which is quite incredible if you think about it, and very bad news for NGOs.

## The Problem with the Word

Even the use of the word 'sustainability' can mean different things to people across the world. According to work undertaken by market research firm IPSOS in 34 countries in 2023,[17] there are significant variations in how sustainability is understood, likely shaped by differing political, environmental, and social conditions, as well as by national cultural contexts. Globally, nearly one quarter of respondents (24%) associate sustainability with *"only producing and consuming what is needed and eliminating waste."* This overall figure is driven largely by particularly strong associations in several European countries, including Romania and Hungary (both 36%), UK (35%), and Italy, Ireland, and France (34% each). By contrast, only 15% of respondents across the 34 countries link sustainability with *"full and productive employment and decent work for all"*. It is not that they don't care about these issues, it is that they do not see them as sustainability issues.

But the social-environmental linkage is considerably higher in Argentina and Peru (both 29%) and peaks in Indonesia, where nearly four in ten (37%) make this connection. Similarly, associations between sustainability and *"inclusive and quality education for all"* are much stronger in Saudi Arabia (29%) and the United Arab Emirates (24%) than the global average of 12%. Malaysia demonstrates the most comprehensive understanding of sustainability, with environmental, social, and governance issues all featuring among the five topics most strongly associated with the term. This supports the finding from other research that sustainability is framed mainly in environmental terms in the global north, but there is more linkage to social considerations in the global south.[18]

Research by the communications group *Radley Yeldar* in 2021[19] looked at how international consumer brands used the 'sustainability' term. It showed that ineffective monotonous language is rampant among many of the world's most valuable brands when communicating on sustainability. Rather, the most effective business performers do not rely on the word *"sustainability"* to do all the heavy lifting. Instead, the companies most serious about sustainability use specific words to describe their efforts and avoid over-use of the sustainability term. For most Forbes

Top 50 known brands, the word "*sustainability*" is repeated 10 times on each sustainability webpage, whilst the true leaders only used it once or twice. This suggests an inverse correlation between the use of the word 'sustainability' and actual action. Radley Yeldar call this problem '*stock sustainability*' and root it back to the start of the sustainable development movement and the Brundtland definition. 'Stock sustainability' is framed by science, numbers, and fear-laden narratives about environmental risks, with its well-known images of melting glaciers, stranded polar bears, and forest fires.[20] There is nothing wrong with this traditional science-based risk-laden approach, in fact it is essential, but it is clearly insufficient in performing the task of public communication on its own.

Better sustainability narratives are therefore not about saying 'sustainability' more; they are about saying things differently. They require facts that feel real and grounded, stories that are rooted in place and culture, and visions of the future that emphasize regeneration, justice, and shared benefit rather than just sacrifice and fear. Products with sustainability claims underperform expectations, public scepticism toward institutions remains high, and sustainability communication often feels repetitive, abstract, or disconnected from everyday life.

There are also many stories of companies launching new products incorporating sustainability-related claims only to find that sales fell short of expectations.[21] Research carried out by YouGov for McKinsey in 2023 showed that only 18% of UK consumers believed that water companies behaved authentically and just 30% of consumers trusted the messaging of renewable energy companies, a serious concern given the nature of their business. YouGov and McKinsey concluded that the findings underlined a profound shift towards the need for authenticity and away from marketing-based approaches.[22] But this gap between stated concern and real engagement is not simply a marketing problem. It reflects a deeper narrative failure. Too often, sustainability is communicated through generic slogans, technical jargon, or catastrophic warnings that fail to resonate with peoples lived experiences.

## 19.3  Delivering the Message

My work on the *Just Transition* has reinforced to me that it is as much about the messenger as it is the message, and that modalities of communication really matter.[23] This is a complex area, but it can be summarised as follows, in particular for climate transitions:

### Operational and Relational Media (the Most Important)

These include internal briefings, management decisions, procurement rules, investment committees, collective bargaining forums, worker councils, supplier engagement, and community meetings. For most stakeholders, sustainability is 'communicated' through what actually happens: how jobs change, how contracts are written, how risks are shared, how compensation or transition support is provided, and how conflicts are handled. Local engagement forums, town halls, trade union dialogues, and place-based consultations are therefore primary media, not supplements. These channels carry the message through *experience*, not narrative alone.

### Institutional and Governance Media

Formal disclosures, regulatory filings, risk reports, transition plans, financial statements, and board-level communications act as credibility anchors for investors, regulators, and policymakers. Sustainability reporting, stress-testing outputs, supply-chain due diligence disclosures, and audit processes are all media in this sense: they signal seriousness, discipline, and consistency. Their function is not inspiration, but assurance. When these channels contradict public messaging, trust collapses quickly.

## Public-Facing Narrative Media

This includes speeches, interviews, opinion pieces, documentaries, mainstream journalism, social media, and corporate communications. These channels matter, but they are no longer primary drivers of legitimacy. Their role is to contextualise decisions already taken, explain trade-offs, and maintain coherence across audiences. Used well, they reinforce delivery; used poorly, they expose gaps between words and action. In this phase, effective sustainability communication relies less on broadcast campaigns and more on aligned signals across these different media, so that what people hear, read, and experience tells the same story under pressure.

The modality through which stories are told has obviously changed radically since the 1960s and much is written today about the risks of social media in particular. But work published by The Reuters Institute and Oxford University in 2022 reviewed decades of social scientific research on 'echo chambers', 'filter bubbles', and 'polarisation'.[24] The core finding is that many common assumptions about these phenomena are exaggerated or misunderstood. For sustainability communicators, this underscores that simplistic messages about how audiences are "trapped" in monolithic information environments aren't accurate. Communicators should avoid assuming audiences are isolated and instead recognize the nuanced ways people consume and engage with information.[25] Thus, *building trust, engaging credible voices, and fostering inclusive dialogues* are essential for sustainability communication. Instead of assuming audiences ignore opposing viewpoints, communicators should highlight common ground, clear information, and respected voices across communities.

## 19.4  A Social Licence to Implement

The 'social licence to implement' is where the sustainability stories for society as a whole, and those explaining the implementing organisation, coincide. There needs to be a strong level of coherence. Narratives that survive under adjudication share several characteristics. They are anchored in material outcomes: they align claims with impacts that matter at system and place level, and they acknowledge where evidence is incomplete or contested. They are explicit about trade-offs: rather than smoothing over conflict, they name costs, distributional effects, and uncertainty. Credibility increases when narratives reflect the complexity decision-makers encounter in practice. They are adaptive rather than definitive: they frame sustainability as an ongoing process of adjustment rather than a destination. Progress is presented as conditional and revisable, not guaranteed. They are institutional rather than heroic: they emphasise governance, coordination, and capability over individual leadership or technological salvation. Finally, they are consistent across time and context. They evolve as conditions change, but do not reverse without explanation. Consistency becomes a signal of integrity under scrutiny.

These requirements do not make narratives weaker. They make them harder to maintain, but more resilient. Under adjudication, narratives no longer sit alongside operations; they shape them. They influence investment horizons, regulatory engagement, workforce expectations, and social licence. In this sense, narratives function less as communication tools and more as operating conditions. When narratives diverge from evidence, systems respond by correcting signals: through repricing, enforcement, or exclusion. When narratives remain aligned with material outcomes, they stabilise coordination under uncertainty. The difference is not rhetorical skill, but structural fit. This reframing closes the space for sustainability storytelling as aspiration management. What remains are narratives that help organisations and societies live with constraint, negotiate trade-offs, and act without guarantees.

The era of sustainability narratives as persuasion is over. Exaggeration fails under scrutiny. Silence fails under uncertainty. What remains is a narrower set of narratives capable of surviving adjudication. These narratives do not promise certainty or speed. They do not resolve conflict or eliminate risk. They acknowledge limits, adapt to evidence, and persist under pressure. Their credibility lies not in inspiration, but in endurance.

*Remaking Sustainability* does not require better stories alone. It requires organisations capable of operating under constraint, making trade-offs visible, and behaving consistently when conditions tighten. Sustainability remade, is no longer a narrative-led project. It is an operating condition. The next chapter is the final one and concludes *Remaking Sustainability*: how it will indeed will emerge stronger after the current pushback

## Notes

1. Edmund Burke, *Reflections on the Revolution in France*, 1790.
2. See the work of Plato, George Orwell, and Noam Chomsky, amongst others.
3. Nicole Seymour, *Bad Environmentalism: Irony and Irreverence in the Ecological Age*, 2018.
4. Many great examples of humour being used to mock authoritarian leaders, none better than Charlie Chaplin in *The Great Dictator*, 1940.
5. Futerra, *Stories to save the world: Imagining new climate narratives*, July 2023.
6. Futerra, *Stories to save the world: Imagining new climate narratives*, July 2023.
7. Futerra, *Stories to save the world: Imagining new climate narratives*, July 2023.
8. John Morrison, *The Social License: How to keep your organisation legitimate*, 2014.
9. John Morrison, *The Social License: How to keep your organisation legitimate*, 2014.
10. Mary Johnstone-Louis and Charmian Love, *The Myth of the Hero CEO*, The Beautiful Truth, 22 June 2021.
11. Lindsay Hooper, *How business can escape the sustainability trap*, Cambridge Institute for Sustainable Leadership, 20 January 2025.
12. For example: Institute for Human Rights and Business, *Just Stories*, (website), December 2025.
13. Kathy Willis, *Good nature: improve your health and happiness with nature—one simple step at a time*, 2024.
14. Evana Said et al., *The US Clean Energy Transition Isn't Equitable—But it could be*, World Resources Institute, 29 November 2021.
15. Kathy Willis, *Good nature: improve your health and happiness with nature—one simple step at a time*, 2024.
16. Edelman, *2025 Edelman Trust Barometer*, January 2025.
17. IPSOS, *Sustainability: All on the same page?* 20 July 2023.

18. IPSOS, *Sustainability: All on the same page?* 20 July 2023.
19. Radley Yeldar, *Words that work: Effective language in sustainability communications*, 2022.
20. Radley Yeldar, *Words that work: Effective language in sustainability communications*, 2022.
21. Jordan Bar Am et al., *Consumers care about sustainability—and back it up with their wallets*, McKinsey & Company, 6 February 2023.
22. Green Business Journal, *Why green brands can't afford to ignore authenticity*, 2025.
23. John Morrison, *The Just Transition: A systems-thinking approach to managing climate action*, 2024.
24. Amy Arguedas et al., *Echo chambers, filter bubbles, and polarisation: a literature review*, Reuters Institute, University of Oxford, 19 January 2022.
25. Amy Arguedas et al,, *Echo chambers, filter bubbles, and polarisation: a literature review*, Reuters Institute, University of Oxford, 19 January 2022.

# Part VII

## Conclusion

# 20

# Sustainability Remade

People get the need for sustainability. The concept has been translated into most languages and has a place in the public imagination, particularly amongst the young.[1] But the sustainability movement is faltering and hence the impetus for writing this book. It is suffering a crisis in confidence.[2] The reasons for this are multiple and complex but are in part a result of the scientifically based and silo-ed approach to managing the sustainable development process, and a failure to communicate and connect with the real lives of most people. This has opened a significant gap between intention and reality, an arbitrage that is being exploited by those wishing to 'short' the current system. As I have argued, we have all been complicit in this to some extent. The 'shorting' of sustainability should be seen as a symptom rather than a cause. And it is an opportunity for reform. We should have initiated the pushback ourselves several years ago against excesses such as performative CEO speeches, the over-extension of ESG, greenwashing, greenhushing, and guilt-ridden narratives. The fact that it has arrived in this manner should not be seen as the end of sustainability but rather its true beginning: as an operational and not only a values-driven or scientific enterprise.



J. Morrison, *Remaking Sustainability*, https://doi.org/10.1007/978-3-032-23755-2_20

## 20.1  A New Social Licence

This book began with an uncomfortable premise: that sustainability has become an orthodoxy. Not in the sense that environmental degradation has been halted or social inequalities resolved, but in the more consequential sense that sustainability has become one of the dominant organising ideas of our time. It is now starting to influence markets, investment flows, trade rules, and industrial strategies.[3] It provokes loyalty and backlash in differing measure. And, like all orthodoxies, it now carries power—it is part of the new modernity, as Marshall Berman might have put it.[4]

I do not see the fact that there has been a backlash against sustainability as evidence of our weakness even if we have made mistakes. The pushback exists precisely because sustainability is no longer marginal. It is contested because it matters. It is resisted because it now influences who pays, who benefits, who decides, and who bears risk. The question is no longer whether sustainability should shape the economy, but how and to what extent. The sustainability movement, as it has grown over the past 70 years, is poorly equipped for this next phase. Movements thrive on clarity of purpose and moral urgency. Orthodoxy demands something different: restraint, operational competence, and legitimacy in the eyes of those who did not choose it. Many of the fractures explored in this book—from finance and insurance to trade, industrial policy, infrastructure, and security of supply—reflect a failure to adapt to this shift. Sustainability has often been framed in utopian or morally self-evident terms. It is neither of these things.

## 20.2  Delivering Sustainability

This book's attempt to 'get real' is premised on delivery. *Remade sustainability* must be both purposeful and consequential. It needs to think about sustainability not in silos but in systems. Delivery must be about both the 'what' and the 'how' of sustainability. Its approach to managing systems must be dynamic and agile, knowing when and how to convene, align and leverage the assets of different actors—governments, businesses, financial institutions, trade unions, civil society, and others. Multilateralism is key to this, but the current multilateral architecture is largely ill suited to systems-based approaches. There is a need to disrupt, experiment and catalyse new forms of delivery, that can harness the global but be seen to deliver locally.

I have described the 'what' of *Remaking Sustainability* in 'bedrock' terms. The first two-thirds of this book draw on developments across investment, value chains, and technology, to give some indications as to where sustainability can and should sit within a broader range of economic and geo-political considerations. A systems-thinking approach to sustainability requires this. Many of the bottlenecks that the delivery of sustainability faces are complex nodes and cannot be solved by siloed sustainability. I hope some of the bedrock insights are helpful in demonstrating what I mean. My overall conclusion from doing this brief inquiry is that sustainability is already deeply embedded in many strategic considerations but is not being prioritised most of the time. Opportunities for building leverage are being missed. The symbiosis goes in both directions: the failure to address climate change and other issues will deeply impact trade, global insurance, and food security, whilst the emergence of AI and new forms of financial investment stand to benefit sustainability if channelled appropriately.

The 'how' of *Remaking Sustainability* is the remaining third of this book and it looks specifically at business environments, in terms of leadership and governance, delivery systems and metrics, as well as retelling sustainability by addressing greenwashing and greenhushing as well as better narratives. Cumulatively, these chapters are only a start in thinking on how businesses themselves might move forward. What this book does not have space to address is the wider questions surrounding multilateralism and international governance. It might be that the multi-polar world into which we are moving will be webbed by a complexity of institutions and networks. There are better minds writing on these issues[5] and the business-sustainability nexus needs to sit within them. Hopefully some of the reflections can cross over in either direction. Whilst I am a life-long supporter of the United Nations and many other intergovernmental organisations, I feel they still tend to either idolise companies and their 'sustainability hero' CEOs—on the one hand—or demonise the entire business community, on the other. Reality lies somewhere in-between, and I hope the international community develops a much more sophisticated approach to working with (and sometimes against) business.

An organisation that has genuinely remade sustainability can be recognised not by its commitments but by its behaviour under constraint. Sustainability is operational when capital allocation decisions explicitly price climate, nature, and social risk even when this suppresses short-term returns; when growth strategies accept physical, regulatory, or social limits rather than treating them as externalities; when leaders make consequential choices without waiting for perfect data or consensus; and when accountability extends beyond disclosures to real-world outcomes across value chains. This is not a lowering of ambition but a hardening of it. Accepting constraint is not an excuse for retreat; it is the condition for ambition that survives contact with reality. In this phase, legitimacy is no longer granted once through alignment with values or expertise but earned repeatedly through credible action in the face of competing pressures from markets, governments, workers, and communities. Trust will not be rebuilt through reassurance or narrative control, but through decisions that are visibly difficult, consistently applied, and experienced as fair by those who bear their consequences.

## 20.3  Living with Monsters

The monsters will always be with us. Things will always be messy. Living with monsters requires a different mindset from traditional risk management. It accepts that uncertainty is not temporary and that stability will not return to previous baselines. Instead of optimisation around a single option, it demands preparedness across multiple plausible futures.

This shift has profound implications for leadership and strategy. First, it reframes resilience. Resilience is not the ability to bounce back to 'normal', because normal is gone. It is the capacity to function under conditions of ongoing disruption. That means designing systems that degrade gracefully rather than fail catastrophically; organisations that can reconfigure rather than freeze; cultures that reward learning rather than denial. Second, it challenges the illusion of control. Many of the forces shaping outcomes—climate systems, geopolitical alignments, technological diffu-sion—are not controllable by any single actor. What *is* controllable is posture: how exposed an organisation is, how quickly it can respond, how transparently it can communicate, and how credibly it can act. Third, living with monsters requires abandoning the false comfort of lin-ear planning. Linear forecasts break down in non-linear systems. Small changes trigger disproportionate effects. Feedback loops amplify shocks. Under these conditions, strategy becomes less about prediction and more about adaptation.

This is where earlier themes of systems leadership and leverage become critical as businesses navigate bottlenecks and constraints. Leaders must be able to hold multiple truths simultaneously: that decarbonisation is urgent but constrained by minerals and grids; that AI drives efficiency but accelerates energy demand; that resilience investments raise costs in the short term but reduce existential risk in the long term. Living with monsters also exposes the limits of purely voluntary action. Many of the challenges discussed in this book—climate risk, water stress, nature loss—exceed the capacity of individual businesses or organisations to manage alone. Collective frameworks, policy alignment, and shared infrastructure become not ideological preferences but operational necessities.

Crucially, living with monsters does not mean surrendering to pessi-mism. It means replacing naïve optimism with durable confidence. Organisations that thrive in this environment will not be those that promise certainty. They will be those that demonstrate competence under pressure and consistency of action even as conditions change. In an age of monsters, credibility becomes the most valuable asset of all.

## 20.4 Stronger Stuff by 2030

Sustainability is stronger than the current pushback, much stronger. But the pushback has yet to reach its zenith and we will have lost several years by the time we have gathered new momentum. Therefore, *Remaking Sustainability* must be much more than a 'course correction'. Coming back to 'business as usual' by 2030 won't be enough and we will have lost the opportunity that this crisis brings. It is too early to tell, but the push-back is likely to have a lasting legacy in both negative and positive terms. It is possible that parts of the US will have lost so much momentum on climate transition, that issues such as a carbon market, and a carbon price, remain partisan issues between US states for a generation or more. Geopolitical instability might be such that an orderly transition to global Net Zero by 2050 recedes from being a viable prospect. Short-term pressures for food security, water, critical minerals and land have resulted in some non-sustainable decision-making, and the number of conflict-affected countries has continued to rise. More countries might be prone to the toxic mix of self-interested elites, geopolitics, and foreign commercial interests that currently blight Ukraine, Sudan, Myanmar, the DRC, or Venezuela. New opportunities to short sustainability will remain, there will still be money to be made in oil and even coal investments. All of this is possible, some would say likely.

But, at the same time, sustainability is likely to be resurgent. The world will have added *over 5500 GW* of new renewable capacity by 2030—roughly three times the growth seen in the last decade—with solar power driving most of the expansion, and a tripling of overall renewable energy capacity.[6] We will have overshot 1.5C global warming but will have stabilised within a 2.4–2.7C predicted range for the century, based on current trends, with the possibility of contracting back in the decades ahead to 1.5C by 2100.[7] The rate of biodiversity loss will remain far too high[8] but more countries might have developed long-term strategies to protect ecosystems, support cleaner air, and ensure sustainable land and water use.

By 2030, some important sustainable development milestones will have been reached, but most will lag, and some will be in reverse. The SDGs will not be abandoned but will need to evolve to encompass some of the systems-thinking and outcome-focused ideas of the many people and organisations covered in this book. Business behaviour cannot be an afterthought. Climate concerns will remain at the forefront, with greater emerging clarity on net-zero pathways and timelines, carbon budgets aligned with 1.5C, climate adaptation and resilience metrics, and loss and damage mechanisms (including all forms of insurance). Countries that can remain within national carbon budgets will start to receive trade and investment benefits for doing so, those unwilling or unable will lose competitive access to parts of the global marketplace. Whilst climate concerns will continue to lead, they will be less dominant, with issues of biodiversity, land and water-use more present as will the nexus issues that bind them to the energy economy and food-systems. 'Planetary Boundaries' will replace broad goal lists and future systems will track issues such as climate stability, biodiversity loss, land-use change, freshwater use, nitrogen and phosphorus cycles.

Whilst social sustainability issues will still be overshadowed by the environmental, particularly in the Global North, there will be renewed focus on the local impacts of resilience, well-being and issues of equity everywhere. There will be an acceptance that societal opposition to sustainability transitions is one of the biggest sustainability challenges of all—whether this is labelled as 'just transitions' or not.[9] We will also be living with the consequence of our failure to act on many sustainability issues to date, with greater wealth inequality within countries causing unrest, climate-driven migration, food, water, and health insecurity, in a world where extreme weather events are increasingly the norm. This will bring place-based approaches increasingly centre stage and the understanding that the role of cities and sub-national entities are critical and need for the local to be directly aligned with the global.

## 20.5  Business Will Be Central

Unlike the Millennium Development Goals in 2000 or the Sustainable Development Goals in 2015, the launch of what comes in 2030 can no longer leave business as a side issue. Without private capital there will be no development capacity and there will be significant opportunities for businesses prepared to be true sustainability implementers. But there will also be expectations in terms of transparency and accountability. The scrutiny of elites and how they protect each other, as characterised by the Epstein files in 2026, might maintain some momentum. Despite, or perhaps because, of the current pushback against sustainability, by 2030 I think we can expect more focused and rigorous ESG frameworks with mandatory disclosure across most markets, climate-risk stress testing for business operations, more supply-chain due diligence laws, and global sustainability reporting standards. Federated data and AI will drive this agenda and no single corporation, or government, will be able to control its sustainability narrative in isolation from others. Businesses that wish to avoid this kind of scrutiny will be restricted to smaller corners of domestic markets and legacy industries such as coal and oil. Several circular economy trends, within apparel, the built environment and furnishings, will bring consumer behaviour into sustainable business models and make them direct stakeholders in ways which has not been true to date.

Global attention to food systems will be more closely aligned with failing health systems. Health concerns and overwhelming health care budgets will drive much more attention to lifestyle and food-related choices everywhere, again bringing sustainability closer to daily conversation. In richer countries, food and nutrition will increasingly be seen as services and not just products. The health consequences of poor nutrition and unhealthy lifestyles—which have driven many business profits for decades—will be an unacceptable burden for the taxpayer, bringing in stricter laws to reform the food industry. Meanwhile, AI and emerging quantum computing will make choices about human agency and autonomy a key element of many sustainability discussions.

From 2030 onwards, sustainability will no longer be something that boards can delegate, marginalise, or brand their way around. There will be fewer "sustainability hero" CEOs, but there will be no serious executive team or board without sustainability competence embedded across finance, operations, technology, procurement, and strategy. Sustainability will not sit alongside the business; it will be part of how business is done, as integral as accounting, risk management, or corporate law.

So, as always, humanity will stumble forward. The world ahead will be marked by greater volatility, weaker predictability, and more frequent disruption. In that sense, sustainability will not deliver the comfort or certainty that some once promised. But paradoxically, it will become one of the most predictable elements of our collective future. Not because outcomes are assured, but because sustainability's direction of travel is now deeply embedded in how things need to be.

This does not mean the world will be on track for all that was promised. We will still be living with monsters. This will include the consequences of delaying and mismanaging the transition: higher temperatures, degraded ecosystems, deeper inequalities, and more frequent geopolitical shocks. Some opportunities will have been missed, and some damage will be irreversible. But it does mean that sustainability will have moved decisively from aspiration to infrastructure. The act of 'shorting sustainability' will not disappear, nor will the even greater risk that democracy itself might be shorted. There will always be incentives to arbitrage complexity, deny responsibility, or externalise risk. But over time, those strategies will become narrower, more fragile, and less defensible, at least where sustainability is concerned. The deeper sustainability becomes embedded in how economies function, the harder it will be to bet against it without betting against stability itself.

If this book has one purpose, it is to help reposition sustainability where it now belongs: not as a movement seeking attention, nor as a set of abstractions to be defended, but as an operational discipline to be practiced. The future of sustainability will be decided less by declarations or debates than by the everyday decisions of those who design systems, allocate capital, manage risk, and lead organisations under real constraints. *Remaking Sustainability* is therefore not a project with an endpoint, but a responsibility that must be exercised continuously, imperfectly, and in full view of its consequences. The work has already begun.

## Notes


1.  IPSOS, *Sustainability: All on the same page?* 20 July 2023.
2.  Lindy Fursman, *Why we need to reset action on climate change*, Tony Blair Institute for Global Change, 29 April 2025.
3.  Cambridge Institute for Sustainability Leadership, *Competing in the age of disruption*, University of Cambridge, 7 April 2025.
4.  Marshall Berman, *All that is solid melts into Air*, 1982.
5.  See for example, the work of Adam Tooze.
6.  International Energy Agency, *Massive global growth of renewables to 2030 is set to match entire power capacity of major economies today, moving world closer to tripling goal*, 9 October 2024.

7. Graham Madge, *1.5C still alive, but most likely in 2100*, Met Office (UK Government), 16 November 2022.
8. Christopher Johnson, *Past and future decline and extinction of species*, The Royal Society, (website), December 2025.
9. John Morrison, *The Just Transition, A systems-thinking approach to managing climate action*, 2024.

# Index[1]



---

[1] Note: Page numbers followed by 'n' refer to notes.

© The Editor(s) (if applicable) and The Author(s), under exclusive license to Springer
Nature Switzerland AG 2026
J. Morrison, *Remaking Sustainability*, https://doi.org/10.1007/978-3-032-23755-2

GPSR Compliance
The European Union's (EU) General Product Safety Regulation (GPSR) is a set of rules that requires consumer products to be safe and our obligations to ensure this.

If you have any concerns about our products, you can contact us on

ProductSafety@springernature.com

In case Publisher is established outside the EU, the EU authorized representative is:

Springer Nature Customer Service Center GmbH
Europaplatz 3
69115 Heidelberg, Germany